JIMMIE LEE & JAMES

JIMMIE LEE & JAMES

TWO LIVES, TWO DEATHS, AND THE MOVEMENT THAT CHANGED AMERICA

"THIS IS THE STORY BEHIND THE HISTORIC 1965 VOTING RIGHTS MARCH FROM SELMA TO MONTGOMERY.

A well-written, well-reported page turner about our collective struggle for equality and justice … hopefully the last chapter in the American Revolution." —**MORRIS DEES, founder Southern Poverty Law Center**

Steve Fiffer & Adar Cohen
NEW YORK TIMES BESTSELLING AUTHOR   OF *CIVIC LEADERSHIP FOUNDATION*

Regan Arts.
NEW YORK

Regan Arts.

65 Bleecker Street
New York, NY 10012

Copyright © 2015 by Steve Fiffer and Adar Cohen

All rights reserved, including the right to reproduce this book or portions thereof in any form whatsoever. For information address Regan Arts Subsidiary Rights Department, 65 Bleecker Street, New York, NY 10012.

First Regan Arts hardcover edition, May 2015

Library of Congress Control Number: 2014955556

ISBN 978-1-941393-48-2

Interior design by William Ruoto
Jacket and Cover design by Richard Ljoenes

Printed in the United States of America

10 9 8 7 6 5 4 3 2

To those who marched, and those still marching.

*It was the killing of **Jimmie Lee Jackson** that provoked the march from Selma to Montgomery. It was his death and his blood that gave us the Voting Rights Act of 1965.*

—CIVIL RIGHTS LEADER AND U.S. REPRESENTATIVE JOHN LEWIS

*Dr. King's murder was the most momentous among those of the dozens who died in the cause of civil rights for African-Americans. While all could be said worthy of remembrance, one in particular—**the Rev. James Reeb**—may be worth recalling now, because the events surrounding his death helped hasten passage of the federal Voting Rights Act, a crowning achievement of the civil rights movement.*

—NEW YORK TIMES RELIGION JOURNAL COLUMNIST GUSTAV NIEBUHR

CONTENTS

AUTHOR NOTE . . . . *xi*

PROLOGUE . . . . *xiii*

CHAPTER ONE   "I WAS HALF DEAD ANYWAY . . ." *1*

CHAPTER TWO   "I GOT HIM . . ." *24*

CHAPTER THREE   "WE ARE GOING TO SEE THE GOVERNOR!" . . *42*

CHAPTER FOUR   "YOU AND THE TWO GIRLS ARE NEXT . . ." . *64*

CHAPTER FIVE   "HOW DO YOU MURDER PEOPLE?" *87*

CHAPTER SIX   "THEY JUST FLUSHED OUT LIKE BIRDS . . .". *112*

CHAPTER SEVEN   "ONE GOOD MAN . . ." *136*

CHAPTER EIGHT   "WE HAVE A NEW SONG TO SING . . ." *157*

CHAPTER NINE   **"HE HAD TO DIE FOR SOMETHING . . ."** *180*

CHAPTER TEN   **"A MOST UNUSUAL OCCURRENCE . . ."** *193*

CHAPTER ELEVEN   **"HE'S GONNA HAVE TO GO TO JAIL . . ."** . . . *218*

CHAPTER TWELVE   **"A DAGGER INTO THE HEART"**. *236*

ACKNOWLEDGMENTS 245

NOTES 247

INDEX 287

AUTHOR NOTE

Over the years, many award-winning journalists and respected scholars have written about the march from Selma, Alabama, to the state capital of Montgomery and the passage of the Voting Rights Act of 1965. As the fiftieth anniversary of these historical landmarks approached, we sought a fresh way to consider the movement that changed America. We eventually decided to focus on the foot soldiers of the day, the largely unknown men, women, and children who were willing to put their lives on the line to win the right to vote and, with that right, the opportunity to change their circumstances. Two of those individuals, Jimmie Lee Jackson and James Reeb, were killed within two weeks of each other. We believe that the lives and deaths of these two men are key elements in a powerful story about America and American justice, then and now.

To tell this story, we traveled to Selma, Montgomery, and nearby Marion to talk with many of the men and women who participated in the movement, and we interviewed dozens of others, including witnesses to the murders of Jackson and Reeb. We secured hundreds of pages of FBI documents, as well as private papers and diaries. We read memoirs and oral histories by civil rights leaders and lesser-known figures from the era, along with countless newspaper and magazine articles. Not surprisingly, the accounts of particular events from all these sources are often at odds with one another: People see things differently as they happen; memories change over the years. We have striven to reconcile these different accounts and write a book that is as factually accurate as possible.

We have also worked to reconcile the struggle for racial justice during the tumultuous days of 1965 with contemporary events. Today, persistent poverty, unprecedented rates of incarceration, and access inequalities disproportionately afflict African Americans. As we wrote, protests over the use of excessive force by the police in the deaths of Michael Brown, Eric Garner, and many other African American men were widespread as the country stumbled into a new installment in the conversation about race, justice, and racial injustice.

Quieter but no less destructive developments are afoot. The same voting rights Jimmie Lee Jackson, James Reeb, and so many others struggled and even died to secure are now being undermined or undone.

It is our hope that this book can help us remember the great promise of American democracy—that everyone has a voice, that everyone can participate—and in honoring two of its heroes, recommit us to its promise.

PROLOGUE

"I don't remember how many times I pulled the trigger, but I think I just pulled it once, but I might have pulled it three times. I don't remember. I didn't know his name at the time, but his name was Jimmie Lee Jackson. He weren't dead. He didn't die that night. But I heard about a month later that he died."

—*JAMES BONARD FOWLER*

March 6, 2005

The *Anniston Star* is barely off the presses, and Michael Jackson's phone is already ringing. *Did you see what Fowler said? What are you going to do about it? Can you reopen the case?*

Jackson has been in office for only two months, but as the first African American elected to serve as district attorney in the west-central Alabama jurisdiction that includes Selma and Marion, the town of 3,800 where state trooper James Bonard Fowler shot Jimmie Lee Jackson (no relation) forty years earlier, the forty-one-year-old prosecutor has heard the story of the death that changed the civil rights movement:

How, since the beginning of 1965, blacks in Selma and Marion, with the help of Dr. Martin Luther King and the Southern Christian Leadership Conference (SCLC), had intensified their efforts to win the right to vote.

How, on the night of February 18, 1965, state and local police turned off the streetlights in Marion and, along with deputized white citizens, attacked scores of men and women as they marched out of Zion United Methodist Church to peacefully protest the arrest of SCLC organizer James Orange.

How, in the chaos that followed, many were beaten as they knelt in prayer, while others hid under cars to avoid billy clubs and baseball bats, and still others sought refuge in nearby Mack's Café.

How, when one of those who had been in the church, Jimmie Lee Jackson, entered Mack's in search of his injured eighty-two-year-old grandfather, he saw his mother wrestling with an Alabama state trooper and rushed to her defense.

How the trooper shot Jimmie Lee in the stomach.

How Jimmie Lee ran out of the café and was immediately attacked by several white men, including, it was believed, other police.

How the wounded and beaten 26-year-old farmer and pulpwood chopper was left on the street to die.

How he was finally taken to a hospital in Marion and then to a hospital in Selma, where he passed away eight days later.

How Dr. King eulogized him at a funeral attended by thousands of outraged African Americans and a handful of whites.

How his death directly inspired the march from Selma to Montgomery for voting rights for blacks.

How, five months later, Congress passed one of the most important pieces of legislation in U.S. history, the Voting Rights Act of 1965.

And how, despite eyewitness testimony to the contrary, state and federal grand juries had accepted James Bonard Fowler's explanation that he had been acting in self-defense when he shot Jackson, and had refused to indict the trooper.

District Attorney Jackson also realizes that it is almost impossible to mount a case forty years after the fact. Witnesses are dead or impossible to find, or they no longer remember enough to be reliable. Documents, if there ever were any to begin with, are long gone. Potential jurors don't necessarily have the stomach to send an aging man to prison for something he may have done so many years earlier.

Still, Fowler's remarks are so offensive that they have re-opened an old wound. It's not just that he reveals he never cared enough to inquire about the health of the man he shot. It's not that he boasts, "I don't think legally I could get convicted for murder now . . . 'cause after forty years there ain't no telling how many people is dead." No, speaking publicly for the first time since the shooting, the seventy-one-year-old retired trooper has shared deeper, darker thoughts with the *Star*'s editor at large, John Fleming. His pronouncements include:

[Blacks] always fared better when they stayed in their place. . . . I think that segregation was good, if it were properly done. Now, you got to give equal funds and they got to be handled right. I don't believe in completely mixing the races. I don't think that is gonna help anything. . . .

I'm on the side of J. Edgar Hoover. I think [Martin Luther King] was a con artist. I don't think he's got a snowball's chance in hell of getting into heaven. No more chance than I do. His goal was to screw and fuck over every white woman that he could.

And so the district attorney fields calls from angry black leaders, including many state legislators; from ordinary citizens who remember the times when they could not vote and the police could get away with murder; and from relatives of Jimmie Lee Jackson who seek justice and closure.

Jackson tells them all that the odds are against gaining an indictment, but that he will try. Several years later, he will explain: "I can't emphasize enough the importance of the case. This was the murder that led to the strategy of the Selma–Montgomery March, and also the Bloody Sunday situation. So, but for Jimmie Lee Jackson's death who knows how things, history, could have been totally different."

A few weeks after the newspaper article appears, the district attorney drives the twenty-eight miles from his office in Selma, heading west on U.S. Route 80, then north up County Road 45 until he reaches Marion. Along with Selma and the state capital, Montgomery, the town is part of Alabama's "Black Belt," so named because of the color of the rich topsoil so amenable to farming, not the majority of its inhabitants, whose ancestors came to America on slave ships.

Marion is the seat of Perry County, whose chamber of commerce today proclaims, "If one word could describe Perry County, Alabama, that word would be Diversity! Its people, its land, its weather and its location are all balanced by the contrasts they provide." According to the 2010 census, the town is about 64 percent black and 33 percent white. More than one-third of the population lives below the poverty line; the median household income is only $24,000.

Originally inhabited by Choctaw Indians, the town was initially called Muckle Ridge in celebration of its first white settler. Four years later, in 1823, the name was changed to honor Revolutionary War hero Francis Marion, aka "the Swamp Fox."

During the Civil War, Marion was a Confederate bastion. Indeed, the first Confederate flag was designed by a teacher at the Marion Female Seminary. So, too, was the traditional gray Confederate uniform.

Dr. King knew Marion well. His wife, Coretta Scott, grew up there, and the couple was married on her front lawn in 1953. Four years later the town gained international notoriety when an African American named Jimmy Wilson was sentenced to death for stealing $1.95 from a white woman. The Alabama Supreme Court upheld the sentence. Bombarded with newspaper headlines and letters from around the world disparaging the United States and its justice system, Secretary of State John Foster Dulles successfully pressured Alabama's governor, "Big Jim" Folsom, to grant Jimmy Wilson clemency.

Michael Jackson, who was just a year old when Jimmie Lee Jackson was shot, begins his quest for justice on a sidewalk by the town square. Zion United Methodist Church sits on the corner, across from the Perry County Courthouse. Nearby is the Lee and Rollins Funeral Home. In the funeral home's parking lot, where Mack's Café once stood, is a plaque bearing the likeness of Jimmie Lee Jackson in cap and gown and the inscription, "Gave his life in the struggle for the right to vote."

Without a list of witnesses or police files, the district attorney is starting not just at ground zero, but at square one. As older black people walk by, he politely stops them. "Excuse me," he says in a slow, deep drawl. "Do you know anything about the night that Jimmie Lee Jackson was shot?"

CHAPTER ONE

"I WAS HALF DEAD ANYWAY . . ."

February 18, 1965

Willie Nell Avery doesn't like what she is seeing. The twenty-seven-year-old insurance agent is standing near the town square when the first of the state troopers drives in to Marion. Fifteen minutes later, another trooper arrives and fifteen minutes after that another. Soon there are nine or ten state police cars parked by the Perry County Courthouse.

Encounters with law enforcement are nothing new to Avery. Since the beginning of the year, when the SCLC came to town, the Marion Police Department and Perry County Sheriff Department have regularly monitored the nighttime meetings that Avery and scores of her fellow black citizens attend to discuss tactics for winning the right to vote. Just two weeks earlier, a cop thrust a billy club across her chest and pushed her to the ground. She was then arrested along with hundreds of other peaceful protestors who refused to disperse.

But the arrival of Governor George Wallace's state troopers on this cool February afternoon suggests something more ominous. Each of their cars has a long rod across the backseat, and on each of the rods there hang several police uniforms. "Something strange is happening," Avery tells her husband, James, "because they can only wear but one uniform."

Strange, but not unheard-of. Officials across the South have been known to deputize and, on occasion, outfit local white citizens who volunteer to help control African Americans marching for civil rights. Dressed as policemen and free of supervision, these volunteers need no hood or sheets to terrorize blacks.

Why would a citizen posse be needed in Marion? Earlier in the day, the authorities arrested and jailed James Orange on charges of disorderly conduct and contributing to the delinquency of minors. The twenty-two-year-old SCLC organizer stands accused of enlisting teenagers and "sub-teens" to participate in protests—albeit nonviolent ones—instead of going to school.

Fearing that Orange might be harmed while in police custody, the SCLC and others in Marion's voting rights movement have announced plans to march peacefully to the jailhouse after this evening's meeting at Zion United Methodist Church. There they will pray and sing freedom songs. Nighttime protests are rare, as organizers know the police are more disposed to attack under cover of darkness. Although the church is only one block from the jail, the march will be dangerous.

Avery knows that whites in town can be cordial to blacks willing to accept their status as second-class citizens, but not those who challenge the power structure. Just a few days ago, some of these men beat up two fellow whites who proposed negotiating with blacks over voting rights. The black community's recent boycott of white-owned businesses in Marion has created additional tension between the races.

Although aware that the evening might be dangerous, Avery

insists on going to the meeting, where she is scheduled to help lead the assembled in song. She and her husband will, as always, take their young children to her stepmother's house before heading to town. And, as always, she will tell them, "Look, it's going to be rough tonight, and we may or may not come back home."

"It didn't really matter at that time whether I lived or whether I didn't," Avery explained years later. "I told people, 'I'm half dead anyway. So until I can get my freedom and have equality, I will just keep fighting and keep pushing.'"

Even as a child, Avery was infuriated by inequality based on the color of one's skin. She grew up in Orrville, a town of less than three hundred, about thirty miles southeast of Marion in neighboring Dallas County. After sharecropping for many years, her father and his brothers were able to buy a few hundred acres of their own to farm. "There were ten of us children. I was the eighth. My parents were hard workers and they made us work hard," she says.

Whites, many of them much younger than her parents, would come to buy produce or vegetables that the family canned. "My parents would thank them and say, "Yes, ma'am,' and, 'No ma'am,' and, "Yes, sir,' and, 'No, sir.'

"I've always been kind of outspoken, so I asked my parents, 'Why would you have to say, "Yes, ma'am" and "No, ma'am" to them, and they can just say yes and no to you?' There didn't seem to be any justice or equality in that.

"They told me I couldn't ask those kind of things. That was my parents. They would just say, 'Shh,' and I would honor that. So I said, *Okay, when I get old enough, I'm going to tackle or challenge some of those things, what I feel is not right.*"

Newly married, Avery and her husband moved to Perry County in November 1961, settling on land about twelve miles outside Marion. Blacks outnumbered whites 60 percent to 40 percent in the county, but not at the polling place. Only 5 percent of African Americans over twenty-one years of age were registered to vote, as opposed to 94 percent of whites. And so, in Perry County, as in similar counties throughout the South, whites elected by whites held all the political power.

This imbalance in voter registration and political power had existed since the beginning of the twentieth century, when Alabama and other southern states rewrote their constitutions to disenfranchise blacks. In the eyes of most whites in the region, such rewriting was necessary because of post–Civil War political changes. In 1865, the Thirteenth Amendment abolished slavery. In 1868, the Fourteenth Amendment extended citizenship to those who had been slaves. And in 1870, the Fifteenth Amendment gave African American men the right to vote. At the same time, the U.S. Congress required the former states of the Confederacy to pass their own constitutions embodying these rights. Alabama did so in 1868.

When Alabama's Democratic Party—home to the white segregationists—regained control of the state legislature and statehouse in the mid–1870s, it took steps to eliminate the political and economic gains made by blacks during Reconstruction. "Democrats feared losing local and state offices to Republicans, however, so they developed creative ways to reduce the influence of blacks, who overwhelmingly voted for Republicans," explains the *Encyclopedia of Alabama*. Literacy tests were established. Registration was limited to May, the busiest month for farmers. Elected positions were eliminated in favor of appointments.

These tactics succeeded in keeping many black men off Alabama's election rolls, but the state's Democratic leadership wanted to go further. Just as Mississippi, South Carolina,

Louisiana, and North Carolina had already taken steps to disenfranchise their black citizens, Alabama held a constitutional convention in 1901 with the aim of eliminating the black vote as fully as possible. Disenfranchising was legitimate if done on the basis of one's "intellectual and moral condition," and not because of race, the convention's president, John B. Knox, suggested. The delegates—none of whom was black—agreed. They proposed requirements for literacy tests, property ownership, and employment, even as a separate clause granting the vote to veterans and their descendants grandfathered in many poor or illiterate white Alabamans.

The proposed new constitution also denied the vote to those convicted of minor crimes, the morally corrupt, and the mentally deficient, while instituting a poll tax for those ages 21 through 45. Despite opposition from white populists and blacks, it was approved by Alabama voters in November 1901.

When Willie Nell Avery arrived in Marion some sixty years later, there was, she said, "a movement going on where people were trying to become registered voters, but were being denied." When she went to the courthouse to register in February 1962, she was told that one had to reside in the county for six months before becoming a registered voter. "When the six months was up, I was allowed to fill out a registration form. You had to take a test at that time, but it had lots of questions on there that really wasn't pertaining to becoming a registered voter."

The registration office was only open for a few hours every other Monday, hardly a schedule designed to encourage a larger electorate. "Whenever they were open, I was back asking had I passed the test, but they didn't grade my test for maybe a year." Eventually, Avery asked the registrars if they had they lost her test and would allow her to take another one.

"I think they knew my walk," Avery recalls. "They wouldn't even look up when I would come in. But I was persistent. Every time they opened, I would be back trying because I didn't feel that I was a first-class citizen not being a registered voter. And so they would say, 'Well, we haven't graded yours.' And it just went on and on."

Why the tests? Those states that required them—almost exclusively in the South and the West—explained that voting was not a right and that those casting ballots must demonstrate a requisite amount of literacy, civic knowledge, and general knowledge. These states did not explain why their registrars had tests of varying degrees of difficulty and almost uniformly administered the toughest ones to blacks. To demonstrate his or her understanding of how government works, a black registrant in Alabama in early 1965 would be asked questions such as:

* A person appointed to the U.S. Supreme Court is appointed for a term of _____.

* When the Constitution was approved by the original colonies, how many states had to ratify it in order for it to be in effect?

* Does enumeration affect the income tax levied on citizens in various states?

* A person opposed to swearing in an oath may say, instead: (solemnly) _____.

General-knowledge questions were even more problematic. An applicant might be asked how many jelly beans filled a jar, or how many bubbles a bar of soap produced, or how many seeds a watermelon had.

As was the case throughout the South, blacks wishing to register to vote in Alabama were also required to find an already registered voter to vouch under oath for their qualifications. Although the pool of "vouchers" was limited—Perry County had just 265 registered black voters in 1961—registrars often capped the number of people one person could vouch for at two or three. Those determined to register despite these hurdles risked more than failure; because their names were listed in the newspaper, they were subject to threats from landlords, employers, and others wishing to keep them off the voting rolls.

While trying to register, Avery joined the newly formed Perry County Civic League (PCCL), an organization dedicated to winning equality for blacks. Its bold, charismatic founder, Albert Turner, was the college-educated son of a local sharecropper. PCCL initially held its meetings in a small church in rural West Perry, then moved to Zion United in downtown Marion. "We pooled our little resources and began to go and ask people to become registered voters to make a difference. It was a nonviolent thing," says Avery. The organization also helped would-be registrants prepare forms and study for the tests.

With the assistance of the U.S. Department of Justice, PCCL went to federal court and won an injunction in late 1962 preventing the county registrars from engaging in "any act or practice which involves or results in distinctions based on race or color in the registration of voters." In July 1963, Avery, her husband, and about thirty other Perry County blacks became registered voters. But over the next eighteen months, the number of black voters in Perry County did not increase significantly. Neither did the number of people willing to protest for the right.

The lack of participation was understandable. Many African Americans in the Black Belt lived and worked on farms owned by whites or sharecropped on white-owned land. And the vast majority of the landowners were unsympathetic to a movement they perceived as a threat to their own power.

"When Dr. King came to Marion, the first thing that the white landowner, plantation owner, did was threaten: 'You and your kid get involved in it, then you got to move,'" explains Walter Dobyne, an African American who grew up a few miles outside Marion on a white-owned "plantation" called Sprott Estate. "They had this pact: 'If blacks participate in the civil rights movement and demonstrate in Marion, we're gonna run them off our place.' And they did."

Dobyne, who as a teen hunted, fished, and shared food and drink with many white friends, noted an unmistakable cooling of relations once King came to Perry County early in 1965. "Prior to that we would pass a person in a car or walking and they'd throw their hands up and wave at you. But after the movement came in, you'd pass a white and he would throw his hand up out of habit, but then he'd think about what he was doing and take it down. He didn't want to wave at you anymore."

The situation was just as bad in nearby Dallas County, where blacks over the age of twenty-one accounted for 51 percent of the population, but only 2 percent of registered voters.

Just as the PCCL had been active for some years in Marion, so, too, had the Dallas County Voters League (DCVL) been active in Selma.

Nicknamed the Queen City of the Black Belt, Selma sits on the banks of the Alabama River in the lower western part of the state. Its name, which means high seat or throne, derives from "The Songs of Selma," epic poetry written by the Scotsman

James Macpherson. A major Confederate manufacturing center during the Civil War, Selma was a target of several Union
attacks. On April 2, 1865, General James H. Wilson captured
the city and some 2,700 soldiers who were under the command
of General Nathan Bedford Forrest, who later served as first
grand wizard of the Ku Klux Klan. Wilson's men burned the
rebel arsenal and foundry as well as many private homes and
businesses.

In 1963, local black activists including Frederick Douglas
Reese and Amelia Boynton began working with Bernard and
Colia Lafayette of the Student Nonviolent Coordinating Committee (SNCC) to register those who had been constitutionally
disenfranchised since the early 1900s. SNCC had been founded
in the spring of 1960 by leaders of sit-ins in Greensboro, North
Carolina, and had gained credibility through its involvement in
the 1961 Freedom Rides. By the end of that year, it was organizing voter registration efforts in Mississippi.

Reese was president of DCVL, pastor of a Baptist church,
and taught mathematics at all-black R. B. Hudson High School.
He also headed the all-black Selma Teachers Association, which
was among the earliest groups to march in support of voting
rights. Inspired by the teachers, high school students and groups
representing beauticians, undertakers, and other professions had
soon joined the drive.

Boynton, who had been a teacher in Georgia and then an
agent for the U.S. Department of Agriculture in Alabama, had
cofounded DCVL in the 1930s. With her husband, Samuel, she
had long worked for civil rights and the right to vote. In 1964,
a year after Samuel's death, she had become the first African
American woman, as well as the first female Democrat, to run
for Congress in Alabama. Her home was the base for movement

activity in Selma, used by Dr. King and others for meetings and lodging.

DCVL's effort was hindered in July 1964 when an Alabama state court judge, James Hare, issued an injunction barring any meeting of three or more people under the umbrella of organizations such as DCVL and SNCC. At great risk, Reese, Boynton, and fellow blacks Marie Foster, Ulysses Blackmon, Earnest Doyle, James E. Gildersleeve, Rev. J. D. Hunter, and Rev. Henry Shannon Jr.—known as the "Courageous Eight"—continued to meet and plan. Later in the year, after SNCC experienced internal difficulties, the Courageous Eight asked SCLC to come to Selma and push for voting rights.

SCLC had been debating such a push for well over a year. After September 1963, when four young black girls were killed in the infamous bombing at Birmingham's 16th Street Baptist Church, husband and wife activists James Bevel and Diane Nash had designed a voter registration effort that came to be known as the Alabama Project. As Nash later explained in a television documentary, "We felt that if blacks in Alabama had the right to vote, they could protect black children."

Born in Chicago in 1938, Nash graduated from Fisk University in Nashville. There she attended workshops led by James Lawson, who as a Methodist missionary in India had studied Gandhi's approach to nonviolent resistance. Summoned south by King himself, the charming minister led workshops training activists in the tactics of nonviolent action.

Along with Bevel, who attended the American Baptist Theological Seminary in Nashville, and others including John Lewis, C. T. Vivian, and Bernard Lafayette, Nash led the Nashville Student Movement. In 1960, the movement organized sit-ins that resulted in the integration of Nashville's downtown establishments. Under Lawson's tutelage, the Nashville sit-ins became a demonstration of the movement's strategic acumen.

After helping found SNCC with other student leaders and longtime activist Ella Baker, Nash and Bevel married and moved to Birmingham. There Bevel organized SCLC's Birmingham Children's Crusade. On May 3, 1963, the day after a thousand students were arrested during a nonviolent march for civil rights, Bevel led a second march. As children came out of the same church that would be bombed four months later, Birmingham's commissioner of public safety, Eugene "Bull" Connor, ordered that high-pressure fire hoses and German shepherds be used on them. Caught on film, the police action resulted in some of the most disturbing (and iconic) images of the civil rights era and sparked international outrage.

Approached by Bevel and Nash to launch a voting rights project in Alabama, SCLC initially chose to focus its efforts elsewhere, principally a nonviolent effort to bring St. Augustine, Florida, in compliance with federal civil rights laws and court decisions such as *Brown v. Board of Education*. The St. Augustine Movement involved weeks of protests and clashes with white segregationists and focused valuable national and international attention on the civil rights movement.

After passage of the Civil Rights Act in November 1964, a voting rights bill seemed the next logical step. But President Lyndon Johnson opted to defer introducing such legislation until he could win congressional approval of his Great Society agenda, a broad social welfare program. He explained that he could not get the southern votes necessary to pass that initiative if voting rights were included.

Dr. King was not happy. Returning from Oslo, Norway, with the Nobel Peace Prize in December 1964, he said he would travel to "the valley filled with literally thousands of Negroes in Alabama and Mississippi who are brutalized, intimidated, and sometimes killed when they seek to register and vote." At a meeting with the president, he explained, "Political reform is as necessary as anything if we are going to solve all these other problems."

On January 2, 1965, SCLC launched an initiative in Selma and Marion. This would be step one of a larger plan. "We wanted to raise the issue of voting to the point where we could take it outside of the Black Belt," King's trusted lieutenant Rev. C. T. Vivian later said. "We were using Selma as a way to shake Alabama . . . so that it would no longer be a Selma issue or even an Alabama issue but a national issue." Nash and Bevel came to Selma, too.

Soon King was behind bars. On February 1, he and Rev. Ralph Abernathy were arrested as they led 250 people protesting the slow pace of voter registration in Dallas County. As he had done so famously in 1963 in Birmingham, King sent a letter from jail, where he was held for five days. In all capital letters, he noted: "THIS IS SELMA, ALABAMA. THERE ARE MORE NEGROES IN JAIL WITH ME THAN THERE ARE ON THE VOTING ROLLS."

While King, Vivian, Bevel, Nash, Reese, Boynton, and other leaders, including Hosea Williams, Andrew Young, and Bernard Lafayette, were shaking things up in Selma, James Orange was roiling the waters in Marion. A formidable man who stood well over six feet tall and weighed three hundred pounds, Orange had helped Bevel organize the children's demonstrations in his hometown of Birmingham. On February 3, he led hundreds of Marion youngsters in a school boycott to protest the previous day's arrest of sixteen blacks.

The sixteen had been jailed after staging a sit-in at a

segregated restaurant. Years later, one of those arrested, Lincoln High School senior Walter Dobyne, remembered trying to get service at a different establishment, Marion Drugs, earlier that day. "Five of us went in and sat down [at the lunch counter]," he said. "At first, they were reluctant to come over and wait on us. But we didn't leave, and they finally took our order. We all ordered Cokes, and when they came, the first person who tasted it said, 'Something's wrong.' Each one of us tasted our drink and they had put salt in it."

Orange's army of approximately seven hundred students gathered in front of the jail where the sixteen were being held and began singing freedom songs. "Sing one more song and you are under arrest," a trooper told them.

As the *New York Times* reported: "James Orange . . . turned to the students and said, 'Sing another song.' They did and the troopers held them under arrest and loaded them into school buses. . . . They were charged with either unlawful assembly or disobeying an officer, hauled off to a work camp sixty miles away, and held under bonds of $100 each."

The arrests and detention of the Perry County schoolchildren changed the mind-set of many adults who had been cautious about getting involved. Richard Bryant, a local Baptist pastor, would explain: "We have a saying that you don't mess with a black woman's children. . . . So then you got the black women involved because they have to figure out where their children was—some were in cells in jail and different places. So the women went [to the meetings], then that means the men had to go. They forgot about whose place they was on and who they was working for."

Orange's strategy of engaging schoolchildren was not novel— it had been employed in Birmingham—but it was calculated.

He correctly figured that the students' arrests would set off the type of chain reaction vital to so many local campaigns throughout the civil rights movement:

First, dramatize the grievance with a nonviolent protest. Next, anticipate and accept being arrested, harassed, or abused. As the injustice in question takes center stage in the media, sympathy for the cause will grow, often accelerated by ugly responses to peaceful protests. Meanwhile, continue building the ranks by finding ways for everyone to get involved.

Reflecting on the successful lunch counter sit-ins in Nashville, James Lawson noted that involvement of "the whole community" was crucial to success. "In the nonviolent movement, everyone can be a participant," he explained. "Children can participate, women can participate, men can participate. Young people, old people. Everyone can do the work."

After the arrests, Avery recalls, "the parents came to the meeting that night looking for their children. We told them that to see their children, they'd have to come to town the next day. So they did, and they chose to march."

These adult marchers were also arrested and taken to detention camps. Avery describes the conditions: "It was terrible— eighty-five women in a room with no heat and one commode that didn't even work. But there was a plunger in there, and we finally got the commode open. Any water we wanted had to come from the commode."

After several hours without food, the prisoners were given black-eyed peas and corn bread for dinner. "It was plain cornmeal, without any baking powder or anything," Avery remembers. "So we took the bread, and when we took the crust apart there was rat manure in it. So I didn't eat. Most of us didn't eat that night. So they gave it back to us the next morning."

After everyone was released from the detention camps, Orange continued to engage Marion's youth. On February 15, the final day of the month for registration, some four hundred teens stood outside the courthouse in support of three hundred adults who had gone inside to register. Dr. King soon arrived and was met with applause.

Earlier in the day, King had been in Selma, where eight hundred young people marched in support of 1,400 adults standing in a line that stretched five blocks. According to the *Times*, "There was no violence and there were no arrests, but only a few names were added to the registration books."

On Thursday, February 18, Orange again leads a protest in Marion. FBI agents are on the ground and on the second floor of a nearby building monitoring the events—as they do throughout Alabama and wherever else the movement is active. One of those agents, Archibald L. Riley, compiles an official log for the Bureau.

Riley notes that at 10:56 a.m., Orange joined "about 125 Negroes," most of them students, who came out of Zion United church and headed toward the courthouse across the street. "Chief of Police was taking names, addresses, dates of birth, and who they lived with."

At 11:55 a.m., as the protestors stand by the courthouse, the chief announces that he is "going to send a letter to the State Board of Education and to families." Riley adds: "May get ORANGE and SHAW [another organizer] for contributing."

Thirty minutes later, Orange is observed "inducing them not to attend school. 3 were under 16 and are witnesses." Within the hour, he is under arrest.

Word of the arrest quickly reaches SCLC and SNCC headquarters in Selma. At 2:30, another FBI agent reports to Riley
via radio transmission that "a new crew" has arrived. The group
includes "WILLIE BOLTON [*sic*] SCLC, LEROY MOTON
of SNCC," and "GEORGE BAKER, SCLC (white), Downers
Grove, Illinois." (Bolton is in fact Bolden.)

George Baker has been in Alabama for only two days. Raised
in the Quaker tradition, he has taken a leave of absence from his
studies at Blackburn College in downstate Illinois to participate
in the movement. After the SNCC office in Chicago turned
down his offer to volunteer, he spoke with Lafayette, a family acquaintance who had previously worked with the American Friends Service Committee. Lafayette got him a job in
the SCLC's Selma office and a bed in Amelia Boynton's home,
where many activists were fed and lodged.

During his stay in the South, Baker has kept a diary. His first
day, February 16, was eventful:

> Was listening to someone talk to King (de lawd) on the
> phone. Called for another march to county courthouse.
> Asked me if I wanted to come along and get arrested. I said
> I wanted to get settled first.
>
> As it turned out C.T. Vivian led 60 people to
> courthouse. . . . [Sheriff Jim] Clark told them to leave, but
> [they] wouldn't, saying they had legal business. Vivian was
> smashed in the jaw by Clark's fist and smashed in the teeth
> by a billy club. All this time Vivian said, "Don't beat us,
> if we're wrong arrest us." I was in the office when the call
> came in and they called a doctor and a dentist to go to the
> jail 'cause Vivian was arrested. Later on met Andy Young,
> King's chief assistant . . .

Sent to Marion with Willie Bolden by Hosea Williams after Orange's arrest on the eighteenth, Baker sees about one hundred children standing in a line singing freedom songs. State troopers and local police, "all in helmets and carrying billy clubs," surround the youngsters. After conferring with local leaders in the church, Baker goes back outside. There he is approached by three men in suits—two investigators for Governor Wallace and one FBI agent—and asked for personal information. "They were very pleasant," Baker writes. But, he notes, Marion's chief of police, T. O. Harris, who followed them, was "a little colder."

As 7 p.m. approaches, Zion United begins to fill up. Willie Nell Avery takes a seat on a bench near the front row so she can help lead the singing. Albert Turner sits up front, too. He will run the meeting, at which Willie Bolden and C. T. Vivian will be the featured speakers. Baker sits towards the back. So, too, does Rev. James Dobynes, a local minister who will be at the head of the march with Turner and Bolden.*

Several hundred men and women and teens—almost all of whom are black—soon fill the nondescript brick church. Among the assembled is a typical family moved to protest by the events of a lifetime and of this day: eighty-two-year-old Cager Lee; his fifty-year-old daughter, Viola Jackson; her twenty-six-year-old son, Jimmie Lee; and her sixteen-year-old daughter, Emma Jean. None has a voter registration card.

All things being equal, Cager Lee, a farmer, would have first been able to vote in 1904, when Theodore Roosevelt defeated Alton B. Parker for the presidency. But he has been denied the right to cast a ballot in that election and the fifteen presidential

---

*Although Walter Dobyne and Rev. James Dobynes spell their last names differently, they are cousins.

contests that have followed, as well as congressional, state, and local races. Jimmie Lee Jackson, a graduate of Lincoln High School who farms and chops pulpwood for six dollars a day, has tried to register several times over the last few years, without success. His grandfather has often accompanied him to the registrar's office.

An Alabama state investigator monitoring the meeting at the church sends periodic messages to the FBI's Riley.

6:58: Started singing in church.

Steeped in the history of slave songs and the traditions of black church music, freedom songs played a central role in the civil rights movement. The soaring voices and thunderous clapping of the assembled punctuated impassioned oratory and frank discussion at mass meetings across the South.

Freedom songs helped spread the word about the movement and drew reticent folks into the fold. For the many who were unfamiliar with political gatherings, but very familiar with church services, the music-filled mass meetings were a gateway to political involvement. And once involved, freedom songs fired people up, fostering courage before, during, and after dangerous protests, marches, and other nonviolent actions.

Sung collectively, freedom songs embody the vision of a shared, participatory movement. The songs don't emphasize star performers and virtuosic solos (although there are stunning exceptions), but focus on the melding of voices ("If you can't sing, sing louder" is the saying).

7:10: Crowds have been going in and singing loud and enthusiastic. ALBERT TURNER is running the program.

"I witnessed for the first time a real Negro, gospel fundamental prayer meeting," Baker writes in his diary. "About four people had happiness spasms as they received the spirit. I was very moved by the emotion present."

7:13: About 300 were in church at this time.

At 7:36 Riley observes three cars driven by white males pass by, and at 7:47 "eight state trooper cars parked by the courthouse." Over the next twenty minutes, more cars driven by white males drive past the church.

8:19: About 400 in church. WILLIE BOLTON [*sic*] spoke some. C. T. VIVIAN supposed to be here, but hasn't shown up yet.

The twenty-six-year-old Bolden met King in Savannah, Georgia, four years earlier. Before coming to Alabama, he had been involved in the St. Augustine Movement. In his speech at Zion United, Bolden recalls King's post-Oslo conversation with President Johnson about the mountaintop and the valley as well as the SCLC leader's promise that there would be a voting rights act.

Bolden then challenges everyone in the church to join the effort: "It is time that you stand up and be men and women and stop scratching when you ain't itching and grinning when you ain't tickled."

Vivian has arrived from Selma by the time Bolden finishes. He wasn't excited about coming, as many of the SCLC leaders have left Selma for a few days and he is, in effect, in charge there. But Orange's arrest was important, and the opportunity to exhort a huge crowd to keep up the good fight cannot be ignored.

As Baker noted in his diary, the slight, forty-year-old Vivian was struck and jailed just two days earlier after leading would-be registrants to the Dallas County Courthouse. His attacker, forty-two-year-old sheriff Jim Clark, is a beefy World War II veteran and cattle rancher, who often dresses in military garb and carries a cattle prod. Clark wears a button that proclaims his timetable for integration: "NEVER." Since the beginning of the year, he has ordered the arrest of hundreds of peaceful protestors in Selma.

In late January, Clark had another well-publicized encounter on the courthouse steps with a fifty-four-year-old African American woman. After Annie Lee Cooper and others waited in line for hours to register, Clark ordered them to go home. Then, according to Cooper, the sheriff pushed her with his cattle prod. Cooper, who weighed more than two hundred pounds, responded with a right hook to Clark's jaw. The punch knocked him to the ground. Cooper was quickly arrested.

Not content to simply use his own men within his own jurisdiction, Sheriff Clark has also recruited Klansmen and others as possemen, a "mobile anti–civil rights force" to harass movement participants outside Dallas County. On the night of February 18, he is again outside his jurisdiction. He stands near Zion United in street clothes carrying a nightstick. "Don't you have enough trouble of your own in Selma?' someone asks the sheriff.

"Things got a little too quiet for me over in Selma tonight and it made me nervous," he replies.

Vivian and others would later hear rumors that Clark, still seething over the events at the courthouse, came to Marion seeking vengeance. Although never verified, word was he had talked with his friends at the state police and was hoping for the opportunity to harm or even kill Vivian when the protestors marched out of the church.

The civil rights leaders counted on law enforcement officials like Clark and Bull Connor of Birmingham to show the true, vicious colors of those who oppose integration. These men were ticking time bombs and when they exploded—which they inevitably did—the world became more sympathetic to those in the movement who were able to act peacefully and with dignity when confronted with bare fists and billy clubs or dogs and fire hoses. Enough sympathy might pressure President Johnson and Congress to enact a voting rights bill.

Vivian, who participated in his first sit-in at a cafeteria in Peoria, Illinois, as a teenager, knows men like Clark well. After attending Western Illinois University, he, like James Bevel and John Lewis, studied for the ministry at American Baptist Theological Seminary in Nashville. And like them, he took Lawson's workshops and helped lead sit-ins. After moving on to SCLC, he also participated in the St. Augustine protests.

Speaking almost fifty years after the Selma and Marion campaign, Vivian remembers Clark as a "bully," but emphasizes that the sheriff was hardly unique. "His society, his culture allowed bullies," he says. "Look at the values that the churches they went to taught. You can't be good under those circumstances."

When Clark angrily denied Vivian and his contingent of would-be registrants entry to the Dallas County Courthouse on February 16, Vivian asked him, "What do you tell your wife at night? What do you tell your children?"

Clark grew angrier as cameras recorded Vivian's refusal to back down. "We have come to be here because they are registering at this time," Vivian said.

"Turn that light out," Clark told a newsman. "You're blinding me, and I can't enforce the law with the light in my face."

Vivian continued, "We have come to register and this is our reason for being here. We're not—"

Clark interrupted: "You're blinding me with that light. Move back." He then hit Vivian, knocking him down the courthouse steps to the sidewalk.

The minister never lost his composure. "You can arrest us. You can arrest us, Sheriff Clark. You don't have to beat us," he said. Rising, he continued, "If we're wrong, why don't you arrest us?"

A policeman said, "Why don't you get out of in front of the camera and go on. Go on."

"It's not a matter of being in front of the camera," Vivian responded. "It's a matter of facing your sheriff and facing your judge. We're willing to be beaten for democracy, and you misuse democracy in this street. You beat people bloody in order that they will not have the privilege to vote. You beat me in the side and then hide your blows. We have come to register to vote."

The confrontation did not surprise Vivian, but his own words did. "When I started that day, I had no idea what I was gonna say. I wasn't even thinking about that," he says. "I just knew when the time came, I would say something. I had no idea it would be that great. But it just kept coming out, almost as though I was in the courtroom."

He wasn't thinking about the cameras. "When you're being beaten up, you don't think about that." But he did remember the training he'd received from Lawson in Nashville. "We can never allow violence to defeat nonviolence. You have to resist the impulse to turn in the other direction and leave. You have to stay. Leaving is the last thing you want to do. If you turn away, what are you gonna tell the people on the line with you?"

Anxious to get back to Selma, Vivian exits Zion United by the back door into a waiting car after speaking to the crowd— now estimated at four hundred by law enforcement officials. Albert Turner then takes the stage. Twenty-eight-year-old "Big

Al," the fifth of twelve Turner children, graduated at age sixteen from high school—where, his brother Robert remembers, he was never hesitant to challenge his teachers. After graduating from college, the five-foot-nine-inch, 210-pound Turner worked as a brick mason. A few years later, Big Al told his brother: "I'm gonna lay this trowel down and work for the people."

Robert Turner remembers frequent debates with his older brother. "Our arguing was this: He said politics, and I said economics. He thought voting and politics was the key to black survival. And I said, 'No, we need an economic base so that we can hire folks and don't have to beg and scratch.' And he said, 'No, we gotta vote.'"

Big Al tells those assembled at Zion United that they will march to the jailhouse in a line, two by two, and sing freedom songs. If stopped by the police, Dobynes, a thirty-eight-year-old Baptist minister born and raised in Perry County, is to offer a prayer. Then they are to turn around and march back inside the church.

As always, Turner emphasizes that anyone who doesn't think he or she can remain peaceful should stay in the church. "All you all standing here, march and go out the front door first," he says. "But if you have a weapon, leave your weapons inside. We gonna be peaceful, and we don't want nobody starting no riot."

And if the police start a riot? Most in attendance have already been trained to remain nonviolent when attacked. "If we were to get beaten, all of us knew how to fold and let them hit our backs instead of our heads or brains," says Avery.

In just a few minutes, that training will prove to be essential.

CHAPTER TWO

"I GOT HIM . . ."

February 18, 1965

As the meeting inside Zion United comes to an end, George Baker and his fellow SCLC workers move outside and sit on the church steps to discuss strategy.

Zion sits on the northeast corner of Jefferson and Pickens. The protestors will exit the front door onto Pickens and march one block north to the jail. On their way, they will pass the bus station, the post office, an office building, and a Ford dealership on the right, and the Perry County Courthouse on their left.

From his vantage point, Baker can see about fifty or sixty "helmeted police with billy clubs all over in the street." State troopers are stationed twenty feet apart from each other. The Marion police and Perry County sheriff's men are out in full force, too. Afraid that these officers as well as those they have deputized might attack, the organizers tell Baker that he is not to march. In case anything happens, he is to phone SCLC headquarters in Selma.

Now the line forms with Albert Turner, Willie Bolden, and Rev. James Dobynes at the front. They have only marched about fifty feet when they hear a voice over a loudspeaker. "You are hereby ordered to disperse," announces Marion chief of police T. O. Harris. "Go home or go back in the church." He tells them that they are breaking the law by having an "unlawful assembly."

Harris will later tell the FBI that earlier in the day he learned leaders were coming in from Selma and there were reports "they planned to put on a show that night." He and Perry County sheriff William Loftis then asked for additional help from the state police. Governor Wallace obliged by sending in troopers who, Harris said, "would not take the initiative, but would back local officials up and follow our direction."

Harris will also say that he witnessed newsmen coming in larger numbers than usual and felt "their presence was an indication that something was planned that they considered newsworthy and presumably things could get out of hand." As a result, he and Loftis devised a plan "to stop the march before it got too far from the church to prevent it being spread over too large an area to control."

Hearing the order to disperse, Rev. Dobynes kneels on the sidewalk. "May we pray before we go back?" he asks.

Suddenly the streetlights go out. "While I was praying a trooper struck me across the head with his stick, opening a bloody wound," Dobynes will later say in a sworn statement.

They drug me off and carried me to jail, beating me all the way. I was charged with unlawful assembly. I kept praying all the way to jail. They kept telling me to shut up, but I kept praying. When I got to jail, blood was streaming down my face like water. Someone at the jail said, "You black ____ ____, you ought to bleed to death."

Dobyne's line mates are also attacked. A cop grabs Bolden by his jeans and delivers him to an unnamed official. "What's your name, nigger?" asks the man, whom Bolden later calls "the sheriff." Before the young organizer can respond, "the sheriff" sticks his pistol in Bolden's mouth and cocks the gun. "If you breathe, nigger, I'll blow your f—in' brains out."

Self, don't breathe, Bolden tells himself.

The sheriff accuses Bolden of being an outside agitator who has come to town to "upset my negroes, my niggers." The police, as well as the white establishment, believe everything was fine before SCLC came to town and organized the local blacks. The sheriff then pulls the pistol out of Bolden's mouth, cracking one of Bolden's teeth. Bolden is hit on the head and carted off to jail.

While the sheriff deals with Bolden, a trooper confronts Turner, asking, "Are you an outsider?" Turner identifies himself as a "local leader." A Marion policeman vouches for him, but the trooper still wants to see some identification. As Big Al reaches for his driver's license, he, too, is clubbed.

Baker never gets a chance to call Selma. As the attack begins, he sees three police officers pointing in his direction. He turns away for an instant and the next thing he knows "they have surrounded me and are hitting me all over." His glasses are knocked off and fall to the ground.

One officer grabs Baker's left arm and one his right. A third cop walks behind him. "They started taking me to jail," Baker later writes. "As we got further away from the commotion, they started hitting me with their billy clubs."

On the way to the jail, the police push Baker "very hard" into a hurricane fence. Once inside the jailhouse, they push him into a brick wall. "Right outside my cell, they let go of me and I received a blow on my head from behind that sent me right to the floor."

Baker is put into a cell with Dobynes. "[Rev. Dobynes's] skull was split and I tried to give him first aid as well as I could," he recalled. "Then I felt my own head and realized it was bleeding very freely. There was blood all over my clothes. The bleeding stopped around 4:00 in the morning. I used toilet paper for a bandage. [Rev. Dobynes] was a diabetic and had some sort of epilepsy. He needed medicine for both conditions daily. Neither of us received *any* medical attention for our entire stay in jail." Baker later requires seven stiches to "sew up my head."

At 9:20 p.m., just five minutes after he noted the march began, FBI agent Riley records: "Troopers put rest back in church midst loud yelling and screaming. Some Negroes yelling and cursing and saying, 'You can't take all of us.'"

Willie Nell Avery and several other men and women who had been sitting on the benches farthest from the door are still lined up waiting to leave Zion United when many of those who did get out begin to return. A policeman on the front steps clubs some of them as they reenter the church.

Turner returns and takes charge. Years later, he will say that the protestors' commitment to nonviolence ended at that moment: "We weren't going to have anybody come into the church and beat folks about the head."

After the men line up in a row by the front door, Turner tells the troopers at the church's entrance, "If you get by one, the next one will get you." The troopers try to enter, but, Turner remembers, "After we busted a couple of heads, they stopped attempting to get through the door."

The troopers settle for surrounding Zion United and busting

a few heads of their own. Seeking refuge at the church and finding the front blocked, Albert Jackson (no relation to Jimmie Lee
or Michael Jackson) tries the back entrance. There he is struck
across the head from behind with a nightstick. The wound requires three stitches.

Where is the press? When the newsmen first arrived, the chief
instructed them to remain across the street from the church, in
front of City Hall. They were not to use lights, as those might
blind the police or interfere with their work.

Now reporters and cameramen are also under fire. White
townspeople knock them to the ground. The vigilantes spray-
paint camera lenses so there can be no images of the attack.
NBC's Richard Valeriani is hit so hard with an ax handle that
he thinks he is going to die. His attacker stands over him and
snarls, "We don't have doctors for people like you." Valeriani is
finally rescued from the mob and taken to the hospital, where he
is stitched up and kept for observation.

United Press International (UPI) photographer Pete Fisher
is struck on the head with what he believes is a nightstick by
a white male in a brown uniform. As he seeks refuge in City
Hall, he is punched in the face "five or six times" by another
white male wearing a white twill shirt with the lettering of a
local service station. Fisher tells the FBI that, when attacked, he
was within four feet of uniformed law enforcement officials who
observed the incidents but did nothing to prevent or stop them.

Valeriani and Fisher, like other newsmen, abandoned plans
for a quiet evening and hurried from Selma to Marion after receiving a heads-up from the SCLC. Neither the civil rights leaders nor the media hoped for bloodshed on this or any evening.
At the same time, however, they realized that images of police
or vigilante violence served their respective agendas.

Whenever an event had the potential to explode, the movement wanted the press present. In this symbiotic relationship, the participants sought public sympathy for their cause from northerners witnessing southern brutality on the evening news. Those covering the participants sought more viewers or readers. The more eyes watching, the better for all . . . except those armed with cans of spray paint and ax handles seeking to maintain the status quo.

After a long wait, Turner asks the troopers if they are "intending to keep us in the church all night." The troopers say that everyone can go home. At his car, Turner is again surrounded by police. "I was about half-mad then," he will recall. "I threw [the car] in reverse and came back like there was nobody there . . . hoping somebody was back there." As he speeds off, the police pound his car with their nightsticks.

C. T. Vivian, who has also sped off in a car, does not immediately make it back to Selma. "We were going down the hill towards the highway when we saw these police cars coming up the hill [heading into Marion]," he later says. "I was trying to figure out what was going on. Then, when we got near the intersection that runs into the road to Selma, I saw this big policeman standing there with a flashlight directing the police cars where to turn. I was wondering, 'What is this?' So I hesitated and thought about it, and decided to go back up the hill."

When Vivian gets back to town, Zion United is dark and empty. He goes to the funeral home a few doors down from the church on Jefferson to find out what is going on. Its owner, Hampton Lee, a longtime civil rights activist, tells him that the police attacked the marchers. Vivian then hurries back to SCLC headquarters in Selma. Later, the police come looking for him at the funeral home.

In the days that follow, rumors will circulate that Jim Clark and the state troopers planned the attack with one goal in mind: to get C. T. Vivian. And if they couldn't get the minister? Get another black man.

Plenty of black men do feel the troopers' billy clubs after the streetlights go out. Some are marchers. But many are not.

John C. Lewis (no relation to the civil rights leader) is married and the father of six children. Born and raised in Marion, he works at the Marion Institute (a military junior college), is on the board of trustees of a local Baptist church, and has never served any jail time. Driving home from work about an hour after the march was halted, he is pulled over by a state trooper about a quarter mile outside Marion. The trooper asks to see his driver's license. (This random stop suggests the troopers may have been looking for a particular person, perhaps Vivian.)

A second trooper arrives almost immediately. "Who you have there?" he asks his fellow officer.

"He's a pretty good boy. He's just off his job," replies the first trooper.

The second trooper asks where Lewis works. After Lewis replies, the trooper says, "Let's beat him anyway." And he does, striking Lewis with his nightstick several times.

"I fell out on the ground for dead," Lewis will say in a sworn statement. "I was badly hurt, but I thought it best to act dead lest they kill me."

The troopers debate whether to leave Lewis where he is, lying partly on the highway. They drag him to his car, then put his head and shoulders on the backseat and leave his legs on the ground. They know he is badly injured, but they drive off.

At the hospital, he needs six stitches for his head wound and is treated for a broken wrist. "I was not arrested or charged with anything, but just beaten and left on the highway," Lewis says.

Elbert Johnson is also attacked. As he leaves a restaurant near the town square with friends, a trooper tells him to get off the street. Johnson tries to get into a friend's car, but there is no room so he starts back to the café. The trooper hits him in the stomach with his nightstick.

Johnson tries to explain that he is going to get off the street. Now the trooper delivers a hard blow to the side of the head with his nightstick. "I don't know why he hit me," Johnson says.

George Sawyer has a notion why the police hit Lewis, Johnson, and several others, including himself. Sawyer is standing outside the Piggly Wiggly store two blocks from the church when troopers attack with nightsticks. "I fell down into a deep ravine which seemed 100 feet deep. I was glad to get to the bottom. They might have killed me if I had not." Sawyer, who will require three stitches in his head, walks along a stream at the bottom of the ravine. "Several times I had to hide from the troopers who were racing around in their cars—looking for Negroes I guess."

Chief Harris will claim to be unaware of the troopers' wanton brutality away from the church. And the confrontation with those who marched out of Zion United? "It appeared to me that the front of the Negro line made a surge forward and someone motioned those behind to go forward," Harris will later tell the FBI. He will also say that he saw three men (presumably Dobynes, Bolden, and Turner) taken out of the line, but "since they were in custody I didn't watch them."

His men and the troopers did "push [the protestors] back toward Zion Methodist church" with their billy clubs. But Harris will say he saw no officers attacking anyone with a club. Sheriff

Loftis will add that he saw no one struck by a club or any of the troopers, but did see someone throw a piece of concrete at the troopers.

Harris and Sheriff Loftis also tell the FBI that, contrary to reports from the protestors and the press, the streetlights were never turned off. They insist that the light over the church steps was turned off before the marchers emerged. That light, they say, was controlled exclusively by the church.

The press sees and experiences something far different than the chief of police and the county sheriff. In a front-page story in the *New York Times*, under the headline NEGROES BEATEN IN ALABAMA RIOT, John Herbers describes seeing troopers struggling with someone at the front of the line of marchers. "The other Negroes in line refused orders to move," Herbers writes. "Then state troopers moved, shouting and jabbing and swinging their nightsticks. The Negroes began screaming and falling back around the entrance of the church."

"Troopers armed with billy-clubs stormed into a group of 100 Negro men and women to break up a protest demonstration at the town square," John Lynch of UPI reports:

> Then came the attack on newsmen by white spectators. "We've got permission to kick the —— out of them," one man shouted. . . . The Negroes were driven back, screaming and praying, into a church where the demonstration originated. Blue helmeted troopers, wielding sawed-off shotguns, kept the crowd in the church for 45 minutes before letting it disperse.

Unlike Sheriff Jim Clark, Chief T. O. Harris did not wear a "NEVER" button on his uniform. In his remarks to a group of students at the University of Alabama several months after the police intervention in Marion, Harris seemed to regard himself as a moderate, tolerant—even enlightened—in his view of African Americans. He acknowledged "that there have been some injustices suffered by the Negro," but added, "the Negro race does not have a monopoly on injustice."

He also acknowledged that Alabama's voting rights standards were too high, but criticized the tactics of those seeking to change those standards. Civil disobedience has no place in America, he argued. "The progress the Negro has made has been made legally in the courts and not in the streets. We have legal processes in this country and things must be done legally." He made no reference to Alabama judge James Hare's ruling barring meetings of more than three blacks under the auspices of civil rights groups.

Harris challenged the students to "go up and down the scale and see where you draw the line" at integration. Which of the following were they willing to do, he asked: "Sell to negroes in a store, work with negroes, work for negroes, live next door to negroes, go to school with negroes, go to church with negroes, attend sporting events, concerts and other public functions with negroes, go swimming with negroes, go to dances with negroes, have negroes attend private socials in your home, date negroes, marry negroes."

He did not reveal where he placed himself on this spectrum, but told his audience there were different "type negroes" to consider: "the cultured, educated, well dressed negro; or the uneducated, uncultured, laboring negro; or . . . the shiftless, unemployed, dirty field hand."

Despite his personal feelings, Harris told the students, he was a "professional law enforcement officer dedicated to . . .

enforcing the law fairly and impartially without regard to race, religion, creed, or color." And the police's actions on the evening of February 18 had been necessary, he explained, "to stop the night-time march . . . and what we had been informed would be a large scale riot."

While Harris's men and the state troopers are driving many of the marchers back into Zion United, some seventy-five to a hundred protestors branch off and run around the side of the church onto the sidewalk and street. Harris will tell the FBI he lost track of them.

The troopers do not lose track of them. Many marchers hurry along the west side of the church and head toward Mack's Café. Before Jerry Brown can enter, he is surrounded by state policemen, who beat him, opening two wounds on his head. Brown passes out. When he comes to, he heads for his truck. Again troopers jump him. A friend finally rescues him and drives him to the hospital. One wound requires six stitches, the other eight.[*]

Jimmie Lee Jackson's grandfather, Cager Lee, is also beaten. Standing in the backyard of the church, he is struck on the back of the head and knocked to the ground by an officer wearing a blue helmet. As the slight eighty-two-year-old tries to stand up, the officer kicks him twice. When he finally rises, Lee is pushed to the sidewalk and knocked down again.

Another officer arrives. "Goddamn, this is old Cager. Don't hit him," he says.

The cops leave and Cager heads to the café, three doors down from the church on Jefferson Street.

---

[*] Two days later, Brown was told by his employer that his services were no longer needed. Ned Evans Jr. was also beaten after marching, then dismissed from his job at Breland Saw Mill; his wife also lost her job as a housemaid in the Breland home. "We were both fired because we wanted to register to vote," Evans said.

Except for a sign out front that reads MACKS CAFÉ under a Coca-Cola logo and another handwritten sign over the front door that simply reads "Café," the two-story building looks more like a residence than a business. There's a small front yard with a modest tree. Six steps lead from the sidewalk to a front porch and the door. A second-floor balcony looks over Jefferson Street.

Upon entering you see a narrow dance hall to your right. Continuing on, you find an eating area with a handful of old wooden tables and booths and a food counter. A cigarette machine sits up against a wall near the front of the counter. Behind the counter is a small kitchen with a stove, and behind the kitchen is a storage room. Upstairs is a room used for recreation by the local VFW and others, a getaway to play cards and drink beer in after a hard day.

Over the years that follow, several different versions of what happened at Mack's Café on the evening of February 18, 1965, will emerge. The citizens of Marion who were there or who knew somebody there or heard about what happened say a state trooper brazenly shot an unarmed young man who posed no imminent threat, Jimmie Lee Jackson. The state troopers who were there acknowledge that James Bonard Fowler shot Jackson, but say he did so in self-defense.

Fowler and three other troopers provided statements to their superiors within hours of the shooting. According to state trooper Corporal B. J. Hoots: "A large group of Negroes were in front of a café just east of the court house and were throwing bottles and making insults toward the officers at the scene." The troopers advised the crowd to disperse and go home. "Instead, they went into the café and started throwing bricks and bottles at us," said Hoots.

The troopers followed the bottle throwers into the café

to arrest them. "I went in and saw a trooper trying to take a drink bottle away from a Negro woman and two Negro men were trying to take him away with bottles. I started toward the trooper to help him and I turned to see where it came from," Hoots continued. "The bottle apparently had been thrown from the rear of the building and when I turned around and started toward the trooper again, Corporal Fowler was wrestling with one of the Negro men who was on the trooper."

Hoots said, "The Negro had a hold of Corporal Fowler's gun in his holster apparently trying to get it out. I grabbed another Negro and threw him out of the way and about then I heard a shot and when I turned around the Negro that Corporal Fowler was wrestling with was on the floor. Another trooper had blood running down his face and I went to see about him. The Negro that Corporal Fowler had been wrestling with must have got up and left at this time."

The bloodied trooper was Frank E. Higginbotham. He reported: "I saw a tall black Negro in a light colored jacket standing across the room from us throw something in our direction. Something knocked my helmet off and this object this Negro threw hit me on the left forehead. I reached to draw my pistol and the blood blinded me. I stumbled outside." Higginbotham said a fellow trooper took him to Perry County Hospital, where "eleven stitches were required to close the wound on my forehead."

State trooper Corporal R. C. Andrews's account was slightly different: "Two colored males began beating Trooper Higginbotham with their bottles. Corporal Fowler tried to pull the two men away from Trooper Higginbotham, as Trooper Higginbotham had blood streaming down his face, and appeared to be falling."

At this point, said Andrews, "One of the Negroes hit Corp. Fowler on the head with a bottle and at the same time appeared to try and get his revolver. Corporal Fowler then threw up his arms and shoved the Negro backward, and the Negro again advanced toward Corporal Fowler, who drew his revolver and fired. Corporal Fowler shouted for someone to get a doctor, that someone had been shot."

Fowler did not acknowledge drawing his revolver:

I and three other officers went inside the café to arrest the bottle throwers and the bottles continued to hit us after getting inside. One trooper was attempting to arrest a woman with a bottle and trying to take the bottle away, when two men assaulted the officer from behind. I started to the assistance of the officer and had pulled one of his assailants off him, when he started assaulting me and trying to take my gun away and had got it approximately halfway out.

My assailant, being taller, heavier, and longer-armed than I, had struck me twice with a drink bottle and with his left hand had my pistol halfway out, when I ordered him to "Halt, you are under arrest," and I staggered backwards yelling "Get off, get off, you are under arrest." My backward movement away from him pulled my gun free from him and free from the holster. He hit me across the head, still coming toward me, and on the next blow which struck my hand the gun fired.

My assailant fell backwards and sat down. I continued backward 'til I got my balance and my assailant got up and ran out the door, knocking over several people and still cursing in a loud voice. I went over and picked up the unconscious officer who was bleeding about the head and assisted him to the car where other officers sped him to the hospital.

The Jackson family and others in the café gave statements to the FBI and sworn affidavits to a civil rights organization within days of the shooting. Cager Lee said that after arriving at Mack's, he saw his grandson and told him the police had hit him. "Jimmie took me out to get me to the hospital, but the troopers forced us back into the café." There, Lee said, they beat him again. He did not witness the shooting.

Emma Jean Jackson said that troopers were hitting her brother on the head and shoulders as they pushed him back into the café. Once inside, he moved near the counter. "Jimmie did not have anything in hand that I could see," she said. "I kept talking to Jimmie to calm him down. He did not appear as if he were going to cause trouble."

Frightened, Emma went to the rear of the café. "I picked up one bottle and threw it at a trooper, but don't believe I hit any of the troopers or anyone else," she told the FBI. "As I threw the bottle, I turned to go back into the storage room and fell on the floor. As I was on the floor, I heard a noise like a balloon breaking which could have been a shot."

Charles Pryor, who tried to help Emma Jean calm down her brother, said Jimmie Lee saw the troopers hit his mother. Then two troopers clubbed Jackson over the head. "Jackson picked up a bottle, but his sister took the bottle from him and put it back in the empty bottle case," said Pryor. "More troopers came in and started using guns, clubs, and their shotguns to force people out. Several Negroes were hit. I saw a trooper draw his revolver and heard two shots but couldn't see anything as there were four or five state troopers close to Jimmie Lee Jackson. Jackson fell against the lunch counter."

Willie Lee Smith did see the shooting. "A state trooper hit Jimmie Lee Jackson over the head with a club. The same state trooper drew his revolver out of his holster and fired one shot at Jimmie Lee Jackson. He had a look of pain on his face as he was hit by the bullet. He said nothing."

Jackson was unarmed, Smith told the FBI, adding, "The trooper that shot Jimmie Lee Jackson was about thirty years of age, about six feet tall, and slender. I believe I would recognize him if I should see him again."

Jeff Moore provided a similar account: "A trooper had used his club and hit Jimmie Lee Jackson over the head. Four troopers surrounded Jimmie Lee Jackson and I heard a gun go off two times. I did not know who was shot, but Jimmie Lee Jackson fell to the floor. I heard one trooper say, 'Who got him?' A trooper answered, 'I got him.'"

In all the chaos, Jimmie Lee's mother could not be certain of what happened. "All I know is that white men came into the café pushing and beating. One of them struck me in the head with a stick opening a wound that required several stitches. They knocked me to the floor and continued beating me," Viola Jackson said in her affidavit. "They had Jimmie on the floor of the café beating him also. When I got up I did not see Jimmie any more. I did not know he was shot until the next morning."

She added: "I have not given up yet. I still want my freedom and the right to vote."

The FBI interviewed Jimmie Lee Jackson, who it was noted had "no prior arrests," at Good Samaritan Hospital in Selma five days after the shooting:

Jackson stated he had gone into Mack's Café and was to pick up his grandfather Cager Lee to take him to the hospital as Lee had been hit on the head. As the two were leaving, they were forced back into the café and two troopers kept striking him on the side, arms, and head with their clubs.

Jackson stated he had been drinking a coke in Mack's Café after returning and saw a state trooper hitting his mother. He recalled having a coke bottle in his hand, but does not recall throwing the bottle. He does recall being held back by his sister Emma Jackson as he was going to assist his mother. He does recall being close to the door leading to the dance hall when a state trooper shot him in the stomach. He did not fall, but immediately ran out of Mack's Café and recalls being hit by troopers with their clubs several times until he was finally stopped in the front of the bus station.

Jimmie Lee Jackson exhibited the gunshot wound reflecting he was shot in the stomach and the bullet came out the left side. He also exhibited bruises on his right side. He had a cut on his head requiring three stitches.

Exactly what happened at Mack's Café? Did Jimmie Lee Jackson strike a trooper or throw a bottle? Did James Bonard Fowler's gun go off accidentally as he claimed? Or did Fowler draw his revolver as Trooper Andrews and others in the café stated? The fog of battle makes it impossible to say with certainty what transpired, other than that innocent marchers attacked by club-wielding local and state police sought refuge in a café—and when the troopers came in a young man was shot.

Before the state or local police interview any of the

townspeople who were in the café, including the beaten and shot Jimmie Lee Jackson, Perry County Sheriff Loftis, who was not at the café, acts swiftly to bring justice to Marion. As the FBI will later report:

A warrant was issued February 18, 1965 charging JIMMY JACKSON [*sic*], also known as JIMMY LEE JACKSON [*sic*], with "Assault with intent to murder." LOFTUS [sic] stated no bond or date for a hearing has been set as JACKSON is in Good Samaritan Hospital. This warrant was in connection with the Trooper being injured with a coke bottle and the shooting of JACKSON on February 18, 1965. The warrant reflects witnesses for the State to be W. H. LOFTUS [sic] and F. E. HIGGINBOTHAM.

Jackson is apparently the "tall black Negro in a light colored jacket standing across the room from us" whom Trooper Higginbotham observed "throw something in our direction."

The warrant will be served on Jackson as he lies fighting for his life in the only hospital in nearby Selma that will admit African Americans.

CHAPTER THREE

"WE ARE GOING TO SEE THE GOVERNOR!"

February 19, 1965

James Bell is hobbling away from Mack's Café on his crutches when Jimmie Lee Jackson runs past him. State troopers follow in hot pursuit. Bell sees the troopers catch Jimmie Lee and throw him to the ground. Jackson begs not to be beaten. "I didn't hit anyone," he cries.

Charles Pryor also sees the troopers grab Jackson down the street from the church, by the bus station. Pryor watches in horror as Jackson is knocked down, kicked, and clubbed.

Perry County deputy sheriff William Perkins tells a different story. Having just arrived at Mack's from the jailhouse, he sees "a Negro run out of the cafe and knock two or three troopers down" as he comes down the steps. Perkins and another trooper try to stop the man, but he rushes past them toward the church. The man then runs around the corner onto Pickens Street.

When Perkins gets to the corner, "the Negro [is] lying on

the sidewalk in front of the bus station hollering that he's been shot." Seeing that Jackson has been wounded in the stomach, the deputy sheriff drives him to Perry County Hospital. In his statement to the FBI, Perkins makes no mention of troopers kicking or beating Jackson on the ground.

The drive takes about five minutes. When Perkins and Jackson arrive around 10 p.m., the hospital is busy. Doctors and nurses are already treating Trooper Higginbotham, NBC reporter Valeriani, a Marion policeman, and several black townspeople injured on the street outside Zion United.

Walter Dobyne, the Lincoln High School student arrested during the sit-ins earlier in the month, is at the hospital visiting his great-aunt Mary. By the time Jackson gets there, Dobyne has heard about the attack on the marchers and seen a few of the injured. He knows Jackson from Sprott Estate and from church.

"When Jimmie Lee came in, some of the nurses wouldn't go up in the area he was," Dobyne remembers. "They just had him up in the front of the hospital on a gurney, blood all over him, and he was crying out in pain, and he stayed there. I could hear them talking, saying they weren't gonna put their hands on that nigger; he could just lay up there and die before they give a shit."

Dr. Arthur Wilkerson, who will later insist there was no delay in treatment, cleans Jackson's bullet wound and sedates him. It would be best to remove the bullet immediately, the doctor concludes, but such a procedure requires having a blood supply on hand. Perry County Hospital has no blood bank and there are no donors available. The doctor thinks Jackson should be transported to a better-equipped hospital in Selma.

Robert Tubbs, of Tubbs Funeral Home and Ambulance Service, transports Jimmie Lee Jackson the twenty-five miles from Perry County Hospital to Good Samaritan Hospital in Selma.

Tubbs will later tell the FBI that Jackson "was in pain and praying, but mentioned nothing concerning where he had been shot, why he had been shot, or who shot him."

Two young black men from Marion are able to shed light on those unanswered questions. Leeandrew Benson works at Perry County Hospital. His friend, Hardis Jackson (no relation to Jimmie Lee), has come to pick him up at about 11:30 p.m. Earlier, Benson saw Jimmie Lee Jackson in the hospital hallway. "I've been shot," Jackson said. "Don't let me die."

As Leeandrew and Hardis walk to the parking lot, they see three state troopers who have just left the hospital. Benson hears a trooper—a slender man with a bandage on his head—say: "I tried to kill that black bastard when I looked up and saw my blood."

Hardis Jackson is unsure which of the troopers is speaking, but he hears: "When I saw blood, I tried to kill the son-of-a-bitch."

In Alabama, Jim Crow trumps Hippocrates. Jimmie Lee Jackson is taken to the only hospital in a nine-county region that will accept him. Good Samaritan Hospital was opened in 1964 by the Fathers of St. Edmund to help Selma's African Americans. Staffed by the Sisters of St. Joseph, it sits on the site of an old, run-down infirmary that once served blacks.

Admitted shortly before midnight, Jackson is in "very critical condition" according to Good Samaritan's administrator, Sister Michael Ann. She does not expect him to live. "His insides are torn up" because he was shot in the stomach and the bullet came out the left side of his body. He's also cut on the head and bruised all over his body.

The hospital's night supervisor, registered nurse Vera Booker, files a report:

Male per ambulance stretcher. In acute pain stating he was shot by a State Trooper after he had attended a mass meeting at a church and stopped at a café where a riot started between State Troopers and people who had attended the mass meeting.

He stated that the riot was started by a State Trooper who said that he [Mr. Jackson] threw a bottle. Mr. Jackson could not identify the State Trooper that made the "accusation" and shot him. Mr. Jackson stated that he did not throw a bottle, nor attempt to hit anyone.

An operation is needed. Good Samaritan summons Dr. William Dinkins, an African American, from the nearby Burwell Infirmary. Dinkins, who has experience with gunshot wounds, performs an exploratory laparotomy. Opening up Jackson's abdomen, he traces down the intestinal track, sewing up any wounds he finds and removing any bullet fragments.

As Jackson fights for his life, Perry County sheriff William Loftis blames "outside integration leaders from Selma" for the disturbance. Marion's mayor, R. L. Pegues, agrees: "We're sorry that someone was struck," he says. "Actually very little went on. It all happened in a very short time." Pegues emphasizes that previous demonstrations in Marion have been without incident. "But last night they got outside leadership from Selma and they were determined to take the town. Of course we can't have that."

Such finger-pointing is consistent with a long-standing theme in the region: everything was fine and everyone was happy until the "outside agitators" came in and stirred things up. One hundred years after the Civil War ended, the local schoolchildren are still taught this. It is in the 1965 edition of their elementary school textbook, *Know Alabama*, which suggests all was idyllic until the North intervened:

> Now we have come to the happiest way of life in Alabama before the War Between the States. Now suppose you were a little boy or girl and lived on one of the plantation homes. . . . You like the friendly way the slaves speak and smile; they show bright rows of white teeth. "How's it coming, Sam," your father asks one of the old Negroes. "Fine, Marse Tom, jus' fine. We got 'most more cotton than we can pick." Then Sam chuckles to himself and goes back to picking cotton as fast as he can.

The textbook goes on to describe the pernicious effect of ceding power to blacks or outsiders in the Reconstruction era:

> The things that happened in these years caused bad feelings—many more bad feelings than the war had caused. . . . The state legislature in Montgomery was made up of carpetbaggers, scalawags, and Negroes. The loyal white men of Alabama saw they could not depend on the laws of the state government to protect their families. A band of white-robed figures appeared. . . . The Klan did not ride often, only when it had to.

The *Montgomery Advertiser*, no friend of Martin Luther King Jr. and SCLC, does not agree with the sheriff or the mayor. "What happened in Marion last night was a nightmare of state police stupidity and brutality," a February 19 editorial, "The Marion Massacre," states. "Let's not hear apologies or denials for this horror. The state is sick and tired of King and his sensation-seeking campaign, but that does nothing to excuse the terrible night in Marion. It cannot be explained away by excuses because of 'outside agitators,' or provocation, which was present. It is the inside agitators in uniform who have disgraced Alabama."

Within hours of the "massacre," Dr. King wires U.S. attorney general Nicholas Katzenbach to ask for federal protection of civil rights workers in Marion. "This situation can only encourage chaos and savagery in the name of law enforcement unless dealt with immediately," he writes.

Katzenbach responds that Justice Department policy is to investigate and prosecute all violations of voting rights. FBI director J. Edgar Hoover has already told the attorney general that his agents in Marion "observed no police brutality," but did see attacks perpetrated by "an unruly mob."

Hoover does not like King. An FBI memo circulated after King's "I Have a Dream" speech at the March on Washington in 1963 characterized the civil rights leader as the "most dangerous and effective Negro leader in the country." Why dangerous? Certain that the communists were behind the civil rights movement, Hoover was committed to discrediting King among officials in the Justice Department and at the White House. The bureau even sent a packet of secretly recorded tapes of King engaging in extramarital sex to top government officials and to King's own home, where it was opened by Coretta Scott King.

John Doar, head of the Justice Department's Civil Rights Division, presents his superiors with a more balanced and comprehensive morning-after. "At one point during the evening, a State Trooper was struck on the head by a bottle and severely cut," Doar writes. "Shortly thereafter a Negro, one Jimmy [*sic*] Jackson, was shot once or twice in the stomach by a State

Trooper. Jackson is reported to be in Good Samaritan Hospital in Selma in critical condition."

The forty-three-year-old Doar—a graduate of Princeton and the Boalt Hall school of law at the University of California, Berkeley—had earned his civil rights bona fides by February 1965. In 1962, he was the Justice Department's man on the ground when James Meredith attempted to become the first black to enroll at the University of Mississippi; he helped calm the citizens of Jackson, Mississippi, after civil rights leader Medgar Evers was assassinated in 1963; he was the first federal official informed that civil rights workers Michael Schwerner, James Chaney, and Andrew Goodman were missing in Mississippi in 1964; and he helped the Perry County Civic League with its voting rights lawsuit in 1962.

Doar now requests an investigation "to determine whether law enforcement officers (in Marion) inflicted summary punishment, arrested and detained persons knowing they had no lawful cause, or deliberately withheld police protection from certain persons. . . ." Katzenbach tasks Hoover, who sends an additional four agents to Marion to interview police, those arrested, those injured, and other witnesses.

The bureau will not be able to ask the state troopers about their actions on the evening of February 18, however. "Director Alabama Department of Public Safety AL LINGO, after advising troopers could be interviewed, subsequently changed mind and refused interviews with troopers," reports FBI special agent Robert Frye. Hoover tells Katzenbach that Lingo "does not trust 'the damn [Justice] Department.'"

On the evening after the shooting, the people of Marion hold another mass meeting at Zion United and come close to abandoning their nonviolent approach. "It was my responsibility to see that nobody got hurt, but I knew what was going on," Albert Turner would recall later:

> I knew everybody had stuff in the trunk of their cars. That night they put the women and children in the church, and the men stayed in their cars, even the trunks of their cars, where they had shotguns and stuff. History would have been different if anybody had attacked us that night. It would have been a Bogalusa.* If anyone attacked the march the second night it wasn't going to be like the first night. But we went out and marched and came right back in, and nothing happened.

Turner will also characterize the attack in Marion as "worse than Bloody Sunday on the bridge in Selma. Nobody knew about it, though, because there was no TV coverage."

Three days after the shooting, the *New York Times'* John Herbers files a story from Selma. "Three generations of one Negro family were in Selma hospitals today as a result of Thursday night's assault by state troopers on a crowd of demonstrators in the Marion Town Square," he writes. He interviews Cager Lee and Viola Jackson, who remain in Burwell Infirmary "with broken scalps and bruises they say had been inflicted by the troopers' night sticks and feet."

Viola Jackson, five stitches in her head, lies in bed. Sitting in a chair beside the bed is Cager Lee, "a small stooped man" with a bandage that "covered the knot on his head." Lee tells Herbers,

---

*Earlier in February 1965, members of the black community in Bogalusa, Louisiana, began to arm themselves against threats of violence by the Klan, leading to one of the tensest standoffs of the civil rights era.

"Voting is what all this is about. I've tried [to register] five times and they keep turning me down. The last time the voting referee asked questions so fast I couldn't understand them."

Herbers is not able to interview Cager Lee's grandson, who remains in critical condition at Good Samaritan Hospital. Who is Jimmie Lee Jackson?

The hospital accurately describes him as a five-foot-eleven, 180-pound black man of muscular build.

The media accurately describes him as a farmer and pulpwood chopper who earns six dollars a day. Chopping wood is dangerous; one has to be careful of snakes and falling trees. But Jackson likes the fact that he receives a steady paycheck. Those who pick cotton often have to wait until the crop is in to get paid.

The FBI and others often spell his first name inaccurately. They refer to him as "Jimmy," an error that persists to this day.

Most accounts describe him as an army veteran; some say he served in Vietnam. While such a history may in the eyes of some make his shooting all the more tragic—*he risked his life for a country that wouldn't let him vote*—it appears to be inaccurate. Several family members today say he was never in the military.

Family and friends remember Jackson as an ordinary fellow who grew up under modest circumstances. He lived in a "shotgun house," says his cousin Florence Lauderdale. "You can see straight through the whole house. It had some holes in it. Some cracks in the walls. When they built houses in that time, they didn't always do it right. They didn't have any plumbing indoors. They would draw water from the well."

Media accounts accurately describe him as a graduate of Lincoln High School and as the youngest deacon in the history of St. James Baptist Church in Marion. Reports that he left Alabama briefly sometime after high school to find work in the

North—specifically Indiana—are also true. Family and friends believe, however, that after his father died in a car accident, Jimmie Lee came home to take on the role of primary provider for his mother, young sister, and aging grandfather.

He was not married, but had a young daughter, Cordelia, by a girlfriend named Addie Heard.

"He was a real quiet, orderly, mannerly, clean guy that did what most of us did at that time, and that was work," says Robert Turner Sr.

"He was kind, gentle," adds Jackson's cousin James W. Oakes. "He was never violent. I knew him since he was six or seven years old, and I never saw Jimmie start a fight. He would try to walk away if you'd let him."

Jackson tried to register to vote on several occasions after he turned twenty-one. Having failed each time and having witnessed his grandfather Cager Lee denied the right to vote, he attended mass meetings in Marion after SCLC launched its registration drive. Jimmie Lee's desire to vote was hardly unique, says Florence Lauderdale: "He went to register, but *everyone* went. We knew that we should have been voting. We were becoming educated. It was like a period of enlightening." She adds:

> It's an honor that people have taken the time to look back at Jimmie and to remember him for what went on and how he impacted things at that time. But there's a period where I question who they're talking about. Is this Jimmie? He didn't set out to be an activist. He ended up protecting his family. Protecting Cager Lee. His dad was dead. He had to play that part. The protective role. Not to take anything away from him. Because he did do a lot of those things and his actions were a springboard.

Another black man is shot three days after Jimmie Lee Jackson. The thirty-nine-year-old Muslim minister and civil rights activist Malcolm X is assassinated by three Nation of Islam members as he prepares to speak to a large gathering at the Audubon Ballroom in Harlem. A who's who of civil rights leaders attends his funeral: John Lewis, Andrew Young, Bayard Rustin, James Forman, and James Farmer.

Dr. King is not present, but sends Malcolm's widow, Betty Shabazz, a telegram:

> While we did not always see eye to eye on methods to solve the race problem, I always had a deep affection for Malcolm and felt that he had a great ability to put his finger on the existence and root of the problem. He was an eloquent spokesman for his point of view and no one can honestly doubt that Malcolm had a great concern for the problems that we face as a race.

At the invitation of SNCC, Malcolm had spoken to a crowd of five hundred at Brown AME Chapel in Selma just seventeen days before his death. On February 4, he had urged blacks of all classes to participate in the movement. Drawing the distinction between "field negroes" and "house negroes" in the antebellum South, he had said, "If I can't live in the house as a human being, I'm praying for that house to blow down, I'm praying for a strong wind to come along. But, if we are all going to live as human beings, as brothers, then I am for a society of human beings that can practice brotherhood."

Following the speech, Malcolm spoke with Coretta Scott King, who was in Selma to visit her jailed husband, at the behest of Andrew Young. He told her that he was not trying to step on

SCLC's toes. His point was to warn intransigent whites in Alabama "that an alternative philosophy awaited them if they did not negotiate with her husband."

The push for such negotiations is intensifying. In his diary entry for Saturday, February 20, George Baker writes about possible talks in Selma "between [the] white power structure and civil rights leaders." A march, "maybe the biggest yet," is called for February 22 "unless certain demands made by Movement leaders are met." Those demands include more jobs for blacks, removal of Sheriff Jim Clark, and faster voter registration. An economic boycott of all white businesses in Selma will also go into in effect until the demands are met.

On the twenty-second ("FREEDOM DAY"), Baker participates in a door-to-door drive "to get people to register." He observes: "I never saw such poor living conditions." At the same time, because the demands have not been met, King leads two hundred people to the Dallas County Courthouse "to sign the book" and begin the registration process. Baker will note that most people had already signed up a week earlier: "The people I was trying to get this morning were the 'Uncle Toms,'" he wrote, "those who were afraid for various reasons and hadn't already signed. It was so funny—actually tragic—to hear all of the people who had just gotten sick or were too busy cooking. All would admit that they would like to register, but they still had their excuses."

In the wake of the violence in Marion, Selma is on edge. State troopers now patrol the city. The *New York Times* notes "a marked increase in the number of hostile-looking white men gathered on the street as the Negroes marched by." The newspaper also reports on increasing support from the white community for Sheriff Clark's militant tactics. Newly elected mayor

Joseph Smitherman, considered a moderate by southern standards, announces he will not meet with local leaders from the
black community until King and other outsiders depart Selma.*

Governor George Wallace, not considered a moderate, takes
an equally tough stance. He orders a ban on nighttime marches
in Selma and Marion. King calls the edict "clearly unconstitutional." Nevertheless, he and Albert Turner suspend such
marches until, says a SCLC spokesman, the protestors are better
prepared for what might befall them.

From the Dallas County Courthouse, King goes to Good
Samaritan Hospital to visit Jimmie Lee Jackson. It is now four
days after the shooting. Jackson remains in critical condition but
is said to be improving. According to King, who prays with
him, "he seems to be in very good spirits."

An hour later, King is in Marion. There he finds Zion United
packed with black townspeople. They sing, "Who's our leader?
Doctor King."

"We have now reached the point of no return," King tells the
assembled. "We must let George Wallace know that the violence
of state troopers will not stop us."

Back in Selma that evening, King speaks to seven hundred
people at Brown Chapel. "We are going to have a motorcade to
Montgomery in the next few days," he announces. "We hope
to have our forces mobilized to have carloads of people from all
over the state to march on the Capitol."

---

*Smitherman, a former home appliance store owner, served as Selma's mayor
for thirty-six years. In 2005, five years after his retirement, he told the *Selma
Times-Journal*: "I fought change and all the while I was for it. A political stance
is often different from your personal beliefs. I had to politically lose as I was
winning. You can sometimes win by losing. In retrospect there were thousands
of things I could have done to have helped the situation or even stopped it, but
my political strength then, my immaturity and the actors involved decided it."

Jackson's family has placed his high school graduation picture at his bedside. Sister Barbara Lum is one of his nurses. Each day, Jackson takes her hand and says, "Sister, don't you think this is a high price to pay for freedom?"

Five days after the shooting, Dr. Dinkins tells the FBI that Jackson is in good mental condition and "physically able to be interviewed." But he adds that the young man "is still in grave condition in view of the fact that infection may set in." Otherwise, "his progress is very satisfactory."

On the evening of February 25, that progress halts. When Dr. Dinkins visits him at 9 p.m., Jackson is sitting up in bed, talking with his nurses. He is not running a temperature and a stethoscope to the abdomen indicates normal bowel sounds.

Dinkins goes home, but he is called back to the hospital within an hour. Jackson, he is told, experienced trouble breathing and then slipped into shock. Emergency surgery in the early morning hours of February 26 reveals the massive infection Dr. Dinkins feared. At 8:10 a.m., twenty-six-year-old Jimmie Lee Jackson is pronounced dead.

An autopsy performed by state toxicologist Dr. Paul Shoffeitt states that Jackson's death is due to peritonitis, a bacterial or fungal infection of the abdominal lining. Dinkins concurs with this verdict.* Good Samaritan's administrator, Sister Michael Ann, speculates that the infection may have been exacerbated by the delay in getting Jackson adequate treatment and surgery after he was shot.

L. C. Crocker, the chief deputy to Sheriff Clark, blames civil

---

*Almost fifteen years later, however, Dinkins told interviewers for the documentary *Eyes on the Prize* that he believed the anesthesiologist at the emergency surgery gave Jackson too much oxygen, and that this was what killed him.

rights leaders for Jackson's death. "I believe they wanted him to die," he says. "They wanted to make a martyr out of him, and they did." C. T. Vivian dismisses the notion. "Nobody needs martyrs," he says. "Nobody in America is going to ask someone, 'Will you die for us today?' That's ridiculous. But when [a death] does happen, it has an effect."

While witnesses have told law enforcement officials and the press that a state trooper shot Jackson, local prosecutor Blanchard McLeod has yet to publicly identify the man. Within hours of Jackson's death, McLeod finally acknowledges that he has a signed statement from the individual who pulled the trigger. McLeod still refuses to name the shooter or say whether he is a trooper, but tells the press that the man is cooperating with police and claims he acted in self-defense. He adds that the man "was struck several times." The prosecutor says he will let a Perry County grand jury decide whether an indictment is in order.

On the evening of the twenty-sixth, James Bevel preaches to six hundred people who have gathered at Brown Chapel in Selma. "I tell you the death of that man is pushing me kind of hard," he says. "The blood of Jackson will be on our hands if we don't march. Be prepared to walk to Montgomery. Be prepared to sleep on the highways."

Earlier in the day, Bevel and Bernard Lafayette had visited Viola Jackson, Emma Jackson, and Cager Lee in the home they had shared with Jimmie Lee Jackson by a small creek in the woods, a few miles outside Marion. It had no running water or electricity. Even Lafayette, who had seen much poverty over his lifetime, was shocked at the primitive state of the family's living conditions. During the visit, Lee gave his blessing for future marches.

The idea to walk to Montgomery—as opposed to drive, as Dr. King had previously suggested—came from an elderly civil rights activist from Marion, Lucy Foster. Described as the "bravest woman I've ever met" by Willie Nell Avery, Foster worked closely with Albert Turner for several years. Movement people who came to Marion usually stayed at her home, just as they stayed at Amelia Boynton's home in Selma.

Foster originally proposed that the people of Marion carry Jackson's casket from their small town to Montgomery—an eighty-mile march. There they would place it in protest on George Wallace's doorstep and demand a meeting with the governor. Bevel and others, however, decided Selma was a more logical point of departure for a five-day march. It would be easier for participants to meet there, and the journey would, at fifty-four miles, be less demanding. They also determined that carrying the casket for five days was impractical, particularly because Jackson's funeral would have already taken place.

Though the movement's leadership crafted the overall strategy, participants like Lucy Foster often rose to the occasion at critical junctures like this. The nature and pace of events suited this subtle power-sharing approach. When leadership needed coordinated, disciplined, nonviolent action, they could count on their rank and file. When events like Jackson's death shook and aroused the people, their spontaneous ideas and actions could carry the day.

Would this be a march for voting rights or something else? "The Selma to Montgomery march was prompted more by ethical concerns than political considerations," Wally G. Vaughn and Mattie Campbell Davis argue persuasively in their introduction to *The Selma Campaign, 1963–1965*. "A man of African heritage was killed by white people, and local residents expected the normal turn of events to be repeated regarding those who committed the offense—that is, the killer or killers would not be held accountable. This reflected a concern that was deeper than politics, a concern that a ballot could not conquer."

Two days after Jackson's death, on Sunday the twenty-eighth, Bevel again speaks to a packed church. This time he is at Zion United in Marion. Chuck Fager—a white activist, author, Quaker, and SCLC worker based in Selma—is among those present. He later writes that Bevel began by citing a passage from the New Testament, Acts 12:2–3: "Herod killed James, the brother of John, with a sword, and when he saw that it pleased the Jews, he proceeded to arrest Peter also."

"I'm not worried about James anymore I'm concerned about Peter, who is still with us," Bevel tells the crowd. "James has found release from the indignities of being a Negro in Alabama, and no longer can he be cowed and coerced and deprived of his rights as a man. . . . I'm not worried about James. I'm concerned with Peter, who must continue to be cowed and coerced and beaten and even murdered."

Bevel then cites another passage, this time from the book of Esther. After a decree was issued to kill the Jews, he recounts, Esther made supplication unto the king to save her people. Now, the preacher says, "I must go see the king. We must go to Montgomery and see the king." The king is Governor Wallace.

The movement does not rest in the days leading up to Jackson's funeral on March 3. On the same Sunday that Bevel preaches at Zion United, George Baker chauffeurs Lafayette to four churches. At each church, Lafayette announces another registration drive scheduled for the next day.

The congregations listen. Although only twenty-five, Lafayette is already a veteran of the movement. In 1960, he studied nonviolence at American Baptist Theological Seminary in Nashville with James Lawson. He also took classes with Myles Horton at the Highlander Folk School, which offered leadership training for civil rights activists, black and white. As a Freedom Rider in Mississippi and Alabama, the following year, he was attacked and arrested.

In 1962, Lafayette joined SNCC as an organizer in Selma. Within a year, he was badly beaten by whites. When SCLC launched its voter registration drive in Alabama, he signed on.

After nine hours of driving Lafayette and others, Baker returns to the Boynton home, where he makes his diary entry while listening to the music of the folk-singing duo Ian & Sylvia. "The boy who was shot in Marion died this weekend. . . . The boy stated before he died that state troopers shot him, and they are trying to say someone else did it. The whole thing is really sad." He continues:

> A march on Montgomery is being planned. . . . Marching will take place only during the day, but we will be marching through Lowndes County, which is one of the worst counties in Alabama in terms of racial hate and potential violence. Participants will be those who have been either beaten or have gone to jail. I believe that many will be hurt and some will be killed if the march takes place. Personally, I hope it doesn't. This is part of SCLC's non-violent strategy. To push right up to crises so that public opinion and Congress fall on their side when the racists strike out.

March 1 is another "FREEDOM DAY" in Selma. John Lewis speaks to several hundred people at Brown Chapel, then moves to the courthouse, where one hundred more people are lined up in the rain to begin the registration process. King then speaks to a crowd of five hundred at the church. After the speech, those in attendance march to the courthouse. "We didn't have a permit to parade, so the people were to march in groups of five to avoid arrest," Baker recalled. "I stood out in the rain for about 45 minutes organizing and spacing the people, although I didn't march."

Baker also recorded a story he overheard: "Last week John Lewis was in Marion. After he was through he was chased back to Selma at speeds up to 100 m.p.h. No one in his car was hurt, however."

Baker has his own trouble in a car while driving three people home from a meeting the following night. "I got stopped by the police," he later writes. "The only thing I was guilty of was having on my bright lights. I was arrested and charged with reckless driving." While waiting for Mrs. Boynton to bail him out, Baker is put with black prisoners instead of fellow whites. "This act very likely saved me from a beating."

There are two funerals for Jackson on March 3. The first is at Brown Chapel, the striking church with twin towers, built in the Romanesque Revival style in 1908. "This was a Christian funeral, strong with the Fundamentalist theology of the Black Belt," reports the *New York Times'* Roy Reed.

As a light rain falls, mourners enter under a banner that reads, RACISM KILLED OUR BROTHER. Music fills the hall. The choir sings "In the Sweet By and By."

> *There's a land that is fairer than day,*
> *And by faith we can see it afar;*

For the Father waits over the way
To prepare us a dwelling place there.

In the sweet by and by,
We shall meet on that beautiful shore;
In the sweet by and by,
We shall meet on that beautiful shore.

The assembled then rise, hold hands, and sing "We Shall Overcome."

We shall overcome, we shall overcome,
We shall overcome someday;
Oh, deep in my heart, I do believe,
We shall overcome someday.

"As the service began," Reed observes, "Viola Jackson sat gazing tearfully and balefully into the eyes of television cameras. The coffin sat surrounded by flowers and cameramen. Besides Mrs. Jackson sat the slain man's grandfather, 82-year-old Cager Lee, a brittle little man with a face like a weathered walnut."

Rev. L. L. Anderson preaches a spirited sermon. Jimmie Lee Jackson is not dead, he says. "He has just gone home."

SCLC's Ralph Abernathy then delivers the eulogy. "We are gathered around the bier of the first casualty of the Black Belt demonstrations. Who knows but what before it's over, you and I may take our rightful places beside him." Abernathy preaches that Jackson has joined a heavenly pantheon that includes Abraham Lincoln, Emmitt Till, Medgar Evers, the four young girls killed in the Birmingham church bombing, the three civil rights workers killed in Mississippi during the Freedom Summer, and

Crispus Attucks, the African American who was the first casualty of the American Revolution.

After the service an estimated three thousand people file past Jackson's open coffin. The young man is dressed in blue denim overalls, a white shirt, and necktie.

The second funeral is held in Marion. In a prayer to open the service, Rev. J. T. Johnson, a local black minister, says, "We pray for the policemen of this town and this state who would rather see blood in the streets and a man shot down than sit down and talk."

Then, a tear in his eye, Dr. King delivers the eulogy to a filled Zion United: "A state trooper pointed the gun, but he did not act alone," he says. Jimmie Lee was murdered by the brutality of lawless sheriffs, irresponsible politicians who feed "constituents the stale bread of hatred and the spoiled meat of racism," by a federal government more concerned about the war in Vietnam than civil rights at home, indifferent and silent white ministers, and by "the cowardice of every Negro who passively accepts the evils of segregation and stands on the sidelines in the struggle for justice."

The funerals were "very depressing and inspirational at the same time," Baker would reflect in his diary.

After the service in Marion, a hearse carries Jimmie Lee Jackson to a small wooded cemetery by State Highway 14, five miles east of town. An estimated one thousand people follow the hearse on foot. Hundreds more drive. In a pouring rain, Jackson is laid to rest on a pine hill.

The headstone, provided by the Perry County Civic League, features Jesus Christ with palms open toward heaven. It reads: JIMMIE LEE JACKSON, 1938–1965. HE WAS KILLED FOR MAN'S FREEDOM.

Later in the evening, James Bevel announces specific plans for the march from Selma to Montgomery in Jimmie Lee Jackson's memory. Dr. King will lead the five-day journey beginning on Sunday, March 7. "We are going to see the governor!" Bevel proclaims.

The governor has a different idea.

CHAPTER FOUR

"YOU AND THE TWO GIRLS ARE NEXT . . ."

March 6, 1965

On the Saturday before SCLC's march to Montgomery, the Concerned White Citizens of Alabama (CWCA) stages its own action in Selma. The group is not to be confused with the White Citizens' Council, that bastion of the Jim Crow South concerned with maintaining a segregated society. On the contrary, CWCA—composed largely of white professors, teachers, doctors, businesspeople, and housewives—is marching in support of voting rights for African Americans.

The protest was planned before the police action in Marion, before the death of Jimmie Lee Jackson, before Lucy Foster's call for a march to the state capital. It is a collaboration between the interracial Birmingham Council on Human Relations (BCHR) and SCLC. The organizers believe an all-white march can make a powerful statement. "My hope was that our demonstration would play a small role in helping focus the eyes of the nation on injustices that should have been removed long ago," Rev. Joseph Ellwanger, the white pastor of Birmingham's all-black St. Paul's Lutheran Church and CWCA's leader, will later explain. "The fact that I knew many of the Negro Lutheran pastors and people of Dallas and Wilcox Counties personally—and knew that they feared for their lives the moment they thought of registering to vote—deepened my determination to help in lifting up the injustice for all to see so that they could help eliminate it."

Local political leaders have not publicly opposed the demonstration. According to the *Selma Times-Journal*, Dallas County deputy sheriff Crocker and Selma's public safety director, Wilson Baker (no relation to George Baker), have been ordered to ignore the protest. Law enforcement is apparently focused on Sunday's march.

At a press conference on Saturday, Governor Wallace says the SCLC march to Montgomery will not be tolerated because it is not "conducive to the orderly flow of traffic and commerce within and through the State of Alabama. The additional hazard placed on highway travel by any such actions cannot be counterbalanced."

Mayor Smitherman says that he "agrees with the governor that Negroes should not be permitted to make this senseless march. The city will join forces and cooperate fully with the state in stopping the march."

SCLC's Vivian responds: "We shall plan to march. I don't know what he—Wallace—plans to do to stop us, but he has several alternatives. He can beat us, he can arrest us, or any other number of things he might choose."

Andrew Young adds that if halted by the city or state, the marchers will have two options: "One is to go back and get a court order permitting us to march. And the other is to sit down wherever they stop us."

Although the city and state have chosen to ignore Saturday's CWCA protest, a crowd of five hundred white citizens has gathered downtown to threaten and intimidate the seventy-two marchers. Rev. James Rongstad of St. John's Lutheran Church in Selma is also present. Chastising CWCA for coming to Selma, he says, "Why don't you stay in your own town, in your own city, and do your work there?" Again, the enemy is the so-called outside agitator.

Ellwanger answers, "We're not simply pointing the finger at Selma. We're pointing the finger at Alabama and the whole country to bring about a Voting Rights Act that will change things for all of us."

Rev. Edgar Homrighausen, president of the Southern District of Lutheran Church Missouri Synod (LCMS), the branch to which Rev. Ellwanger belongs, also responds. He sends a telegram to Ellwanger affirming LCMS's support for civil rights achieved through the legislative process but criticizing the demonstration as an act of resistance to legal authority.

Dr. King, who earned his PhD in theology from Boston University in 1955, found the inspiration for his nonviolent resistance in Christ and the Christian gospels. When the movement came under fire for taking actions deemed too extreme, he responded that Jesus was also an extremist. "So the question is not whether we will be extremists," he wrote in his "Letter from a Birmingham Jail," "but what kind of extremists we will be. Will we be extremists for hate or for love?"

In Alabama and the Deep South, adherence to Jim Crow doctrine often took precedence over the gospel. Only a handful of local white clergy joined their fellow black ministers in the struggle for civil rights. And while black churches were the movement's heart and soul, most white churches offered only a cold shoulder.

The difference in the attitudes and actions of the churches was evident in Marion. Zion United, a black Methodist church, was the center of civil rights protest activity. First Methodist of Marion, a white church, was the center of protest directed at its own minister, Rev. Joe Neal Blair.

In the past, Blair had supported the Montgomery Bus Boycott and helped organize an interracial group in Pensacola, Florida. In *When the Church Bells Rang Racist*, Donald E. Collins described Blair's difficulties during "the Marion turmoil." First Methodist's board "had the locks on the doors of the church changed without informing Blair. He was not given a key," Collins wrote. "The officials would unlock the door and let him in right before the Sunday service began. The officials took turns guarding the doors during the worship services to make certain no blacks could enter."

Blair took further heat from his congregation for visiting NBC's Richard Valeriani in Perry County Hospital after the newsman was attacked by the white mob on the night Jackson was shot. In addition, "the pastoral relations committee of his church asked him not to use the words 'love' or 'brotherhood' in the pulpit." Blair refused to comply and was subjected to continuous harassment and criticism because he "let his congregation down and was not on their side."

In Selma, the Catholic Church sent mixed messages. The Edmundites and Sisters of St. Joseph established Good Samaritan to treat African Americans denied admission to other hospitals and to train nurses. But, says Sister Barbara Lum, "Archbishop Thomas Joseph Toolen said that any priest or sister in the diocese who marched in the black community would be on the next bus out of Selma."

She describes Toolen as "a good man caught in his time, caught in fear that Catholics were such a small percentage of the population" they would suffer retaliation from the whites in power. Edmundite priests obeyed the archbishop and did not march, but they did open their rectory to the Dallas County Voters League for meetings.

Sister Barbara explains that she never considered disobeying the archbishop "because I wanted to be in the hospital. I thought that was where we were called to be." Marching, she says, "felt very precarious in terms of our needing to be on deck at our best, given what was going on."

Others working at the hospital "talked about the movement but were very fearful of physical violence," the nun recalls. "They were also fearful members of their families would lose their jobs if they were seen at a public demonstration. Fear had quite a claim on the people."

A number of white Unitarians join the CWCA march in Selma, but fear keeps "scores if not hundreds" of supporters from participating, Rev. Ellwanger says. He will later observe:

> Since Jim Clark was in charge there, we knew that there
> was the possibility of arrest, we knew that there was the
> possibility of violence. Given that atmosphere, there was
> no way that we were going to get huge numbers. That's
> why most of us were very satisfied that we had 72. At least
> it was a critical mass that made it clear there was not just
> this six or seven of us from Birmingham, but it was, it
> really was, Alabamans from all over the state, Mobile, Tal-
> ladega, Clanton, Tuscaloosa, Birmingham.

The minister does not sleep well on the eve of the protest. He is worried because his wife, Joyce, who is five months pregnant with their first child, insists on marching. "That shows you how committed she is to the movement and to justice," he reflects years later.

Ellwanger's commitment to justice began in the late 1940s as a young teen attending an all-white school in Selma. "It was very much Jim Crow," he recalls. His minister father, who was president of the LCMS-affiliated Concordia College in Selma and director of Alabama Missions, sometimes took him along when visiting or preaching at rural churches. On such trips the disparity between the opportunities for blacks and whites came into focus.

After attending seminary, Joseph Ellwanger was ordained and installed at St. Paul's in the southwest section of Birmingham in 1958. The church sat in the center of a low- to middle-income black community, and the congregation was 100 percent African American. Ellwanger lived in a parsonage adjacent to the church.

Once settled, Ellwanger joined BCHR. The organization wrote letters to newspaper editors and met with local white officials to call attention to racial injustice. CWCA would spin off from BCHR in 1965.

In 1961, Ellwanger had his first brush with white supremacists. After taking two young black girls from his congregation to a Sunday evening interracial gathering at a white Lutheran church in Tuscaloosa, he learned that the Ku Klux Klan there had beaten the interim pastor who had planned the program for that evening. The Klan then burned a cross in the pastor's churchyard and left a note on the door of the church saying that if there were another interracial youth meeting, something worse would happen.

Ellwanger later said, "I was still reading the account of this event when the phone rang and a rough voice on the other end said, 'Is this the Reverend?' I said, 'Yes,' and he said, 'Well, you and the two girls are next.' Click." Fortunately, the caller did not follow through.

Two years later, the Klan did attack a black church about a mile away from St. Paul's. On the morning of Sunday, September 15, 1963, Ellwanger was teaching an adult Bible class when there was a loud explosion followed by strong vibrations. "I hope that is not what I think it was," said a woman in the class. Within ten minutes, they learned that the 16th Street Baptist church had been bombed.

The horror hit Ellwanger's congregation particularly hard. The wife and daughter of St. Paul's Sunday school superintendent, Chris McNair, belonged to the 16th Street church. Now word came that eleven-year-old Denise McNair was one of four young girls who died in the attack.

Half an hour later, St. Paul's Sunday service began. Ellwanger offered prayers for the victims' families and all the members of the church. "The reaction of our congregation was a lot of shock, disbelief, and then a reaction of anger," Ellwanger remembers. "How could this happen to us? One more act of violence, a vicious act of discrimination."

The mood of the congregation was very much like the mood of a funeral, the minister said. "I can honestly say that every African American, not only in my congregation, but in Birmingham, felt that this was an action that happened to them, not just to those four families that were impacted."

The reaction of the white community in Birmingham was varied. Many knew that the Klan was responsible. "But to show what the Jim Crow culture really fostered in the minds and the hearts of white folks, there was a huge number of people in Birmingham who honestly believed and spread the rumor that this bombing was done by blacks in the movement to garner attention and support for the cause. Unbelievable," says Ellwanger. He adds that many people, black and white, even knew the names of the people that did it "because a couple of them were stupid enough, or just brazen enough, that they were standing around just to make sure that things really happened."

The anger of the black community was palpable. Some spoke of finding a way to get revenge. The families of the victims, however, urged calm. In one television interview, Chris McNair said that those who bombed the church and killed the girls must be found and justice must be done, but that a violent response would drag the victims down to the level of the perpetrators.

The McNair family asked Ellwanger to participate in the funeral and do the committal service for Denise at the cemetery. The minister read from a chapter of the gospel of Luke, in which Jesus weeps over the city of Jerusalem and says, "Would that you, even you, had known on this day the things that make for peace! But now they are hidden from your eyes." Ellwanger then put down his Bible and said, "I am reading this scripture today because the city of Birmingham does not know what makes for peace. And we need to learn that equality and dignity for all is what makes for peace, not violence and not retaliation."

Ellwanger was the only white clergyman to lead the worship. Some seven to eight hundred people sat inside the packed 16th Street Baptist Church, and another two or three thousand stood outside in the street. "It was interesting that there were three or four white clergy, maybe a few more, there," Ellwanger says. "But, the fact that there weren't more white clergy and white people of faith who came to that service is a sign of how polarized the city was before the explosion as well as at this tense time in its history."

Two years later and ninety miles away, the polarization in Selma is evident as Ellwanger and CWCA begin their twelve-block march from the Reformed Baptist Church to the Dallas County Courthouse. Three hundred African Americans who have come to show their support stand across from the five hundred whites. The marchers reach the courthouse and sing "America." The angry white counterdemonstrators call them "nigger lovers" and answer with "Dixie." The African Americans sing "We Shall Overcome."

Despite their desire to ignore the demonstration, the police are forced to intervene. One white townsperson, Jimmy George Robinson, is arrested for chasing and attacking a SNCC photographer. The *Selma Times-Journal* reports: "The photographer escaped from Robinson and two other white men who beat him to the sidewalk. [The photographer] then jumped into an automobile parked at the curb. Several whites attempted to overturn the auto and had two wheels lifted from the ground when police walked up." One month earlier Robinson had assaulted King in a Selma hotel lobby.

The newspaper also reports: "When the taunts came from a crowd of about 500 persons, Wilson Baker worked his way through the mob in an attempt to disperse it. He arrested one unidentified man on a charge of disorderly conduct. 'I told you to quit cursing and I mean it,' Baker said as the heckler was led away by two police officers."

In Selma, as in some other towns and cities, the public safety director was in effect the chief of police. Baker leads the city's police force, while Sheriff Jim Clark leads the county's force. Like Mayor Smitherman, who appointed him in 1964, Baker is considered a "moderate." Early in his tenure, he announces that he will not enforce Judge James Hare's injunction that bars meetings of small groups of blacks from SNCC, SCLC, or DCVL. He also tells the city's white establishment that he wants to "lead Selma into dignity."

Unlike the previous mayor, Smitherman puts the public safety director, not the county sheriff, in charge of dealing with the protests within Selma. Although Jim Clark remains responsible for the Dallas County Courthouse, his turf has shrunk. Years later, in an interview for the documentary *Eyes on the Prize*, Clark will castigate Baker:

> Wilson Baker, as they used to say about him in Selma, was anybody's dog that would hunt with him. He had joined the Klan, Ku Klux Klan publicly back in 1958 . . . was a very active member. . . . Then when Martin Luther King came to town, well he went up and met with him and had breakfast with him every morning and they laid out the day's program for what they were going to do and how they were going to do it. I just did not think that he was the person for the job . . . as far as education and experience he was, but he went along with the wishes of Martin Luther King and the outside agitators that came in.

Some of those so-called agitators disagree that Baker went along with King's wishes. "Baker was a good and smart man, a worthy opponent to Dr. King," observes Quaker activist Chuck

Fager. "If we had faced him alone in Selma, it's a fair guess that he would have routed us. Baker would have beat the movement not with force, but with brains."

Fager explains that Baker was a disciple of Laurie Pritchett, the Albany, Georgia, police chief who "outsmarted and out-maneuvered a vigorous protest campaign" three years earlier. Like Pritchett, Baker "understood the reporters' stereotypes, and was careful not to reinforce them. Instead, he spoke politely to the reporters, and made sure that when his police arrested the marchers, they did so quietly and without fanfare."

Baker, Fager adds, "had the Pritchett mild-mannered demeanor cold, right down to the nonthreatening title of Public Safety Director he had chosen himself, and his civilian-style suit and fedora, which matched and blended with Dr. King's typical attire."

But, Fager says, "Selma, fortunately for us, was not Albany." Baker did not have the autonomy that Pritchett enjoyed. "In particular, Baker couldn't afford to let us get past him to the courthouse, because his rival, Dallas County sheriff Jim Clark, was waiting there," ready and willing to use force.

On the eve of Sunday's march to Montgomery, James Bevel tells a rally that when he saw the CWCA demonstration, he thought, "Damn the Kingdom's come." Vivian agrees, but then asks the white community, "Where have you been?"

Young George Baker's diary entry for Saturday, March 6, is ominous. "Tension over tomorrow's activities is very high. There is a good chance that people will be killed. We all went out and got drunk and tried to forget, and lose ourselves at a Negro night club in town."

Bernard Lafayette has asked Baker to coordinate the medical staff. Three doctors and nine nurses from the Medical Committee for Human Rights (MCHR) have come down from New York City. Two more nurses have brought in an ambulance from Jackson, Mississippi. "We expect a lot of tear gas from the police," Baker writes.

Governor Wallace's threats to stop the march by whatever means necessary, coupled with threats on Dr. King's life, lead some at SCLC headquarters to question the wisdom of the protest. Hosea Williams and Bevel seek counsel from King, who is in Atlanta. King floats the idea of delaying the march, but Williams and Bevel tell him that hundreds of people are going to show up at Brown Chapel in the morning. These foot soldiers will be expecting to proceed.

Sensitive to the needs of the movement's participants, Bevel argues for providing them with a physical outlet for their emotions, and something to do. At the same time, it is not lost on the men that a march of several days is an invaluable public relations asset to their campaign. Together, the three men decide the march will go on, but that King will stay in Atlanta.

Wilson Baker is also trying to figure out what to do. Fearing that state troopers and Sheriff Clark's men will attack the marchers once they are outside Selma's city limits, the public safety director wants to peaceably arrest the protestors before they get out of town and are subjected to tear gas and billy clubs. Threatening to resign, he tells Mayor Smitherman that he will not permit his men to participate in any attacks, but agrees to a compromise after being told that his worries about violence are overblown. The Selma police will not arrest the demonstrators, nor will they join state or county forces in using those undefined "means" necessary to halt the march.

On Sunday, it is evident that the young man whose death inspired the march has not been forgotten. The RACISM KILLED OUR BROTHER banner from Jimmie Lee Jackson's funeral still graces the entrance of Brown Chapel. The five-day trip is scheduled to begin after church services. Almost half of the expected six hundred participants will be from Marion. Some arrive as early as six o'clock on this chilly morning.

Aware of the danger that awaits them, SCLC leaders in Selma phone Atlanta one last time on Sunday morning. In his Pulitzer Prize–winning book, *Bearing the Cross*, David Garrow writes that King "reluctantly" gave approval when told how many people had come to march. Years later, Albert Turner remembered that King initially opposed marching because he feared someone would be killed. "We have to do something," Turner responded, "because you'll kill the movement if you don't march."

King then told Williams, "Well, Hosea, if y'all are fool enough to march, go on, but I am not going to give my word for people to go and get thrown in that river." Ralph Abernathy echoed King: "If you are fool enough to march, march."

Williams, Bevel, and Andrew Young flip coins to determine who will lead the procession. "Hosea lost," says George Baker, meaning Rev. Williams would lead the march, while Bevel and Young stayed behind to man SCLC'S Selma headquarters.

Hosea Williams, a thirty-nine-year-old Georgian who holds a master's degree in chemistry, is no stranger to battle. During World War II, he served in an all-black unit under General George Patton. Badly injured in a Nazi bombing, Williams was hospitalized for more than a year and awarded the Purple Heart.

Back in the States, he was beaten and left for dead by white thugs at a bus station in Americus, Georgia. He spent eight weeks recovering in a Veterans Administration hospital "crying, 'cause I had fought on the wrong side," he remembered. Several years later, after his children were denied service at a segregated drugstore lunch counter, he began organizing sit-ins and marches in Savannah, Georgia. Now King calls him "my wild man, my Castro."

SNCC refuses to sanction the march because, it says, "we strongly believe that the objectives . . . of the march do not justify the dangers and the resources involved." The refusal is indicative of the tension between the organization and SCLC. That tension was exacerbated when SCLC came to Selma after SNCC had already been on the ground for two years building trust and relationships. SCLC's strategy of swooping in with dramatic maneuvers calibrated for television audiences offended SNCC's principles and was perceived as undermining its efforts.

Adopting a grassroots, egalitarian approach to defeating segregation and racial injustice, SNCC's brand of activism incorporated education. This was at once a principled and a pragmatic position; everyone participated because that was most empowering to the people. In addition, such engagement can outlast the period of time when the leaders were in town.

King's impassioned but restrained oratory was representative of SCLC's patient approach to accumulating broad public sympathy and building toward a grand bargain through federal legislation. This tone and approach was contrasted by SNCC's less patient and more insistent attitude, embodied by executive secretary Jim Forman's take on black disenfranchisement from the democratic process: "If we can't sit at the table, let's knock the fucking legs off!"

Despite its opposition to the march to Montgomery, SNCC allows members to participate as individuals. John Lewis, the organization's president, will march at the front next to Williams.

"I just felt during the period, it was too much, too much, too many, too many funerals, and some us will say, 'How many more?'" Lewis later explained.

Bevel agreed. As he said many years later:

In the nonviolent movement, if you went back to some of the classical strategies of Gandhi, when you have, say, a great violation of the people and there's a great sense of injury, you have to give people an honorable means and context in which to express and eliminate that grief and speak decisively and succinctly back to the issue. Otherwise, your movement will break down in violence and chaos. So agreeing to go to Montgomery was that kind of tool that would absorb a tremendous amount of energy and effort.

The length of the march would, he said, keep voting rights in the public eye. "The whole point was walking from Selma to Montgomery, it'd take you five or six days, which would give you the time to discuss in the nation through the papers, radio, television and going around speaking what the real issues were."

Marchers will be responsible for their own food, water, and sleeping arrangements. They can spend the nights at designated road stops or return home and rejoin the procession the following day. The organizers will send cars and trucks with supplies and portable restrooms. The leaders anticipate returning to Selma each night so they can be well rested for the next day's leg of the journey to Montgomery.

Walter Dobyne is among those gathering in Brown Chapel, as is Willie Nell Avery. "They told us what to expect and what to look for from the white police," Dobyne will recall. "It was stated they would be throwing tear gas on us and they would have dogs that they were gonna put on us. Once they stopped us and said we were under arrest, we were to kneel down, hold our heads down, and cover our head with our hands, and stay there."

Although he insists on marching, Albert Turner is not thinking about where he will be in five or six days. "We really thought half of us were going to get thrown in the river down there," he would write. "We really thought we were going to get killed. I ain't lying, every step I made that Sunday, I trembled. We knew we were walking into hell."

The walk into hell begins at about 1:40 p.m. Williams, Lewis, Turner, Amelia Boynton, Dallas County Voters League cofounder Marie Foster, and SNCC field secretary Bob Mants lead the procession from Brown Chapel. While several well-known leaders are present, the vast majority of participants are unknown. They represent all walks of life and include more than one hundred Perry County residents who attempted to march the night Jimmie Lee Jackson was shot.

The Selma police are waiting outside Brown Chapel. No arrests are made. Wilson Baker tells the marchers they must form their procession in pairs, five feet apart. It takes about thirty minutes to line up properly. Several ambulances and a truck carrying portable toilets and supplies are positioned at the rear.

Now the march can begin. The procession moves slowly along Sylvan Street for about four blocks, then turns right on to Water Street. Within a few minutes the front of the line has reached the base of the Edmund Pettus Bridge. Named after a Confederate brigadier general, the arched steel structure is 1,280 feet in length and carries U.S. Route 80, also known as the Jefferson Davis Highway, over the Alabama River.

As John Lewis will later write, "a small posse of armed white men" stands near the bridge. Wearing hard hats and holding clubs, they smirk, but do not speak as the marchers pass by. The police have closed the road to traffic, so Lewis and those behind him are "careful to stay on the narrow sidewalk."

When Lewis reaches the crest of the bridge, he stops "dead still." So does Williams. "There, facing us at the bottom of the other side stood a sea of blue-helmeted, blue-uniformed Alabama state troopers, line after line of them, dozens of battle-ready lawmen stretched from one side of US Highway 80 to the other," Lewis recalls. Sheriff Clark's possemen are also on the bridge. Armed with clubs and bats and bullwhips, they stand or ride on horses behind the troopers.

Williams looks out over the bridge to the river a hundred feet below. "Can you swim?" he asks Lewis. "No." "Neither can I, but we might have to," Williams says.

George Wallace's man on the ground, state trooper chief Colonel Al Lingo, watches from a car near the bridge. He has assigned Major John Cloud to carry out the governor's orders. When the marchers reach a spot on the bridge about one hundred yards from where Cloud, Clark, and their men have set up their blockade, the officers strap on their gas masks.

The marchers are no longer within Selma city limits, no longer within Wilson Baker's jurisdiction. Cloud gets on his bullhorn and tells them to stop and return to the church or go back home.

The order sounds eerily similar to what Chief Harris told the demonstrators the night Jackson was shot. The marchers respond as they did in Marion. They kneel in prayer.

"Troopers forward," Cloud orders.

The next day's *Selma Times-Journal* will report what happened when the marchers did not disperse:

The troopers stormed into the double column line. This failed to force the marchers back across the Alabama River bridge . . . so the troopers began throwing tear gas grenades. As the troopers moved in . . . a crowd of several hundred white persons which had gathered about 100 yards away broke into cheers. The cheering grew louder and the crowd shouted encouragement as the troopers heaved the grenades. . . . As the grenades exploded, the Negroes . . . knelt by the side of the road to pray. But finally the gas routed them and they began running back across the long bridge that leads into downtown Selma. Some stumbled over fellow marchers as they ran in panic and state troopers hit them with clubs. . . . They were chased by the posse all the way back to the church.

"I was somewhere between twelve and fifteen rows from the front," Dobyne recalls. "When everything got started, I followed the instructions. I kneeled down and covered my head up and I heard all kind of noise and activity going around. There was tear gas and you could hear people hollering and crying out. When I finally decided to raise my head and look, I was in the front then and by myself."

After police arrest the leaders, they begin beating the other marchers. As the tear gas hits, protestors flee toward a nearby farm supply store, or into the river. "It was chaos," according to Dobyne, "crying, screaming and noise and everything. I bumped into one of the ladies from Marion, a cousin, Sandy Ford, and I grabbed her and I told her, 'Come go with me. We gotta find a way back to the church.'"

Having started the march well behind Dobyne, Avery has

just reached the foot of the bridge when the troopers throw the tear gas. She joins those running back to Brown Chapel. "That was a horrible day," she will say later. "My husband really didn't want me to go across the bridge, but I told him that's why we had come." The tear gas was intended to make people jump in the Alabama River, she says. Although she escaped the gas, her friends did not. "They put their pocketbooks up to their faces [for protection] and the pocketbooks got burned."

George Baker rides in an ambulance with two doctors and two nurses. The police won't let any traffic near the bridge. "We parked a block away," Baker later wrote. "I went up to some Negro people and asked what was happening. They said that tear gas was already in use and the marchers had started back across the bridge. . . . A few minutes later the first of the returning marchers were up to us. Two or three people were put on stretchers and into ambulances. . . . Emotional contagion was building rapidly among the Negroes."

Finally, local police, who Baker said were not being violent, let the ambulance through: "We witnessed possemen on horseback driving the marchers back over the bridge," he recalled. "They urged the horses forward with their feet and pulling back on the reins. This caused the horses to kick out high with their front feet . . . so that the horses would kick the marchers. One nurse told me later that she had seen a horse kick one of the marchers in the head. We drove on past the marchers to see if there was anyone left behind and saw bedrolls and purses and shoes and jackets and scarves strewn all over."

Baker sees a lady on the ground. "It turned out to be Mrs. Boynton, and she was unconscious. We helped put her on a stretcher and into the ambulance. Other injured stragglers climbed in. A doctor, nurse, and I stayed behind because there was no room. There were troopers milling all around and I was sort of scared, but they left us alone."

As Clark and his posse chase the marchers back into town, a disgusted Wilson Baker orders the sheriff to keep his men back. "Everything will be all right," Clark tells the public safety director. "I've already waited a month too damn long!"

"A bunch of police on horses in the street had gotten us back on the sidewalk going back across the bridge," Dobyne remembers. "They followed us. There was one cop that had targeted me to beat me, and he followed me around and I kept up next to the building out of reach where he couldn't come in with the horse to hit me."

Hearing gunfire, Dobyne runs to the housing project near the church and begins knocking on doors in search of a safe place. "I think both sides were shooting," he said later. "Because when we were in the church before the march, there was a bunch of guys from the Selma area that said, 'I have my gun and I ain't gonna let anybody beat my head.' And once the cops started beating and turning dogs on them, one of those guys was the first one I saw running back. Once they got back in the projects, then the shooting started."

"Thirty minutes after the marchers' encounter with the troopers a Negro could not be seen walking the streets," the *Selma Times-Journal* will report. Many, however, can be found in the makeshift trauma center set up in the parsonage adjacent to Brown Chapel. "Negroes lay on the floors and chairs, many weeping and moaning, the *New York Times'* Roy Reed will write. "A girl in red slacks was carried from the house screaming. Mrs. Boynton lay semiconscious on a table. Doctors and nurses threaded feverishly through the crowd administering first aid and daubing a solution of water and baking soda on the eyes of those who had been in the worst of the gas."

John Lewis is among the approximately eighty injured marchers. He has a fractured skull and concussion. Before seeking treatment at Good Samaritan Hospital, the SNCC leader addresses those who have made it back to the church: "I don't know how President Johnson can send troops to Vietnam. I don't see how he can send troops to the Congo. I don't see how he can send troops to Africa, and he can't send troops to Selma, Alabama. Next time we march, we may have to keep going when we get to Montgomery. We have to go to Washington."

Later, F. D. Reese and Hosea Williams speak at the church to a crowd of seven hundred marchers and others who have come to show their support and anger. Reese feels triumphant despite the attack. He is proud that the assembled challenged the powers that be. Williams says: "I fought in World War II, and I once was captured by the German army, and I want to tell you that the Germans never were as inhuman as the state troopers of Alabama."

Nine-year-old Sheyann Webb, one of the youngest marchers, sits in the church, still suffering the effects of the tear gas. In a memoir written fifteen years later, *Selma Lord, Selma,* she will recall that at first everyone who had returned from the bridge seemed to have given up hope. Later, however, the people start humming a freedom song, "Ain't Gonna Let Nobody Turn Me 'Round." The tune is familiar, but the words are new: "Ain't gonna let George Wallace turn me 'round . . . Ain't gonna let Jim Clark turn me 'round . . . Ain't gonna let no state trooper turn me 'round . . . Ain't gonna let no horses . . . ain't gonna let no tear gas—ain't gonna let nobody turn me 'round. Nobody!"

"And everybody's singing now," Webb writes, "and some of them are clapping their hands, and they're still crying, but it's a different kind of crying. It's the kind of crying that's got spirit, not the weeping they had been doing. And me and [my friend] Rachel West are crying and singing and it just gets louder and louder. I know the state troopers outside the church heard it. Everybody heard it. Because more people were coming in then, leaving their apartments and coming to the church—because something was happening. We was singing and telling the world that we hadn't been whipped."

By late Sunday evening, the entire nation has seen and been horrified by the images of the state of Alabama's attack on the marchers. ABC cuts into its regularly scheduled programming— of all things, the network premiere of the movie *Judgment at Nuremberg*—to show several minutes of film footage. NBC sends the feed to its affiliates across the country for broadcast at 10 p.m. or 11 p.m., as does CBS.

Valeriani, back on the civil rights beat for NBC after his hospitalization the night Jackson was shot, recalls how he covered what has come to be known as "Bloody Sunday."

What I said was, "Dozens of civil rights marchers tried to go from Selma to Montgomery today. They were stopped by state police, and this is what happened." And then I shut up. We watched the film for, like, a minute—just showing them wading into them, tear gas, beating the hell out of them. And I said, "The marchers say they'll try again." And I signed off.

The marchers are going to try again. Those on the ground in Selma provide constant updates of the attack to the leaders of SCLC and SNCC in Atlanta. Each organization agrees that the movement cannot allow itself to be cowed by Governor Wallace, Sheriff Clark, and others of their ilk.

Kwame Ture (then known as Stokely Carmichael) later recalled the reaction of SNCC's executive committee. "Naturally Bloody Sunday rendered, at least for a New York minute, all doctrinal and strategic differences [with SCLC] moot," he noted. "For many in SNCC it was déjà vu all over again, the Freedom Rides revisited, the 'violence-cannot-be-allowed-to-stop-the-movement' reflex."

Jim Forman summons all SNCC members to Selma. Dr. King summons an even larger group to resume the march. On Sunday night, he sends telegrams to hundreds of religious institutions, progressive organizations, and clergy:

> The people of Selma will struggle on for the soul of the nation, but it is fitting that all Americans help to bear the burden. I call therefore, on clergy of all faiths, representatives of every part of the country, to join me in Selma for a ministers march to Montgomery on Tuesday morning, March ninth.

In Boston, a thirty-eight-year-old white Unitarian minister hears King's call. He sympathizes with the cause, but is unsure whether it would be wise to leave his pressing work and his young family for Selma. The decision Rev. James Reeb makes will change history.

CHAPTER FIVE

"HOW DO YOU MURDER PEOPLE?"

March 8, 1965

James Reeb has posted a prayer over his desk at the American Friends Service Committee (AFSC) office on Blue Hill Avenue in the tough Boston neighborhood of Roxbury:

> Grant us peace fearlessly to contend against evil and to make no peace with oppression and, that we may reverently use our freedom, help us to employ it in the maintenance of justice among men and nations.

On the day after the bloody police action on the Edmund Pettus Bridge, the minister turned community organizer is not at peace. A fellow Unitarian has just called to tell him of Martin Luther King's appeal for help some 1,250 miles to the south. Reeb is horrified by the televised images of state troopers beating helpless black men and women, and his immediate reaction is to get on an airplane and join other clergy for the next day's march in Selma.

But he is not certain he should go. He has a wife and four young children at home. What if something should happen to him? He is also embroiled in a contentious fight with the city of Boston over a recent fire in the African American community and the need for better building codes. What message will he be sending to his opponents as well as those he represents if he leaves town?

Over the next few hours, he speaks with several people. He confesses his ambivalence to Herbert Hillman, the head of the AFSC regional community relations committee. Hillman tells him to weigh his options carefully, then adds, "I know it's academic, but you could get hurt."

Reeb also seeks counsel from Rev. Virgil Wood, an African American friend who is SCLC's area representative. Would I be of service if I went? Reeb asks.

Yes, Wood tells him. "I am speaking as a Negro. I think it is important for a white man to stand with the Negro in whatever hellhole he finds himself. It is important for white people to share in the suffering Negroes have had to endure."

Reeb next speaks with John Sullivan, executive director of AFSC's New England region. Sullivan gives his blessing—so long as Reeb thinks his work won't suffer in his absence. Reeb explains that King has asked clergy to come down for twenty-four to forty-eight hours and that he expects to be back in his office by Wednesday or Thursday.

Office mates Dan Richardson and Bob Gustafson tell Reeb they can handle matters while he is away. Gustafson, who is white, has worked in the South and was once attacked by a segregationist thug. He warns Reeb that Selma could be dangerous.

Before leaving the office, Reeb also calls Unitarian

Universalist headquarters in Boston. Although he resigned as associate minister at All Souls Church in Washington, D.C., in the summer of 1964 to take the position with AFSC, Reeb remains a Unitarian. Now he is told that a large number of Unitarians are going to Selma.

At about 5 p.m., Reeb heads to his nearby home, described by his friend Rev. Jack Mendelsohn as "a rambling old frame dwelling on Half Moon Street in North Dorchester, with a shrinking number of white neighbors and a swelling number of Negro neighbors."

Marie Reeb, too, is dedicated to fighting oppression. But her top priority is her husband's safety. She also worries about her family's security. They took a pay cut to come to Boston, borrowed money to buy their home, and gave up their health and life insurance policies. What if he is attacked as the marchers were on Sunday? Who will provide? "There are others to go. You belong here," she says.

"No, I belong there. It's the kind of fight I believe in," he responds. "I want to be part of it. Every man who can go is needed."

She tells him that she understands. The family will "manage somehow" in his absence. "I know you'll be all right. It is important that you go."

After calling friends to get the names of SCLC contacts in the South, Reeb says good night to his four children. John has just turned thirteen. Karen is two weeks shy of her seventh birthday. Anne is five. Steven is three.

Reeb's flight to Atlanta departs at 11 p.m. There will be a layover of several hours. Then he'll board a plane to Montgomery. In Boston's Logan Airport, he sees many Unitarian friends.

About a hundred laymen and clergy from New England are on their way to Selma. Given a registration form, Reeb writes "Unitarian Minister" next to his name.

"Unitarian Minister" only begins to describe the man. "Community organizer" is equally insufficient. Who is James Reeb?

Born in Wichita, Kansas, in 1927, Reeb moved to Casper, Wyoming, when he was a high school sophomore. His father, Harry, was an executive at Western Oil Tool Company. His mother, Mae, was devoted to her son's education and spiritual growth. Jimmie Joe, as Reeb was called in his early years, was an only child. Because his eyes were crossed, he began wearing glasses when he was eighteen months old. Until an operation corrected the condition, he was teased by classmates.

Reeb was raised Presbyterian but developed close ties to a different denomination when in high school. While volunteering at the local Boys Club, he asked Rev. Griffith Williams, the minister of a nearby Lutheran church, to serve as "unofficial chaplain" to the group. Williams later described the young man as "church-minded [but] not strongly sectarian or denomination-minded." The pair taught religion and worked together on sports programs. About this time, Reeb decided he wanted to be a minister.

Reeb led an ROTC unit in high school. After graduating in 1945, he enlisted in the army. He served for eighteen months in California and Alaska. While in the military, he became increasingly devout. In an army chapel in Anchorage, he had a religious experience. "Inside all was blackness, but suddenly there seemed to be light all around him," Reeb's friend and biographer, Rev. Duncan Howlett of All Souls Church, writes. "He did not doubt that it was of heavenly origin."

Following his discharge in 1947, Reeb entered St. Olaf College, an evangelical Lutheran school in Northfield, Minnesota, on the GI Bill. There he was "a literalist as far as belief in the Bible was concerned" and strictly observed the Sabbath. He refused to study on Sundays, because study was work.

Although he found Lutheran theology "better than my own," he still preferred Presbyterianism. "The Lutherans are not sufficiently involved in life for me," he wrote. "The Presbyterians are involved in a greater degree in the lives of people and I think that is as important as sound doctrine."

Shortly after graduating from college in 1950, Reeb married Marie Deason, whom he had met in Casper. One month later they moved to New Jersey, and he entered the Presbyterian-affiliated Princeton Theological Seminary. He was not particularly happy there. "All the Bible minutiae, the church history, and the theology courses seemed tedious to him," Howlett explains. "Because he found them neither intellectually exciting nor practically important, it had become increasingly clear in his mind that he would not take a church after graduation, but would seek a chaplaincy instead."

Reeb had enjoyed doing fieldwork at Philadelphia General Hospital (PGH) under the hospital's Presbyterian chaplain, Rev. Robert Foulkes. Offered a promotion at a different hospital, Foulkes recommended that Reeb succeed him. Reeb accepted, reasoning that the people at the hospital needed him more than Sunday churchgoers.

Reeb would spend almost four years at PGH. During his tenure he took courses at Temple University and earned a master's degree in sacred theology. He and Marie also started a family. John was born in 1952. Whenever possible they vacationed back home in Wyoming. Reeb enjoyed collecting fossils, and his study of the bones contributed in part to his conclusion that the Bible need not be taken literally.

A number of the patients Reeb saw at PGH were people of color with limited economic means. Many believed in prayer. Reeb had his doubts:

> I thought that in many instances prayer was a substitute for actions that could conceivably have more influence than the God who was prayed to. I was particularly impressed that the mortality rate for the newborn fell markedly when the *city fathers* appropriated more money for personnel and better equipment for the maternity wards. I never remember an unexpected change occurring after prayers of *the church fathers*.

The doubts grew. Three years into his chaplaincy, Reeb decided to leave the Presbyterian ministry, having "clearly progressed in my views until I am much more of a humanist than deist or theist." His goal now was to "inspire people to noble and courageous living."

After reading a great deal about Unitarianism and attending Unitarian services, Reeb sought a ministry in that church. "Here were his own thoughts duplicated almost exactly," says Howlett: "The depths of human experience are emotional; it is the task of religion to fathom those depths; each individual must plumb the vastness of experience for himself, yet in community, for there we do it more effectively."

The vetting process to become a Unitarian minister took time. During the interim, Reeb served as youth director of the West Branch YMCA in Philadelphia. Much of his work there was in the black community. During a conversation with an African American on the Youth Board, Reeb said he could identify with how black people felt. The board member pushed back, but Reeb held his ground. "I do feel it," he said. "I feel the pain inside me—physical pain. I have worked among Negroes for several years now. I have seen them in their deepest misery, and I think I understand. But I must agree with you that few people do."

In the spring of 1959, Rev. Howlett began a search for an assistant minister with an understanding of urban and racial issues. He was introduced to Reeb and hired him. Howlett would later explain: "Jim was singularly dedicated to a high concern for all people from all walks of life. This concern expressed itself among the poor living near the church, most of whom were Negroes. This was a man with fresh ideas, bright intelligence, original, yet with an extraordinary amount of modesty."

All Souls, located at 16th Street and Harvard NW in the nation's capital, appeared to be the ideal fit for Reeb. It had been founded as First Unitarian Church of Washington in 1821 by, among others, John Quincy Adams and boasted a long tradition of abolitionist ministers. The church's thousand-pound bell, cast by Paul Revere's son Joseph, was for decades the city's unofficial emergency bell, until it was rung to mourn the death of John Brown after the raid at Harpers Ferry in 1859. After that, it became known as the "Abolition Bell."

During the Civil War, the church served as a hospital for wounded soldiers. Its minister, William Henry Channing, then organized the Freedman's Relief Union to help liberated African Americans. In the early twentieth century, the church was the center of a push for women's rights.

Civil rights also became a priority, and Eleanor Roosevelt would use the church's desegregated dining room to meet

with women of all races. All Souls formally welcomed its first
African American members in 1950, and three years later,
Rev. A. Powell Davies led congregation members in a boycott
of restaurants and entertainment venues that refused entrance
to blacks. In 1954, the church organized the city's first deseg-
regated youth club in the Columbia Heights neighborhood.
Howlett, whose tenure began in 1958, would later lead a thou-
sand congregants from the church to the Lincoln Memorial for
Dr. King's "I Have a Dream" speech during the 1963 March on
Washington.

Reeb quickly became involved in urban matters. He helped
organize a fair housing group, participated with Washington's
Urban Renewal Council, and chaired the University Neighborhoods Council, an inner-city collaboration between Howard
University and neighborhood organizations.

The young minister was also involved with the church's teenage youth group, the Charmian Club. Ron Engel, who met Reeb
while serving as an intern at All Souls in 1962, remembers him
leading an annual midnight trek to Gettysburg. "Once there, we
paid our respects at the eternal flame and then began the ritual
enactment of the battle of Gettysburg. . . . Whenever the group
lagged, Jim revved it up. I remember him sweeping his arm out
over the landscape and pretending Pickett's men were advancing
that minute across the plain."

The two men became fast friends. In the early 1960s, Engel
writes, they and other colleagues were "caught up in this ecumenical movement of church renewal and totally absorbed in an
attempt to redefine the most basic terms of our faith." This was
nothing new to Reeb, who had already redefined himself and
his religious beliefs on several occasions.

"We believed that the first word religion must speak is a word against religion, against the self-satisfied notion that the church exists as an end in itself, that its purpose is to solve the 'spiritual needs' of its members," Engel would say of their new definition of faith. "We could not believe that the church was justified in devoting its resources to bigger buildings and programs when the earth was groaning outside its doors laboring to bring forth a more just social order."

To help deliver that social order, Reeb decided in the fall of 1963 to leave All Souls and take a ministry in the inner city. Unable to find the right match within his church, he searched out urban programs aimed at helping disenfranchised minorities. Engel had become a community organizer with the Center for Urban Ministry on Chicago's north side. Reeb interviewed for a position there, but the center could not find sufficient funding to pay him.

In 1964, Reeb learned that AFSC was launching a pilot program in Boston to assist low-income African Americans in marshaling their own resources to improve their living conditions, particularly their housing. "The emphasis was to be on working *with* people—not *on* or *for* them," said Mendelsohn.

Applicants were asked to explain why they wanted the job. "I have been primarily seeking an opportunity where I could continue to help meet the problems of the people of our great urban centers," Reeb wrote. "I think this is a particularly crucial period. Many Negroes are living in . . . wretched conditions. They see few white people that are interested in their welfare."

After a round of interviews, AFSC hired Reeb as their Boston community relations director. He began on September 1, 1964.

In his final sermon at All Souls in July, Reeb spoke of the current racial climate:

What the Negro now knows is that no man has the right to have his foot on his neck. . . . [The Negro] has a new sense of self-dignity out of which will be born a greater sense of taking responsibility for their own future, but out of which must also be born our sense of understanding what is involved. . . . We must not let the backlash, as it were, increase because we continue to see that Negroes do what people call push. There is going to be even greater pressure for more progress, for now the Negro knows that there is only injustice that stands between him and a better way of life.

In Washington, the church had provided a home for the Reebs in a comfortable neighborhood. In Boston, the Reebs bought a house in the inner city. To demonstrate that they were part of the community, they disregarded the advice of many friends and sent their children to the underfunded public school in the neighborhood rather than private school.

Although willing to fight for his constituents, Reeb remained true to his principles. Once, a member of the Boston Action Group came to the office with a newspaper photo of a white police officer beating a black man. He suggested Reeb hang it on the wall to "show the folks what police brutality is."

Reeb refused. The people already knew, he explained. The man left in a huff. "Had the visitor seen to the heart of the man he was talking to, he would have seen that he was a man of peace who would not hang in his office a picture that might be considered to be inciting in character," writes Howlett. He adds that the incident "plunged Jim into deep despair." Reeb felt that this activist, as well as others in the community and his staff, thought he "was not really an action man."

George Rae, AFSC's assistant executive secretary, took a different view. "Jim was kind, very kind, but there was a point beyond which he could not be pushed. He felt a deep sense of outrage at injustice." He was thorough and deliberate, but "when he made a decision, he moved and moved fast."

Reeb kept a log during his six months in Boston. In it, he chronicled numerous meetings with government officials, civil rights and religious leaders, neighborhood organizations, and local residents. He reported on his testimony before a low-income housing commission and his discussions with SNCC and the Congress of Racial Equality (CORE) about tactics to improve the housing code. He wrote about sympathetic bureaucrats and less than sympathetic white citizens, and vice versa. He also observed:

★ "Tenants evidence a deep frustration over their feeling of being trapped in inferior housing and at the mercy of landlords."

★ "Many residents do not appear to see the relevance of the civil rights movement in their lives."

★ "City officials believe the job of tenant education is the most difficult of all and that no agency is doing the job. They resent suburban residents who criticize things in the city but do not work to change the rules in their own communities."

Reeb faced his toughest challenge early in 1965. 4 DIE IN ROXBURY FIRE, MOTHER KILLED IN LEAP WITH BABY, read the headline above a story chronicling a horrifying blaze shortly before midnight on December 30, 1964. Among the dead in the twenty-nine-unit building were Anna Lou Perry and two of her young children. "A third Perry child, Emmet Jr., 1, was saved when the mother leaped from a fifth-floor window and cushioned the fall with her own body."

Reeb had previously tried, without success, to talk with city officials about a variety of housing and fire code violations. After the Roxbury tragedy—called the Hammond Street Fire—he and others in his office undertook an extensive evaluation of the fire code. They interviewed displaced residents of the building, housing department and fire officials, inspectors, and others.

On March 3, Reeb met with assistant Boston fire chief John E. Clougherty and informed him that he was going to make a report on the fire and call for creation of an independent citizens' committee to study the codes. Reeb would write in his log: "We were mainly concerned about the inadequacy of the exits."

Clougherty went on the offensive. He said the fire had been set intentionally and told Reeb, "You are no expert. You can't say anything about this fire that would have any meaning." The chief accused Reeb of trying to get publicity for his organization and stir up trouble because the victims were black. "If you are wrong, I will murder you," Clougherty said.

"How do you murder people?" Reeb shot back.

In his log, Reeb noted, "This set off a volcano." Clougherty apparently thought Reeb was accusing the fire department of killing people. Reeb explained that he had respect for the department and was simply asking what Clougherty had meant by his remark.

Reeb followed up his account of this meeting with a note in his log that he had asked a photographer to take more pictures of the building. "So long as I may be 'murdered,' to say nothing of AFSC, I thought we should supplement our evidence in every way."

This was James Reeb's last entry before heading to Selma on the evening of March 8. He left it on his desk next to a stack of AFSC pamphlets on nonviolence. One pamphlet was turned to a page that featured words from George Orwell's classic *1984*: "If you want a picture of the future, imagine a boot stamping on a human face—forever."

While waiting to depart from the airport, Reeb sees several colleagues. Among them is Rev. Orloff Miller, the director of the Unitarian Universalists' College Centers Program. Miller, too, saw the images of Bloody Sunday on television. Having previously been to Mississippi, he knows Selma could be dangerous. Just a few weeks earlier he had told another clergyman who was thinking about going to Alabama that he shouldn't go unless he was prepared not to return. Henry Hampton, the Unitarian Universalists' information director, is also present. In the future, he will create one of the largest minority-owned film production companies in the United States and produce the *Eyes on the Prize* documentaries about the civil rights movement.

In California, another Unitarian, Rev. Clark Olsen, kisses his wife and young daughter good-bye and heads for Selma. The thirty-two-year-old minister of the Berkeley Fellowship of Unitarians was driving near the San Francisco Bay when he heard Dr. King's summons on his car radio. Rather than be "a silent witness," he decided he wanted to "stand there on behalf of everyone in decency." But, finding the airfare too expensive, he was resigned to staying home, until two members of his congregation offered to pay his way.

Clergy of all faiths answer King's call. Rabbi Israel Dresner, known as "the most arrested rabbi in America," journeys from Springfield, New Jersey. A close friend of Dr. King, he was first jailed in 1961 while on an interfaith freedom ride. California's Episcopal bishop James Pike, Methodist bishop John Wesley Lord of the National Council of Churches, and Msgr. George Gingras of the Roman Catholic archdiocese in Washington also hurry to Alabama.

The Medical Committee for Human Rights sends additional personnel to join the small contingent that was on hand for Bloody Sunday. There were not enough doctors and nurses to handle all the injuries. Seventeen marchers remain hospitalized.

In his diary, George Baker notes that "one of the doctors from King's party that was coming from the Montgomery airport told me that for the whole trip police cars were weaving in and out following them."

This is not an isolated incident. Governor Wallace has stationed one hundred highway patrol cars in Montgomery. The state troopers wait there, on call to back up the large number of troopers already in Selma. In the meantime, the highway patrolmen, their cruisers bearing the Confederate flag, stop all vehicles driving between Selma and Montgomery to ask drivers their destinations and plans.

Laypersons also converge on Selma. Among those who plan to march are three prominent women. Emily Taft Douglas, a former Democratic congresswoman from Illinois, is active in several social justice causes. Jane Dahlman Ickes is involved in the conservation, women's rights, and civil rights movements. Lillian Crompton Tobey is active in the Red Cross.*

---

*Although these three women were activists, they were almost always referred to as the wives or widows of prominent men. Douglas was the wife of U.S. Senator

The involvement of women in the movement had long been an issue of contention. As women participated in, and in many instances led, the drive for civil rights, they endured injustice and subjugation based on their gender. Race further complicated the picture; white women had an easier time addressing gender disparity, while black women often faced the painful choice between racial justice or their rights as women. Yet despite these difficulties, the contributions of women to civil rights were numerous and transformative.

Beyond the well-known story of Rosa Parks—whose refusal to vacate her bus seat was a calculated step in a long journey as a disciplined activist—there are countless women like Lucy Foster and Willie Nell Avery in Marion, or Amelia Boynton and Marie Foster in Selma, who battled Jim Crow in their own backyard. Many offered leadership beyond their communities.

Ella Baker's vision of broad, deep participation in the democratic process guided her decision making as she established an impressive track record as a community organizer. Baker assumed a critical role in shaping SCLC, including serving as its executive director, and had a part in the formation of SNCC.

The daughter of sharecroppers, Fannie Lou Hamer lent her booming voice and commanding presence to SNCC's efforts. She faced arrests, beatings, and jail time, gaining a reputation for fearlessness and poise during nonviolent protest. As a founder of Mississippi Freedom Summer, Hamer worked to flood her home state with college students from throughout the country

---

Paul Douglas. Ickes was the widow of Harold Ickes, Franklin Roosevelt's secretary of the interior. Tobey was the widow of Senator Charles Tobey of New Hampshire.

to support local blacks on voting rights, education, and community empowerment.

Born far from Mississippi and its unrestrained racism, the Chicago native Diane Nash was, as noted, an architect and tactician of the Nashville Student Movement. Her talent for nonviolence strategy was on display when, as a culmination of the campaign, with equal parts shrewdness and charm, she extracted a televised denouncement of segregation from Nashville mayor Ben West.

Many women and men, black and white, clergy and laity, arrive in Selma on Monday in time for a midnight meeting at Brown Chapel. Few in the crowd are aware that King has spent the last several hours searching his soul. And they have no idea that he plans to tell them that he is postponing the march.

King's inner turmoil began earlier in the day. His lawyers went to federal court seeking an order overturning Wallace's ban on the march to Montgomery. In response U.S. district court judge Frank M. Johnson Jr. scheduled a hearing for later in the week and said the march should be postponed until he issued a decision.

The forty-six-year-old Johnson, raised and schooled in Alabama, is one of just a few state or federal judges in the South sympathetic to the movement. He and Wallace, once friends, have been at odds for some time. The governor has referred to him as an "integrating, scalawagging, carpetbagging liar."

The ruling puts King in a difficult position. The minister is well aware that many of his supporters disdain civil disobedience. If he proceeds with his plans, he will be violating a federal order—something he has never done—and antagonizing allies in Washington. If he postpones the march, he will be disappointing hundreds of people from distant cities who have answered his call to Selma on short notice at significant expense. Practically speaking, SNCC will most likely march anyway, and this will further undercut King, who is already taking heat for not having been at the front of the line on Sunday.

King is also receiving pressure to delay the march from President Johnson and Attorney General Katzenbach, who are sympathetic to the cause but worried about a replay of Sunday's violence. *Give us more time to set up a mechanism to protect you,* they tell King. They weigh the possibility of sending in federal troops, something the National Association for the Advancement of Colored People (NAACP) is now demanding.

The president himself is also under pressure. "Democrats and Republicans complained that President Johnson's promise to eliminate the remaining barriers to Negro voting rights had not yet been sent to Congress," the *New York Times* reports the day after the bloody march. Senator Joseph S. Clark Jr. from Pennsylvania threatens to submit his own bill if Johnson does not act quickly.

Washington lawmakers also condemn the violence. Speaker of the House John McCormack calls Bloody Sunday "a disgraceful exhibition of arbitrary power." Senator Ralph Yarborough of Texas adds: "Shame on you, George Wallace, for the wet ropes that bruised the muscles, for the bullwhips that cut the flesh, for the clubs that broke the bones, for the tear gas that blinded, burned and choked into insensibility!"

The foreign press, too, takes note of Sunday's events. In Great Britain, the *Guardian* writes that "indiscriminate use of [clubs] by forces of law and order against inoffensive demonstrators is a major blemish on the face of American society." The Soviet Union describes Selma as a "bloody pogrom." And Communist China's *People's Daily* opines, "the law and the court are but an instrument of the ruling class for the oppression of the American people."

Still, an FBI assessment of the international coverage notes, "editorials condemn police brutality in Selma, but point out that it is not representative of the country and merely the rearguard action of white supremacists doomed to defeat." The events in Selma appear on the inside pages of foreign papers rather than the front pages, which give "more immediate concern" to Vietnam and U.S. and Soviet achievements in space.

President Johnson does not talk directly to Governor Wallace, with whom he has only a passing acquaintance. Instead, he communicates his concerns through Senator Lister Hill of Alabama and Buford Ellington, the former governor of Tennessee. Each has Wallace's ear if not his heart. Johnson's conversation with Ellington is recorded:

President Johnson: We got a little problem. The biggest problem we have in the Alabama situation is communicating with George Wallace. He apparently has his own very strongly held, positive views on just how this thing ought to be handled. We . . . it would improve the situation a good deal if we could speak freely with him with confidence in each other, but we have nobody who could do that. Do you think that you have that much standing with him?

Buford Ellington: Mr. President, I talked with George, I guess, 10 minutes Friday about the Appalachian Bill. My relationship with George has been very good, but you can't trust him. You talk to him; you don't know what he's going to say. . . . But I can talk to him anytime, but it is an element of danger there in talking with George.

Wallace is unrepentant about the actions of the state troopers. After denying that his men used unnecessary force, he asserts that they actually saved the lives of many on the bridge. He explains that the troopers could not have protected the marchers all the way from Selma to Montgomery. Angry white citizens would surely have ambushed the procession. "There's no telling what would have happened," he says. "There's a good possibility that death would have resulted to some of these people if we had not stopped them." He promises to use the same tactics if there is a march on Tuesday. Responding to rumors that the governor might call out the Alabama National Guard, a spokesman says that a decision has not yet been reached.

Processing all that had happened Monday, King consults with his lawyers before heading to the midnight rally. *Do not march until Judge Johnson rules*, they counsel. Reluctantly, King agrees.

Now, however, standing before those assembled at Brown Chapel, he says, "We've gone too far to turn back. We must let them know that nothing can stop us. Not even death itself."

Why the change of heart? Historian Gary May surmises that the size and makeup of the crowd—"more than one thousand, the veterans of the day before now augmented by distinguished clergymen and others who had just arrived from thirty states"—may have influenced King. "Although King did not explicitly say it, his audience thought his decision was irrevocable. They would march again tomorrow [Tuesday], and this time he would lead them."

But would he? Early Tuesday morning, Judge Johnson denies King's lawyers' request for a temporary restraining order that would allow the march immediately. "There will be no irreparable harm if the plaintiffs will await a judicial determination of the matters involved," says the judge. A hearing leading to that determination will take place in two days, on Thursday, March 11. The judge decrees that the plaintiffs are "hereby enjoined and restrained from attempting to march from Selma, Ala. to Montgomery, Ala. until this court can have a reasonable opportunity to make a judicial determination."

After the ruling, President Johnson issues his first statement about the events in Selma: "I am certain Americans everywhere join in deploring the brutality with which a number of Negro citizens in Alabama were treated when they sought to dramatize their deep and sincere interest in attaining the precious right to vote." He promises to submit voting rights legislation to Congress soon and says that the Justice Department will assist Dr. King in his court battle before Judge Johnson. At the same time, White House press secretary George Reedy says that the president wants civil rights leaders to obey Judge Johnson's current order banning a march.

By the time King reaches Brown Chapel early Tuesday afternoon, a compromise has been brokered by LBJ's emissaries, Assistant Attorney General John Doar and LeRoy Collins, director of the federal government's Community Relations Committee. Collins is a former governor of Florida who bucked southern tradition in 1960 when he said he intended to represent all the citizens of his state, "whether that person is black or white, whether that person is rich or poor, or whether that person is influential or not influential." His current post was created by the Civil Rights Act of 1964.

King agrees to lead his marchers to the spot on the Edmund Pettus Bridge where the police action took place on Sunday. They will kneel in prayer there and then return to Brown Chapel. State trooper chief Lingo and Sheriff Clark promise not to attack the marchers. Collins hands King a map of the route he should follow.

In his speech to those ready to march, King does not mention the compromise. Instead he echoes his remarks from the midnight rally fifteen hours earlier: "I have no alternative but to lead a march from this spot to carry our grievance to the seat of government. I do not know what lies ahead of us. There may be beatings, jail, tear gas. But I would rather die on the highways of Alabama than make a butchery of my conscience."

James Reeb and his fellow Unitarians hear King speak. After the late-night flight to Atlanta, they slept in an airport rental car office. At about 8 a.m., they boarded a plane for Montgomery. Volunteers from SCLC and other organizations met them when their flight arrived and drove them—as well as dozens of other out-of-towners—from the airport to Brown Chapel.

As the would-be marchers began to assemble late Tuesday morning, they learned of Judge Johnson's injunction. Just as King was torn between obeying or disobeying the order, so, too, was Reeb. "Jim believed in a law that was higher than the law of the state," Howlett explains. "But what he sought there, as he had before, was a principle by which to decide when a man might set the law of the state aside in the name of the higher law and when he was merely taking the law into his own hands because of a conviction that might be important to him but might not be to others."

Others, too, weigh the pros and cons of violating the court order. "It seems if we wait two more days, we are losing a great deal of public support," says Emily Taft Douglas. Rabbi Dresner is also in favor of marching: "There is a higher law in God's universe and that is God's law. There is a time when man must choose between man's law and God's law."

Charles Reynolds, a graduate student in ethics at Harvard, argues against going forward. "The civil rights movement owes its life and accomplishments to the good will of the Government of the United States," says the Alabama native. "If it were the truth that there were no hope for the civil rights movement in federal government, there might be reason to go against it. For us to march because we are here is not correct."

Why focus on marches and demonstrations when the federal government and courts held so much power to advance voting rights? Central to the movement's strategy was the dramatization of grievances—staging public displays of dissatisfaction with racial injustice—and activists did so in pursuit of two primary goals. First, to amass broader and stronger sympathy and support from the national majority. And second, to spur segregationist backlashes and outbursts like those of Sheriff Clark, which in and of themselves appealed to the conscience of the nation, broadening support for voting rights and racial equality. More than a symbolic gesture, the street-level nonviolent action taken by the people of Marion and Selma and so many others drove the movement forward.

By the time today's march begins at about three o'clock, Reeb has made his decision. He joins the procession, linking arms with a white minister and an African American from Selma. King, SNCC's Jim Forman, CORE's James Farmer, and Bishop Lord of the Methodist Church lead some two thousand men, women, and children on the same route that was followed two days earlier.

At about the same time, thousands in cities across North America march in sympathy with those in Selma—a thousand people in Washington, D.C.; a thousand in Union, New Jersey; two thousand in Toronto. In Beloit, Wisconsin, about 175 students begin a fifty-mile trek to the state capital, Madison. And in Detroit, Mayor Jerome Cavanaugh and Michigan's Governor George Romney lead ten thousand people on a ten-block march to the Federal Building. The Detroit marchers, mostly white, include civic and religious leaders, helmeted construction workers, businessmen, students, and women with children.

When Reeb and those marching in Selma reach the Pettus Bridge, a state police marshal stops them and reads from the injunction Judge Johnson issued earlier in the day. King announces they plan to exercise their constitutional right to march. The marshal does not stop them.

State troopers form a barrier farther down the bridge, as they did on Sunday. And, as on Sunday, when the marchers reach the crest of the bridge, Major Cloud tells them to halt and return to the church. King asks for permission to kneel in prayer and song. Following the script, Cloud says, yes.

Then, a surprise. As the prayers end, Cloud orders his troopers to pull back and let the march proceed. King again must make a difficult decision. Should he continue and face the wrath of Judge Johnson and President Johnson, or turn around and disappoint those he has rallied to march to Montgomery?

"We will go back to the church now," King says.

Many of the marchers are, like Rev. Miller, "astounded and bewildered." Some are angry. Almost none are aware of the plan brokered earlier in the day. *Time* magazine will later call Tuesday's march a "charade." Gary May will note that "many thought that it was [King's] worst moment as a leader."

Reeb is among the confused who march back to Brown Chapel, where King explains: "We decided we had to stand and confront the state troopers who committed the brutality Sunday. We did march and we did reach the point of the brutality Sunday and we had a prayer service and a freedom rally. And we will go to Montgomery next week in numbers no man can number."

The explanation does not satisfy everyone, including many from out of town who expected an impressive advance toward Montgomery, not a sudden retreat back to Brown Chapel. King suggests everyone go out for dinner and then return to the church to discuss future plans.

Reeb considers going back to Boston that night. He has learned of the death of a close friend, and he has much work to do on the Hammond Street Fire. A minister from Georgia offers to drive him to the airport in Atlanta. Reeb puts his suitcase in the minister's car, then changes his mind when another minister asks him to stay.

A group of clergymen look for a place to eat dinner. They have been cautioned to avoid the white neighborhood near the church, where the residents are not hospitable to outsiders. As Edward G. McGrath, a reporter covering the march for the *Boston Globe*, notes: "This is Selma, where to respect the dignity of man, the worth of a vote, and the courage of those who fight for their rights is to qualify as a 'nigger-lover.'"

At the nearby SCLC office housed in the Boynton Insurance Agency, the clergymen ask Diane Nash for restaurant advice. "Do you prefer to eat with your own kind?" she asks.

They tell her they would like to go somewhere frequented by African Americans. She suggests a place around the corner on Washington Street—Eddie's, which is known more formally as Walker's Café. Reeb heads there with Orloff Miller and Miller's friend Rev. Clark Olsen. After a long day of flying, the minister from Berkeley arrived too late to march.

At Walker's Café, jars of pigs' feet and sausage line the counters. Sam Cooke's civil rights anthem "A Change Is Gonna Come" plays over and over on the jukebox. The place is jammed with other clergy and lay people who have come to march, including Mario Savio, leader of student protests at University of California, Berkeley. By the time Reeb, Miller, Olsen, and Gerald Krick, another minister from Boston, are seated, fried chicken is the only option on the menu.

Despite the disappointment of the march, the mood is jovial. Friends who haven't seen each other in some time reconnect. New friends are made. "Lots of positive energy," Olsen later remembered. "The blacks in the café were surprised and appreciative that so many people had answered Dr. King's call."

Reeb and his companions discuss the day's events as well as a student tour of Russia that Olsen will soon be leading. When finished, Reeb decides to call his wife from a pay phone in the café. Miller goes outside to smoke, while Olsen waits inside. Krick heads back with another group.

"I stood outside the restaurant smoking my cigar as the streetlights were just beginning to come on," Miller will recall years later. "They were these sodium vapor lights, or phosphorescent, and I thought to myself, what a peaceful scene this is, it was dusk and there was nobody on the streets and I thought this could be any Midwestern community like I grew up in [back] in Ohio."

CHAPTER SIX

"THEY JUST FLUSHED OUT LIKE BIRDS . . ."

March 9, 1965

Who knows what would have happened if James Reeb, Clark Olsen, and Orloff Miller had returned to Brown Chapel the same way they had come?

Turn *left* coming out of Walker's Café at 118 Washington Street, walk half a block to Alabama Avenue and turn right, continue on Alabama for four blocks, take a left on Sylvan Street, and proceed four more blocks to the church. That route—the one followed by the dozen or so other clergy who had eaten at Walker's—would have taken them back by way of the friendly black neighborhood through which they had passed uneventfully some ninety minutes earlier.

Instead, when they leave the café they turn *right*. Why? Dr. King has asked all those who participated in the aborted march earlier in the day to return to Brown Chapel at 7:30. "It was getting to be that time, and we wanted to make sure we had decent seats. We chose the shortest route," recalled Olsen. "We didn't know we'd be walking past the Silver Moon Café or any other place that catered to whites who were anti-black."

Darkness is beginning to fall as the men set off for the church three abreast on the wide sidewalk. Olsen is closest to the buildings on their right, Miller in the middle, Reeb nearest to the curb. They are in good spirits. The dinner and the conversation were restorative.

A few doors down from Walker's, the three men cross Hogan Alley. It is empty, quiet, as is the rest of the street. They are approaching Selma Avenue now. They will turn right there and head straight to Sylvan Street and the church.

The Silver Moon Café sits on the corner of Selma Avenue and Washington Street. With its swinging doors and tin spittoons, the place recalls the saloons of the Wild West. The whites-only establishment serves everything "from oatmeal to bourbon," a journalist writes, and is a popular Klan hangout.

Some of the ministers' colleagues have already taken a peek at the Silver Moon. Finding a long line at Walker's, these clergymen had sought an alternative on the same block. "We felt an atmosphere of hatred, anger, hostility, and were aware of unsmiling, unfriendly white faces pointed in our direction," Unitarian minister Richard Norsworthy later remembered. "We heard taunts and jeers. I looked inside at the grim faces there, and suddenly I was afraid."

Reeb and his companions are almost at the corner when they see four, maybe five, men coming toward them from across the street, most likely from the doorway of C & C Novelty Company. One in the pack is carrying a club of some kind—a bat or a pipe, thinks Olsen. "Hey you niggers!" someone yells. Olsen assumes the men saw them leave the café and have pegged them as "outside agitators."

Earlier in the day, before Olsen had arrived from California, those marching to the Edmund Pettus Bridge had been taught how to react to a variety of threatening scenarios. "Just keep walking. Don't look at them. Don't run," Miller and Reeb now whisper to their uninitiated friend.

Within seconds the men with the foul mouths and the weapon have crossed the street. Now they are behind the ministers. Olsen can't help himself. He turns around. He sees four "vicious and intense" faces.

One of the men swings the club like it is a baseball bat and hits Reeb squarely in the left temple. "I heard the sound it made," Olsen later said, his voice quavering. "And I saw Jim fall."

Miller crouches and puts his hands over his head in the prayerlike position nonviolent protestors are instructed to employ when attack appears imminent. At least one of the men kicks him, while another kicks the fallen Reeb. Miller shouts for help. No one comes, although it is later revealed that others at the Silver Moon watched the beating.

While Miller kneels, Olsen runs. His response is no more effective. One assailant quickly chases him down, then hits him. "Here's how it feels to be a nigger down here," the attacker snarls as the minister's glasses go flying.

The thugs take off as suddenly as they came. Miller, who later estimates that the attack took no more than a minute, rises and staggers. Olsen returns from down the street, numbed and bruised, but "basically okay."

Reeb is not okay. Although conscious, he is babbling incoherently and his eyes are vacant. Olsen and Miller help him to his feet and lean him against a building wall. After a couple of minutes, Reeb seems to gather his senses. He says his head hurts. Olsen notices a small cut on the left temple but no bleeding.

Reeb is in no condition to walk on his own. Olsen and Miller drape his arms over their shoulders. Then the three men, shaken and hurting, struggle down the street and around the corner to SCLC headquarters. Diane Nash summons a hearse that doubles as an ambulance from the black-owned funeral home next door. She phones the Burwell Infirmary, Selma's ten-bed black hospital located in an aging frame house on Philpot Avenue a mile and a half away. Three injured ministers are on their way, she says.

The "ambulance," a black station wagon used to carry the dead as well as the living, arrives a few minutes later. As the vehicle pulls out, Olsen and Miller notice they are being followed. *Would it make more sense to go to Brown Chapel instead of Burwell?* they ask the driver.

No, he says. The church is surrounded by police who are monitoring Dr. King's meeting. It will be hard to get through. They speed to the infirmary, where the cut just above Reeb's ear is inspected. "It looked superficial enough," Olsen would tell a fellow minister soon after, "but Jim's head was hurting more and more, and he began to act as if he knew something was seriously wrong; his face showed great anxiety and worry. When the doctor came, Jim took hold of my hand with both hands and squeezed as if to keep in contact with the world he knew."

William Dinkins, the same doctor who saw Jimmie Lee Jackson at Selma's Good Samaritan Hospital three weeks earlier, attends to the ministers. He sends Reeb to the X-ray room. Miller, who has been given a cold towel, ice, and aspirin, calls Brown Chapel and asks to speak to Rev. Homer Jack, who is coordinating the Unitarians' social justice initiative. Miller tells him what has happened. Jack says he will come meet the ministers. Before leaving the church, he passes a note to Dr. King.

The assembly is stunned when King reports that three Unitarian ministers have been beaten and that one may have suffered a brain concussion. "Selma had to show its true colors. It was cowardly work done by night," he says. "The beast had to strike back. Now our [white] brethren know something of what it's like to be a Negro in Alabama."

Sheyann Webb, the young girl who listened to the freedom songs in Brown Chapel after Sunday's march, is again in the church. "Shey, you know who it was that got beat up?" her mother asks her.

"Who it was?" asks Sheyann.

"That one with the glasses that was coming for coffee."

Earlier in the day, Sheyann had invited several of the out-of-town marchers to the Webb home. Reeb had come. When leaving, he promised to return. "Of course he never did come back to my house," Webb later wrote.

Reeb's X-ray is difficult to read, but Dr. Dinkins recognizes the gravity of the injury. At first he is unsure whether the minister's skull is fractured. Now he notes reflexes of the pupils indicating pressure is being exerted on the brain. Olsen feels Reeb's tight grip slip away. The minister has lost consciousness.

An operation might be necessary, Dinkins concludes. Reeb needs a neurosurgeon. Selma's hospitals aren't staffed to deal with an injury this severe. University Hospital in Birmingham, ninety miles to the north, is the best place to treat the minister. Dinkins phones and makes arrangements to send Reeb there. The hospital says the patient will need to pay a $150 entrance fee before admission.

The Selma police, called by a nurse at Dr. Dinkins' request, arrive at the infirmary. They question Miller and Olsen. Miller, who scribbled notes on a spiral pad throughout the evening, writes: "Police seem somewhat sympathetic and indicate that they do not condone this business."

Nobody at the infirmary has $150. After helping put Reeb into the ambulance/hearse on a stretcher, Dinkins drives Miller and Olsen back to the SCLC office, where Nash gives them a check made out to the hospital. The ambulance follows them.

Soon a Volkswagen bus carrying Homer Jack and other Unitarian officials arrives. They decide that Miller and Olsen should accompany Dinkins and Reeb to Birmingham. Dinkins sits in the front with the driver, while the two ministers sit in back with their unconscious friend.

After the ambulance leaves, Rev. Jack makes a phone call. "Marie Reeb had to be notified, if possible before the late-night news," he later wrote.

Rev. Jack reaches fellow Unitarian Jack Mendelsohn, the Reebs' minister and friend. Mendelsohn is in the middle of chairing a meeting of the Massachusetts Committee on Discrimination in Housing. Reeb is a member of the committee, and those in attendance have just been talking about his trip to Selma. Mendelsohn terminates the meeting and hurries to the Reeb home on Half Moon Street in Dorchester.

He sits with a devastated Marie Reeb through the night. They receive periodic updates from Birmingham on James Reeb's condition. The news is not good.

Other friends arrive after seeing the eleven o'clock news and learning of the beating. The Reeb children are asleep and unaware of the attack. Their mother does not wake them. She does call her mother and her in-laws. Then she and James Reeb's father, Harry, who is in Casper, Wyoming, decide they will each fly to Alabama in the morning.

The vehicle carrying James Reeb is no more than two miles out of town when it suffers a flat tire. As the driver pulls to the side of the two-lane road, another car suddenly pulls up behind it. And stops. And waits.

Olsen counts at least four white men in the car. None of them get out to offer assistance. "At that point I became quite afraid," Olsen said later. "We didn't know whether this was part of a conspiracy—the attack on us, the flat tire, the guys behind us. We didn't know whether it was all coordinated."

Fearful of what might happen if they get out to change the tire, Dr. Dinkins picks up the vehicle's radio telephone to call for a backup ambulance. The phone doesn't work. *Is this part of the conspiracy, too?* Olsen remembers wondering. "Everything in me was saying, get out of this ambulance and run as fast as you can. And then I remembered Schwerner, Chaney, and Goodman. If I run, my body might end up in a ditch tonight, I thought."

Or a dam. On the evening of June 21, 1964, civil rights workers Michael Schwerner, James Chaney, and Andrew Goodman were followed by a deputy sheriff as they drove through rural Mississippi. They were stopped, pulled from their car, shot at close range by Klansmen, and buried in a dam on the land of another Klan member. Their bodies were not found until August.

Olsen and the others do not run from their disabled vehicle. The driver tells them that he once worked at a nearby radio station. They can all stay in the car, drive slowly on the tire rim, and roll into the station parking lot. Then the driver will go inside to call for an ambulance with four good tires and one good radio phone.

The ambulance makes it to the radio station without incident, although the mystery car does follow. Once there, Olsen suggests that it would be safer if another vehicle could accompany them. Dr. Dinkins agrees and calls for his own car. He will trail them on the drive to Birmingham.

Olsen waits with Miller inside the ambulance for "an interminable amount of time" until the backup ambulance arrives. Reeb remains unconscious on the stretcher. As they wait, they see the mystery car park nearby.

Four men get out. They circle the ambulance. "Hey, what ya doing in there?" one asks. They knock on the windows, but don't try to open the door or break in.

The backup ambulance arrives, as does a Dallas County sheriff's car. The police surround the ambulance and flash lights on Reeb's face. One policeman opens the right rear door and asks Miller and Olsen who the injured man is and what happened to him. The ministers answer. Olsen's request for a police escort is refused. "We'll radio ahead—that's all you'll need," says the cop.

Olsen, Miller, Dinkins, and the driver of the first ambulance start to transfer the stretcher bearing Reeb to the second ambulance. Several white men have gathered to watch. "What's happening here?" one of them asks. His tone is not friendly.

Half a century later, Olsen still becomes emotional when describing the moment. "All I remember saying to him was, 'Please don't.' That's all I could bring myself to say, 'Please don't,' and in fact they did nothing."

Dr. Dinkins' car arrives. Now they can resume the trip to Birmingham. A state trooper who has come offers to escort them to the interstate highway.

The offer catches Olsen off guard. A trooper shot Jimmie Lee Jackson in Marion a few weeks earlier. And just two days earlier, troopers cruelly beat scores on Bloody Sunday. But on this night, as they leave the radio station, there is no trouble with the police.

There is some trouble in the ambulance. There are no brackets to secure the stretcher on which James Reeb lies. Olsen and Miller have to hold it to make sure he does not fall off on a ride that includes not just long stretches of highway, but twists, turns, and bumps.

Medical experts will later say that Reeb's chances of surviving the blow were slim, and they probably became even slimmer due to delays in getting to Birmingham. When the ambulance reaches University Hospital after these delays—at about 11 p.m., almost four hours after the beating on Washington Street—a team of doctors and nurses is waiting for them. Reeb is rushed to the emergency room.

Within minutes he is in surgery. The three neurosurgeons operating on him find a huge blood clot and observe that his skull has been crushed on the left side. The minister's brain can no longer control breathing or the beating of his heart.

As doctors work on Reeb, Miller and Olsen are escorted to a waiting area. Reporters from local and national news outlets— alerted by Dr. King's announcement at Brown Chapel—descend upon them. Miller wants to tell their story. *If something happens to Jim, we have to let the world know what happened and why it happened*, he thinks.

FBI agents conduct a different kind of interview. They take the ministers to a private room and question them about the attack. The agents are straightforward. FBI director J. Edgar Hoover's animus toward Martin Luther King Jr. is well known, but the interrogators betray no such feelings.

Miller's notes are simple, yet poignant:

Arrive. Jim's personal effects turned over to hospital and recorded. Blue Cross card found. Tracheostomy. Evaluate brain damage. Martin Luther King gave prayer for Jim (all of us). 12:30 A.M. Wednesday. Massive skull fracture. Very large clot. 15th floor room reserved for Mrs. Reeb to stay in Hospital (when she arrives).

The hospital offers the ministers a room where they can sleep. They decline, choosing instead to accept the invitation of a Unitarian couple from Birmingham active in the social justice movement. After calling their own families to tell them what happened and that they are well, Olsen and Miller leave the hospital at about 1 a.m., overwhelmed and exhausted.

Even in the Birmingham home, Olsen finds it difficult to feel completely safe. His hosts' civil rights efforts do not sit well with all in the community. The couple feels sufficiently endangered to employ round-the-clock guards.

Wednesday, March 10, brings action on many fronts.

In Selma, Wilson Baker announces, "We are making every effort to arrest the assailants." The public safety director cautions, however, that descriptions of the perpetrators are "vague." One man who witnessed the beating while in the Silver Moon later said he couldn't identify the attackers because "they just flushed out like birds."

Despite the inability or reluctance of witnesses to make an identification, the police effort—in concert with an effort by the FBI—pays off. By evening, three local men are arrested and charged with the attack. Elmer Cook, forty-two, manages C & C Novelty, a store directly across the street from the scene of the crime. He is well known to the police, having been arrested on twenty-five separate occasions, seventeen times for assault and battery. R. B. Kelley is a thirty-year-old television repairman who has also been arrested previously for assault and battery; William Stanley Hoggle is a thirty-seven-year-old salesman who has been arrested for drunken driving in the past. (Within twenty-four hours, Hoggle's brother, Namon O'Neal "Duck" Hoggle, a thirty-one-year-old auto mechanic, will also be charged.) Frances Bowden, who manages the Coffee Pot Café across the street from the Silver Moon, tells a reporter that those arrested are "mean as a snake—all of them."

After his arrest, Cook briefly shares a jail cell with Robert Dorsett, a marketing writer from Illinois who answered Dr. King's call to come to Selma after Bloody Sunday. "Cook wore a neat double breasted suit, was stocky like myself, and was in good spirits," writes Dorsett, who has been charged with vagrancy after failing to present proper identification when stopped by police. "Cook said he liked black people, though they had their place. . . . He and the others [in the cell] did not think the black educable. They thought the black should be treated as a child."

After making bond on the assault with intent to commit murder charges that will be adjudicated in state court, Cook and the others are arrested by FBI agents and charged with a federal offense: conspiracy to intimidate, threaten, or oppress a person in the free exercise of his rights under the laws and the Constitution. Their attorney promptly declares them innocent: "Their only knowledge of the assault on the ministers has come from reading of it in the papers and hearing about it in news reports."

The threat of a criminal trial in federal court is important. Justice Department attorneys are beginning to aggressively prosecute those who attack civil rights demonstrators, in contrast to the state prosecutors throughout the South who seek to convict the demonstrators.

While some of the Selma police are busy investigating the previous evening's attack, other officers and state troopers are assigned to contain three hundred people bent on marching the ten blocks from Brown Chapel to the Dallas County Courthouse. The group wants to protest the beating of the ministers and the continuing denial of voting rights to blacks. Wilson Baker meets the marchers, led by SCLC's Ralph Abernathy and C. T. Vivian, about two blocks from the church at the corner of Sylvan Street and Selma Avenue. He offers them a choice: they can go back to Brown Chapel or stay where they are, but they cannot continue to the courthouse. They stay.

So begins a vigil that will last for several days. On this first night, the *Selma Times-Journal* reports:

> Many marchers produced blankets and air mattresses and started bedding down on the asphalt street and on the grassy area bordering the street. A searchlight played continually throughout the area searching the tops of buildings and in trees. Security was tight, with few unauthorized persons permitted in the vicinity. The demonstrators prayed and sang.

Later the *Birmingham News* will run a story titled "Lovemaking in open definitely occurred in Selma prayer vigil," quoting Wilson Baker, who says he saw "kissing and loving and drinking." Associated Press writer Kelso Sturgeon will confirm this. "I saw at least three couples involved in intercourse. There was considerable other hanky-panky."

• • •

Early Wednesday morning, Marie Reeb boards a plane at Boston's Logan Airport for Birmingham. Her husband's boss at AFSC, John Sullivan, accompanies her. "It was ironic that as the plane stopped in Birmingham the stewardess said on the loudspeaker . . . 'Have a very pleasant day,'" Sullivan recalls. "This we did not have."

By this time, Reeb has gone into cardiac arrest and is being kept alive by a ventilator. He has not regained consciousness since leaving Selma. Doctors at University Hospital tell the family there is no hope of recovery.

Before leaving, Marie Reeb told her children that their father had been injured, but she did not go into detail. Rev. Mendelsohn recalls how he had been the one to inform the oldest Reeb child, thirteen-year-old John, about the seriousness of the situation. "I will never forget the bewilderment, pain, pride, and courage that mingled in constantly changing patterns on his handsome, adolescent face as we talked," Mendelsohn says. "After that we sat together for a long time while he cried, and when he stood up and squared his shoulders it was as one of the adults in the house who would do everything possible to protect the other children from an awful knowledge their mother wanted them to hear from her."

In the federal courthouse in Montgomery, the Johnson administration fulfills its promise to intercede on behalf of Dr. King and help win a court order overturning Governor Wallace's ban on marches. The Department of Justice files a complaint under the recently passed Civil Rights Act of 1964 accusing Wallace, Lingo, and Clark of "preventing and discouraging Negroes from exercising their full rights of citizenship." The suit seeks to eliminate intimidation of those trying to register to vote, to prevent interference with lawful demonstrations, and to compel the officials to provide police protection to those attempting to register or demonstrate. It is conceivable Judge Johnson will rule on this the next day at the hearing he scheduled before Tuesday's shortened march.

The news from Birmingham's University Hospital Wednesday morning is tragic. "7:30 A.M., cardiac arrest," Miller writes. "Mayo surgeon in constant attention. 9:30 A.M., 'We have lost a patient.' Machine is breathing for him and beating his heart for him."

Olsen can't forget that last squeeze of his hand by Reeb. "I was the last person Jim had contact with while he was conscious in this world," he realizes. The two had known each other for less than two hours.

Miller and Olsen again meet with the press. They also meet with C. T. Vivian and Joseph Lowery. Dr. King has sent the two SCLC leaders to offer condolences.

During a second interview with the FBI, the ministers are not asked to identify the assailants. Olsen will soon see their pictures in the *Selma Times-Journal*. "I had this question in mind—were they the ones, were they not the ones?" They looked familiar, especially Cook, but, the minister wondered, was his judgment clouded by the fact that they were in the newspaper?

Rev. Duncan Howlett of All Souls Church flies in from

Washington. He later described going with Marie Reeb and Sullivan to see the dying minister: "There we saw him, lying on one of those rolling, stretcher-like beds . . . a sheet over his body and an enormous bandage wound round his head. A tube had been inserted in his throat just below the Adam's apple, and all about were machines busily at working sustaining his life."

Marie Reeb moves close to her husband. "For a long time she remained there gazing at him, weeping silently, the epitome of human anguish," wrote Howlett.

As evening falls, James Crank, assistant director of the hospital, tells Howlett that he has been keeping the press at bay by promising an interview with Mrs. Reeb. Impossible, the minister replies; she has already been through too much. Crank is considerate, but insistent. "He pointed out what we, isolated as we were, did not realize—that James Reeb, our Jim, was now a figure of international importance," said Howlett.

Marie Reeb is understandably reluctant. She feels emotionally unhinged and intellectually numb. After much discussion, she agrees to answer a limited number of questions if they are submitted in advance of her appearance in front of cameras and microphones. The press agrees to these terms.

Mrs. Reeb prepares her answers and meets reporters in Crank's office. She sits beside ABC's Edgar Needham, who asks all the questions on behalf of the media. Her short responses are delivered in a clear, low voice. She pauses occasionally to maintain her composure.

Q. Was your husband's decision to come to Selma a mutual decision between you and your husband?

A. I told him that I would prefer that he not go. But he said that he had to go.

Q. Do you think Reverend Reeb was aware of the full potential of violence? Were you?

A. Yes, I'm sure he was aware of it.

Q. Did you have any communication with your husband after the march and before he was injured?

A. Yes. Jim called about eight Tuesday evening. He said the march had not gone as planned, but that everything was fine and he would be home Wednesday morning.*

Q. What have the children been told?

A. I told the children this morning as soon as they woke up that their father had been hurt. The younger ones did not fully understand, but the thirteen-year-old was quite upset.

Q. What were some of the reasons he gave for wanting to come to Selma?

A. One of the reasons was the march that occurred Sunday. After he saw that, he felt he had to go. He couldn't stay home and do nothing when he was so much needed there.

Q. Was the cause worth the risk of death?

A. I don't believe I could answer for myself, only for Jim. For him, any consequence that might occur would merit his coming.

---

*This was the phone call Reeb made from Walker's Café just before the fateful walk.

After the brief interview ends, the room is silent. Marie Reeb exits. "I felt that hardened group of news men and women would have applauded had there been any appropriate way to do so, their sympathy and admiration for the courage and tenderness of this stricken woman had been so great," said Howlett.

Harry Reeb arrives from Wyoming a few minutes later. He and Marie immediately go to see his son. "When I looked at him, I knew he was done for," he said.

Later that night, Olsen and Miller painfully recount Tuesday's harrowing events for Marie and Harry Reeb, Howlett, and other friends and colleagues who have come to the hospital. Howlett later wrote: "Marie sat staring at them, tearless, unbelieving. Jim's father, periodically striking his left palm with his closed right hand, shook his head as if to deny what he heard. The rest of us sat stupefied, numb, and cold."

At the end of their hourlong narrative, Miller says, "Marie, Jim was the right man, in the right place, at the right time." He means it as the ultimate compliment. Reeb is now a martyr whose death may alter history. Later, however, Howlett berates him for making insensitive comments. Miller understands that he spoke too soon.

In Washington this Wednesday, the Justice Department announces that the FBI is investigating several events that have transpired in the Black Belt: the previous night's attack on the three ministers, the Bloody Sunday beatings, and the assault on the marchers in Marion the night Jimmie Lee Jackson was shot.

Later in the day President Johnson speaks with Attorney

General Nicholas Katzenbach. "This minister is going to die, isn't he?" says the president.

"Yes, sir," says Katzenbach.

The president and Mrs. Johnson send a bouquet of yellow roses to Marie Reeb in Birmingham.

Thursday, March 11, is a day of reckoning.

Presidential aide Jack Valenti sends a memorandum to LBJ that morning: "All quiet on the civil rights front. Mostly waiting to see what happens to the beaten minister. Trouble will erupt when he dies."

Trouble erupts sooner than expected, but it is not directly related to the beaten minister. One dozen young men and women from SNCC and CORE enter the White House under the pretense of taking a tour. Once inside, they leave the tour and stage a sit-in near the East Wing. The president, already under fire for what some perceive as a tepid effort on the civil rights front, ignores his advisers who want to expel or arrest the demonstrators. "Let them eat and drink, but don't let them go to the bathroom," he says. First Lady Lady Bird Johnson offers to serve them coffee.

At 5 p.m., Attorney General Katzenbach holds a live televised press conference. The event is noted in the White House Daily Diary, kept by Johnson's secretary.

[Katzenbach] was asked questions concerning the riots in Selma and the legislation from the White House on voter's rights that will be sent to the Hill sometime next week. The President was intently watching the telecast—with his chair pulled up directly in front of the set, and leaning over to get a "good, close look."

A reporter from the *Boston Globe* ventures to Roxbury, where he interviews several families who have been touched by James Reeb and are praying for his recovery. "JIM WAS MY FRIEND," SAYS BOY OF 8 runs the story's headline. "Think Jim will be all right?" asks young Billy Golson. His mother adds: "He was such a kind man, always trying to help with better housing and asking how the kids were making out. He was our friend all right."

Another resident describes how Reeb helped them get better heat and electricity at Christmas. "We loved to see him coming to the house because he was the kindest man I ever met," she says.

Rev. Mendelsohn is also interviewed. "He brought a new sense of hope to the Roxbury area. He encouraged downtrodden people to think more hopefully, to realize that they could do a good deal about their own problems, once they were shown the way."

Doctors at University Hospital tell Howlett that Reeb's heart has stopped twice. They have started it again through stimulation. A pacemaker could keep the heart beating, but for all intents and purposes James Reeb is already dead.

Howlett knows what he would do, but says that it is up to Marie Reeb to decide whether "heroic efforts" should be taken. "Tell her about it in such a way she will not feel that she is called upon to let Jim die," he says to the doctor.

Later in the day, Marie and Harry Reeb and Bob Foulkes, the former chaplain from Philadelphia, go to see Reeb again. Nothing has changed.

When Reeb's heart stops again a few hours later, no effort

is made to save him. At 6:55 p.m. (CST), forty-eight hours after he'd turned right instead of left after leaving Walker's Café, Rev. James Joseph Reeb, thirty-eight years old, father of four, is pronounced dead. His death is attributed to complications following one or more blows to the head.

President Johnson is hosting a White House dinner for congressional leaders. Secretary of State Dean Rusk is briefing the guests on Vietnam when the president receives word that Reeb has passed away. Johnson excuses himself and, with the first lady and Vice President Hubert Humphrey, he calls Marie Reeb and Harry Reeb in Birmingham to offer condolences. As they speak to the dead minister's wife and father, the three can hear civil rights demonstrators chanting outside the White House.

"I will have a private plane waiting for you at the airport tomorrow morning to fly you direct to Boston," the president tells the Reebs. "And when you are ready to fly to Wyoming, I will provide for that flight, too."

Years earlier, James Reeb told his wife that when he died he wanted his body to be cremated and his ashes scattered in Wyoming—at the petrified forest on the prairie in the Shirley Basin. She will honor his wishes, but before heading west, there will be a memorial service in Selma on March 15, a funeral in Washington on March 16, and a funeral in Boston on March 18.

Back in Selma, the standoff near Brown Chapel continues. At 9 a.m., Wilson Baker denies a second request for a march to the courthouse in order to hold a prayer vigil for Reeb. Such a march would endanger the citizens of Selma, he explains. He then strings a rope across Sylvan Street. The Selma police stand by, ready to stop anyone daring to breach the barricade.

Soon the protestors have an anthem:

We've got a rope that's a Berlin Wall,
We're gonna stand here till it falls.
Hate is the thing that built the wall,
Love is the thing that'll make it fall.

The faithful stand behind the rope for hours, singing and offering prayers for both Reeb and Jimmie Lee Jackson.

Some two hundred local residents and out-of-town clergy are praying in the rain outside Brown Chapel when the public safety director announces, "Reverend Reeb has died in the hospital in Birmingham."

Two hours earlier, Baker had learned that the minister's death was imminent. He had then approached SCLC's James Orange, who had been released from jail in Marion, and asked: "Can you control your people when it happens?"

"We can control ours. The question is can you control yours?" said Orange.

Each side does maintain control. The peaceful protestors carry the news of Reeb's death to those attending a rally inside the church. SNCC's John Lewis comes outside. "We will hold one minute of silent prayer for our fallen brother," he tells the demonstrators.

By nightfall, the charges against the four men arrested for attacking Reeb have been changed to murder. Several hundred people remain at the Wall. One of them, Rev. Richard Leonard, a Unitarian minister from New York, later noted that they improvised songs to taunt the police. "One song went, 'I love everybody, I love everybody, I love everybody in my heart,'" he recalled. "In succeeding verses, they would name everybody.

'I love Governor Wallace, I love Governor Wallace . . .' Then it would be 'I love Wilson Baker,' and 'I love Chief Al Lingo' [head of the state troopers], and 'I love Martin King,' and 'I love old Bull Connor' [Birmingham's vicious sheriff], and 'I love Jimmie Jackson,' and 'I love Lyndon Johnson,' and 'I love all the troopers,' and on and on into the night."

Martin Luther King Jr. is in Montgomery when he learns of Reeb's passing. He has already begun talking to Homer Jack about a televised interreligious service on Monday if Reeb dies. Now he calls the Reebs to offer his condolences.

King and other movement leaders have spent the day in Judge Johnson's federal courtroom, seeking the injunction against Alabama's ban on highway and street marches. Before that issue is addressed, however, Sheriff Clark's lawyer, W. McLean Pitts, asks the judge to hold King in contempt because he led the march on Tuesday in defiance of the court order.

Johnson chastises the attorney. "Any contempt proceedings will be a matter between the court and the contemptor and is not any business of James Clark."

The likelihood of the judge finding King in contempt is diminished when King testifies. The civil rights leader acknowledges that he called Judge Johnson's Tuesday order "unjust." He also admits the obvious: that he did lead a brief march.

King explains: "I was very upset. I felt like it was condemning the robbed man for being robbed. I was disturbed. Thousands of people who had come to Selma to march were deeply aroused by the brutality of Sunday. I felt that if I had not [led the march] pent-up emotions could have developed into an uncontrollable situation."

Judge Johnson: Is it correct to say that when you started across the bridge you knew at that time that you did not intend to march to Montgomery?"

King: Yes, it is.

King's courtroom revelation of the secret deal with Alabama officials to stop on the bridge, pray, and return to Brown Chapel assuages Johnson, but it also exacerbates the tensions between King and more militant civil rights activists, both white and black. "Many of these spokesmen," the *New York Times* reports, "have privately charged that they were 'betrayed' by King's behind-the-scenes bargaining."

Testimony by others suggests the necessity for court-ordered protection of those demonstrating. Hosea Williams testifies that on Sunday he heard Sheriff Clark tell his men: "Go get them goddam niggers!" Williams adds that he saw about half a dozen possemen with whips. Asked if he knows what a bullwhip is, he responds: "I'm a country boy. I know what a bullwhip is."

The proceeding grows testy, and Pitts's aggressive conduct prompts King's lawyer, Jack Greenberg, to object to his "insulting manner." Sustaining the objection, Judge Johnson informs the room, "Everybody in this court, regardless of who he or she is, will be treated with common courtesy." A correspondent for *Time* observes: "Pitts sputtered: 'I'm trying very hard, but...' Johnson shot back acidly: 'Try a little harder.'"

On Friday morning, March 12, Mayor Smitherman tells blacks and whites peacefully assembled on Sylvan Street that "no marches or demonstrations will be held in Selma as long as the present threat of violence on our citizens exists." Still, the protestors maintain their vigil at the "Selma Wall" throughout the rainy day.

In Boston, black women kneel and pray outside the Reeb home. "They were expressing their sorrow and the sorrow of millions of others over the death of her husband," reports the Associated Press.

The Boston Symphony changes its program that afternoon to perform "Dance of the Blessed Spirits" in Reeb's memory. The orchestra played the same piece after President John F. Kennedy was assassinated eighteen months earlier.

Marie Reeb flies back to Boston on the four-engine C-140 airplane that President Johnson has sent. Before she leaves, an African American minister brings her a collection taken up for her family by Birmingham's black churches. The Unitarians also announce creation of a memorial fund for the four Reeb children.

"[Mrs. Reeb] is not a bitter woman," says AFSC's John Sullivan, who flies back with her and Harry Reeb. He explains that she has been visibly moved by the "outpouring of support and condolence from the President of the United States on down."

Back inside the house at 3 Half Moon Street, Marie Reeb hugs her four children and asks them to come upstairs with her. She wants to tell them about their father.

CHAPTER SEVEN

"ONE GOOD MAN . . ."

March 12, 1965

On the same day that Marie Reeb returns home to her now-fatherless children, President Johnson meets in the Cabinet Room of the White House for more than two hours with nine white and nine African American civil rights leaders. The meeting addresses the recent events in Selma and the imminent introduction of voting rights legislation. The group includes Dr. King's representative, Rev. Walter Fauntroy, head of the Washington branch of SCLC; SNCC's Lester McKinnie; Rev. Joseph Ellwanger, who led the march of concerned white citizens in Selma just six days earlier; and Rev. Duncan Howlett, who has just returned from the James Reeb vigil in Birmingham. Earlier in the week several of these leaders met with Vice President Humphrey and Attorney General Katzenbach, who are also present today.

The president notes Reeb's death and says he has sent flowers to Birmingham and a plane to bring the Reebs back from Boston. Then, as Rev. Fauntroy makes introductions, Johnson interrupts to say that his "two little girls" also need civil rights. He explains that daughters Lynda Bird, twenty, and Luci Baines, seventeen, "weren't able to study for their exams because of all those pickets outside the White House."

At the president's suggestion, those assembled "go around the table" so that he can "hear from everyone." The NAACP's Carl Moultrie begins with a strong call for a voting rights bill. He is followed by Herbert Woods of CORE and then H. Rap Brown of the Nonviolent Action Group.

Brown, just twenty-one years old, calls out Johnson for his remarks about the picketing. "I'm just so sorry your two little girls were upset, Mr. President," he says. "But the thing is that people in Selma, Alabama, have been beaten and murdered and flogged and here you are concerned about your two little girls. That's a percentage of two people in the White House that lost their civil rights against twenty million people who lost their civil rights every day." LBJ does not respond.

After Rev. Howlett tries to cut the tension by praising the president's civil rights efforts, William Higgs, a white lawyer for the Mississippi Freedom Democratic Party, also challenges the president. "You know Mr. President, there was a black boy killed down there, too, Jimmie Lee Jackson. Reverend Reeb wasn't the first."

In the days that follow, others will also note that the murder of the white northerner overshadows the death of the young black man. "The real moral fervor did not come until Rev. James Reeb died," civil rights activist David Riley writes in the *New Republic*. "The country is really not concerned about the murder of black men."

"There is a sense of national outrage and shame over Reeb's death, but how many people know the name of the young

Negro laborer who died two weeks earlier?" Riley's article, titled "Who Is Jimmie Lee Jackson?," asks. "This young Negro
was killed not by crazed ruffians as Mr. Reeb was, but by a law
officer of one of the 50 states of our country. And we can't recall
his name."*

At the White House meeting, Higgs also presses the president on the measures being taken to protect the marchers. "You
could put badges on the U.S. marshals to prevent violence," he
says. Johnson replies that he has only six hundred marshals and
that he has been advised by expert lawyers not to use federal
troops—although he had them on alert earlier in the week.

When it is Humphrey's turn to speak, the vice president
looks "upset and somewhat emotional." He lauds Johnson, who
he says "has been working day and night" on civil rights matters. Humphrey then yields the floor to the president.

Johnson defends his record on civil rights, citing his role in
passing landmark legislation in 1957 and 1964. He outlines current initiatives to improve education and employment. And he
points out that he was already working on a voting rights bill
before the events in Selma; he had mentioned the need for such
legislation in his inaugural address in January.

"He gave an impressive recitation," writes columnist and
Washington insider Drew Pearson. "Some of those present,
however, still went away unimpressed and dissatisfied."

Later in the day, the civil right leaders brief four thousand
clergy who have come to Washington for an emergency meeting

---

*The activist Rev. Orloff Miller had not heard of Jackson until journeying to
Selma two weeks after the young man's death. Many African Americans in the
South were in a similar position; Hank Sanders, now a prominent state senator
in Alabama, does not recall hearing of Jackson until the first attempted march
from Selma to Montgomery.

of the National Council of Churches inspired by Bloody Sunday. Still angered by Reeb's death, many of the ministers criticize the president for failing to provide a federal presence in Selma.

The following day brings another visitor to the White House. After requesting a meeting with LBJ, George Wallace arrives on Saturday morning in a powder-blue State of Alabama airplane. The president and the governor talk for three hours. They then hold a live press conference in the Rose Garden with two hundred television, radio, and print reporters. LBJ TELLS WALLACE BRUTALITY MUST END, the *Washington Post* headline reads on Sunday. The president says:

> It is wrong to do violence to peaceful citizens in the streets of their towns. It is wrong to deny Americans the right to vote. It is wrong to deny any person full equality because of the color of their skin. . . . I told the governor a few moments ago that when all the eligible Negroes of Alabama have been registered, the economic and the social injustice they have experienced will be righted, and the demonstrations, I believe, will stop.

The president explains that he made three suggestions to Wallace that could end demonstrations: publicly declare his support of the universal right to vote; ensure the right of peaceful assembly in Alabama; and call a meeting between blacks and whites in the state to discuss greater cooperation between the races. Anticipating a court order by U.S. district court judge Johnson that will permit the march from Selma to Montgomery, the president says, "When the court has made its orders, it must be obeyed."

"It was evident that Mr. Johnson was giving Wallace little

comfort and the governor reflected this at the press conference," the *Post* reports. Acknowledging that he and Johnson disagree on the demonstrations, Wallace says, "The president was a gentleman, as he always is. I'm considering his recommendations, and I hope he is considering mine."

Before the day ends, the White House also briefs reporters on bipartisan voting rights legislation the president intends to submit to Congress the following Monday, March 15. It would, says President Johnson, "strike down all restrictions used to deny people the right to vote."

While the president and the governor are meeting in Washington, Judge Johnson holds a rare Saturday court session in Montgomery to address Dr. King's petition for an injunction preventing police intimidation of the proposed march from Selma to the state capital. State trooper chief Colonel Al Lingo testifies that he ordered the use of tear gas on the Edmund Pettus Bridge because he doesn't like to make mass arrests of protestors and put them in jail.

Lingo continues: "Governor Wallace had proclaimed that there was to be no march. I interpreted that to mean that I was to restrain the marchers."

Judge Johnson responds sharply: "Regardless of what it meant to do?"

Colonel Lingo: "No . . . I did not mean to kill them, but to use the least force possible to do it."

Judge Johnson is not impressed: "Regardless of what it is? Where were you going to stop?"

Later Assistant Attorney General John Doar asks Lingo: "Would you say the actions of Major Cloud in sending twenty to thirty troopers against the marchers was a minimum amount of force?"

Lingo responds, "Yes. I do."

Doar moves on to another weapon used on Bloody Sunday. "Is it your testimony that the use of nightsticks would be unreasonable after gas?"

"Well, if you have some people who are just determined to stay and lie there, I think you can use the sticks to give them a little shove," answers Lingo, though he later adds that the use of nightsticks is not appropriate against demonstrators who lie on the ground and don't move. Archival film of Bloody Sunday shows police striking fleeing or collapsed protestors with forceful and frequent swings of their nightsticks.

While Lingo's answers to Judge Johnson and Doar may raise eyebrows, the *Times* highlights other testimony from Saturday. Fifteen days after the death of Jimmie Lee Jackson, Lingo finally acknowledges what all in Marion knew: that a state trooper pulled the trigger. He also says that he has conducted a "full investigation" and that Jackson died of a "massive infection," not of the gunshot wound. He concedes that the case will be settled in the courts, presumably by state and federal grand juries scheduled to meet soon.

Judge Johnson does not make a ruling on Saturday and adjourns his court until Monday. On Sunday, Governor Wallace again takes the stage. He appears on CBS television's *Face the Nation* and then holds a news conference televised by ABC.

The previous day's face-to-face with the president apparently had little impact. Wallace asserts he will only allow the Selma to Montgomery march if a judge orders it and an appellate court then upholds that order. That could take weeks. He adds that beyond his remarks today, he has no plans to provide "detailed answers" to the president.

Those remarks make it clear he will not allow demonstrations in Selma unless ordered to do so. Nor will he hold meetings of groups made up of blacks and whites. His disdain for Dr. King is also apparent. He suggests that King and many other civil rights leaders "belong to many organizations that have been cited by the Justice Department, the House Un-American Activities Committee, and the Senate Internal Security committee as subversive."

The governor also tries to turn the spotlight away from Selma and shine it on the North. He holds up a newspaper showing a clash between blacks and police with raised clubs and drawn guns. "That's not Selma. That's New York," he says.

Wallace's finger-pointing echoes an editorial in the *Montgomery Advertiser* titled "I Am the Law." The same newspaper that termed the police action in Marion a "massacre" does not condone the attack on the three ministers. But it directs more anger at "the hundreds of ministers from other states." By defying Alabama and federal court orders, "they soiled the cloth and demeaned the pulpit. They demeaned themselves as moral preceptors."

The newspaper notes that "forty of the ministerial grenadiers" came from New York City, "where citizens won't phone the police when they look out a window on a rape or murder." This is a city where "gunfire erased Malcolm X," a woman stabbed Dr. King, and "the subways have to be policed."

After citing similar incidents in Philadelphia, Pennsylvania, the editorial concludes with purple prose: "The insensate Pharisees have departed such crimson jungles to make incendiary

Jimmie Lee Jackson
(courtesy of Cordelia Billingsley)

Rev. James Reeb
(courtesy of Unitarian Universalist Association)

On March 7, 1965, state troopers forcibly suppressed a peaceful march out of Selma, Alabama, organized to protest the fatal shooting of Jimmie Lee Jackson. Future U.S. Congressman John Lewis (left center, in light coat) was among the hundreds of civil rights demonstrators attacked in what would become known as "Bloody Sunday."
(courtesy of Library of Congress)

Clergy and others from across the country answer Dr. Martin Luther King Jr.'s call to come to Selma after the events of "Bloody Sunday." (courtesy of Unitarian Universalist Association)

On March 11, 1965, police officers stop a group of protestors attempting to march from Selma's Brown Chapel after the beating of James Reeb. (courtesy of Unitarian Universalist Association)

Dr. King (center) leads mourners at the memorial service for Rev. James Reeb in Selma on March 15, 1965. (courtesy of Unitarian Universalist Association)

Dr. King and his wife, Coretta Scott King, are joined by Andrew Young, James Bevel, Rev. F. D. Reese, and others in the march from Selma to Montgomery. (photo by Mandell Terman, courtesy of Diana Gourguechon)

President Lyndon B. Johnson presents Dr. King with one of the pens used to sign the Voting Rights Act in Washington, D.C., on August 6, 1965. (Yoichi R. Okamato/U.S. Government)

Jimmie Lee Jackson and James Reeb are two of the forty activists whose deaths are remembered at the Civil Rights Memorial in Montgomery, Alabama. (courtesy of Southern Poverty Law Center)

excursions into Alabama to perform lawless acts. This is a moral blindness and a vice."

The photos shown by Wallace do not lie. The examples noted by the *Advertiser* are real. There is racial tension wherever inequality exists, and in 1965 that is virtually everywhere in the United States. King is, of course, aware of de facto segregation in the North that is as insidious as de jure segregation in the South. In a few months, SCLC will initiate the Chicago Freedom Movement to desegregate that city's public schools and fight for open housing. King will eventually move there to draw attention to the plight of blacks. For now, however, the battle is for voting rights and the battlefield is Alabama.

As Wallace goes on the offensive, demonstrations take place from coast to coast. Blacks and whites gather separately and together to demonstrate their support for those in Selma and to remember James Reeb. Prayer vigils, sit-ins, and marches will continue for the next several days.

Reeb's most recent home sees the largest rally. 25,000 MARCH ON BOSTON COMMON IN TRIBUTE TO SLAIN MINISTER, proclaims the front page of the *Boston Globe*. Those present are black and white, young and old, from "the ghetto in Roxbury and the ivy-covered homes in the Back Bay." Many arrive after marching in columns from various points in the city.

"The tempo of the demonstration varied," reports the *Globe*'s John C. Thomas. "It was a memorial service and a civil rights rally, and as such, the crowd could stand silent in memory of Rev. Mr. Reeb and cheer militantly against Alabama's Gov. George Wallace."

Massachusetts lieutenant governor Elliot Richardson, who will later hold several cabinet-level positions including U.S.

attorney general, is among the speakers. He proclaims that Reeb's death "makes us all, North and South, remove every trace of hate and prejudice and replace it with brotherhood and love."

Reeb's superior at AFSC, John Sullivan, also reflects on the last week. In an essay for the *Globe* titled "Rev. Reeb's Spirit Lives," he writes: "James Reeb stirred the conscience and moral responsiveness of the highest officials of the land, of the clergy and the church people of America and of Negro and white men and women who marched and prayed in witness and wept because of his sacrifice. He gave to the human struggle that now goes on without him, but not without his spirit."

Nearby town councils also honor the fallen minister, as do places of worship. In Roman Catholic churches throughout the area, every mass includes a "Prayer for Selma" written by Richard Cardinal Cushing. A Catholic newspaper in Worcester, Massachusetts, proposes Reeb for sainthood.

At the Unitarian's First Church of Boston, Rev. Gerald Krick, who ate dinner with Reeb, Miller, and Olsen on the fateful night, answers those who argue that clergymen should stay home to address problems in their own neighborhoods. "To disregard Alabama is to place all of America in jeopardy. We must fight the battle of injustice wherever it occurs. . . . In a real sense the Selma marchers have been using spiritual swords. . . . The church has been the leader in the struggle this past week."

In Casper, Wyoming, Reeb's boyhood home, hundreds attend a memorial rally at his alma mater, Natrona County High School. Friends eulogize him. NAACP executive director Roy Wilkins travels from Washington to pay his respects.

Crowds of fifteen thousand or more gather in New York

nty Courthouse because there is an injunction against such
ity. "I'm pledged to enforce the laws of the state of Ala-
a," says Clark.

There is to be a memorial service for James Reeb at the
ch later in the day, with Dr. King delivering the eulogy.
s morning march to the courthouse is also intended to honor
b. Rev. Dana McLean Greeley, president of the Unitarian
versalist Association, who leads the effort with SCLC's C. T.
ian, responds to Clark: "And the Constitution of the United
es, is that not right?"

Soon Wilson Baker arrives. Greeley knows that the public
ty director is more reasonable than Clark. "The world is on
side. So are you. How can we resolve this?" asks the min-
r. Negotiations begin on a deal to allow a march after the
norial service.

t a different courthouse fifty miles away in Montgomery,
Judge Frank Johnson continues his hearing on the petition
llow the march from Selma to the state capital. While testi-
g about the actions of his men, Dallas County deputy sheriff
ury Middlebrooks makes a startling revelation. Two of the
r men arrested for the March 9 attack on Reeb had been de-
ed by police in Selma on March 6.

By pouring an oil compound into the carburetor of the car
y were driving, Elmer Cook and one other unidentified sus-
t had set off a smoke screen in front of the Dallas County
urthouse during the rally held by Rev. Ellwanger and the
ncerned White Citizens of Alabama. The men were stopped,
stioned, and then told to move on. No arrest was made, says
ddlebrooks.

City and Washington, D.C. Thousands r
At the front of the procession, a black-an
by a black man and a white man reads, "
SELMA!" Many middle-class whites pa
rights leader Bayard Rustin to hail the
ment" of that population.

In San Francisco, sixteen thousand peo
rally. Later that evening, ten thousand pai
procession that Episcopal bishop James Pi
stiffen the spine of the President of the U

Events also take place in Philadelphia
hassee, Knoxville, and several other cities
testors picket a meeting of southern attorn
Alabama's Richmond Flowers. Considere
tential challenger to Governor Wallace, F.
Selma, "If they want to march, let them n

Some gatherings are met with counte
marching in Seattle to commemorate the
met by white supremacists passing out le
self-proclaimed evangelist" meets movem
sign reading, "Negro Mobs Must Not Ru
Lexington, Massachusetts, birthplace of th
tion and just minutes from Reeb's home, a
on the lawn of a Roman Catholic church. /
the cross reads: "We Hate Niggers."

At 9:45 a.m. on Monday, Sheriff Clark in
clergymen and other would-be march
proceed from Brown Chapel past the Selm

Co
act
ba

ch
Th
Re
Un
Vi
Sta

saf
ou
ist
me

to
fy
As
fo
ta

th
pe
C
C
qu
M

"And one or two days later they allegedly assaulted Reverend Reeb?" asks Peter Hall, one of the attorneys for the civil rights groups.

"Our deputies had their hands full," explains the deputy.

Back in Selma, the service for Rev. Reeb is scheduled to begin at 2 p.m. One thousand people from around the country fill Brown Chapel. Ministers, rabbis, bishops, and priests sit on the altar near a black wreath with purple and white flowers sent by the people of Bucks County, Pennsylvania.

SCLC's Rev. Abernathy presides. Among those in the church is Rev. Leonard of Unitarian Church of All Souls in New York City. Like Reeb and others, he came down for the march on Tuesday with little more than a toothbrush and the clothes on his back. He will end up staying for eighteen days.

In his diary and later writings, Leonard offered his perspective on the memorial. "From the moment the service began, I found myself greatly agitated and sometimes furiously angry at the behavior of my white colleagues," he would recall. "James Reeb's death was described as the most monstrous example of brutality, when in fact it was one more instance in a long series. Men who had not taken the time to meet any young people praised them for their courage. The men and women who had come 'thousands of miles' for the memorial were extolled. I thought that it was not too difficult to come and go in 24 hours and have the vicarious experience of heroism through singing a few freedom songs. When King began to speak, however, it suddenly seemed right that we should all be there."

Dr. King does not arrive until three. President Johnson is to deliver a nationally televised speech on voting rights legislation to Congress this evening. He has invited the civil rights leader to sit in the gallery, but King has chosen to remain in Selma to honor Reeb.

King eulogizes Reeb as "our fallen hero and martyr." He then remembers the fallen Jimmie Lee Jackson. "Truly they lie, black and white together. Their spirit covers the land as the water covers the sea."

Echoing his eulogy at Jackson's funeral, King asks, "Who killed James Reeb?" and places blame on the church, the political establishment, the federal government, and fellow African Americans who refuse to get involved in the fight for justice.

He compares Reeb's life to Schubert's Unfinished Symphony. Now it is up to the living to complete that work, he says. He concludes with thanks to the Lord for Reeb's life, his goodness, and his willingness to sacrifice his life to "redeem the soul of our nation."

As the service ends, Rev. Abernathy says, "God has spoken from the federal court." With the help of Wilson Baker and Le-Roy Collins, U.S. district judge Daniel Thomas of Mobile has worked out a compromise between law enforcement officials and representatives of those wishing to march to the courthouse. As long as the participants follow a prescribed route and march three abreast, they can proceed.

Dr. King, Rev. Abernathy, Andrew Young, and Archbishop Iakovos of the Greek Orthodox Diocese of North and South America lead a procession estimated at between two and five thousand people. Rev. Greeley and United Auto Workers president Walter Reuther are one row behind them. King carries the wreath that was on the church's altar.

Rev. Olsen does not march. Because he got the best view of

the assailants, he and others in the movement fear for his safety. He has flown back to California.

Rev. Miller, who did not get as good a look as Olsen did, returned to Selma after Reeb's death and visited Dr. King at his motel in Montgomery to discuss the fallen minister. He marches in the middle of the pack, as anonymously as possible. He worries that Sheriff Clark or Public Safety Director Baker might take him into custody as a material witness, "an experience he was willing to forego," the *Boston Globe*'s Robert J. Anglin notes wryly.

The line for the eight-block march extends half a mile. Dr. King and those in the front reach the courthouse at about 5:25. Almost half an hour passes before the last of the marchers arrives. As the ceremony begins, Sheriff Clark grabs Mayor Smitherman, pulls him into the building, slams the door, and turns off the lights. Clark's five children can be seen watching the events from a courthouse window.

Accompanied by seven nuns, Rev. Greeley, Reuther, and Archbishop Iakovos, King climbs the courthouse steps and lays the wreath outside the sheriff's door. "We are here to reaffirm our commitment that racial segregation is evil and the nation will never rise to its maturity until we get rid of it," he says. "Here the spirit of James Reeb will dwell until every citizen is free to vote." As the sun sets, the large gathering sings, "We Shall Overcome."

Three hours later, these words echo in homes across the country and around the world. President Johnson pledges to a joint session of Congress and 70 million television viewers that "we shall overcome" America's "crippling legacy of bigotry and injustice." In a forty-five-minute address delivered in the House of Representatives, he invites Americans "of all religions and of all colors, from every section of this country" to join him in passing comprehensive legislation designed "to remove every barrier of discrimination against citizens trying to register and vote." The president continues:

> At times history and fate meet in a single time in a single place to shape a turning point in man's unending search for freedom. So it was at Lexington and Concord. So it was a century ago at Appomattox. So it was last week in Selma, Alabama. There, long-suffering men and women peacefully protested the denial of their rights as Americans. Many were brutally assaulted. One good man, a man of God, was killed.

That "good man, a man of God," is James Reeb. The president does not refer to Jimmie Lee Jackson, but has high praise and admiration for "the Negro" in general: "His actions and protests, his courage to risk safety and even to risk his life have awakened the conscience of the nation. His demonstrations have been designed to call attention to injustice, designed to provoke change and designed to stir reform, and who among us can say that we would have made the same progress were it not for his persistent bravery, and his faith in American democracy."

As the *New York Times'* Tom Wicker will note in his coverage the next day, "No other American President had so completely identified himself with the cause of the Negro. No other President had made the issue of equality for Negroes so frankly a moral cause to himself and all Americans."

In calling for the entire nation to aid in "the effort of

American Negroes to secure for themselves the full blessings of American life," the president stresses the moral imperative of the campaign. "Should we defeat every enemy, double our wealth and conquer the stars and still be unequal to this issue, then we will have failed as a people and as a nation." He explains:

> There is no constitutional issue here. The command of the Constitution is plain. There is no moral issue. It is wrong— deadly wrong—to deny any of your fellow Americans the right to vote. There is no issue of states' rights or national rights. There is no Negro problem. There is no Southern problem or Northern problem. There is only an American problem.

The time for action is now, says Johnson. "We have already waited a hundred years and more. The time for waiting is gone." He calls on the Congress to join him to work "long hours, nights and weekends if necessary to pass this bill."

The legislators interrupt the speech with applause thirty-six times and with two standing ovations. One ovation, lasting almost a minute, follows Johnson's insistence that "[w]e cannot— we must not—refuse to protect the right of Americans to vote in any election in which they may desire to participate."

"*And we . . . shall . . . overcome*," Wicker writes. "To these last words, the title of the great Negro freedom hymn, Mr. Johnson's accent and emphasis imparted an unmistakable determination."

That determination is clear to those watching the speech in apartments throughout Selma's George Washington Carver Homes, the public housing project where many visiting clergy are staying with black host families. When the president finished, "there was jubilation," remembers Rev. Miller, who stayed with a Catholic family, Lonzy and Alice West and their children. Rev. Leonard adds: "Everyone in the room where we had stood throughout was crying, men and women, old and young, black and white."

Those emotions are mirrored in the friend's home where Dr. King, Rev. Vivian, and other civil rights leaders are watching the speech. "There was din everywhere," remembers Vivian. "We were all jumping around. I looked over at Martin, and he was just sitting there, rather staid. He was just sitting in his chair, and a tear started to roll down his face."

Later in the evening King talks to the president on the phone. The following day he tells the press that the president has shown a "great and amazing understanding of the depth and dimension of the problem of racial justice. . . . We are happy to know that our struggle in Selma has brought the whole issue of the right to vote to the forefront of the conscience of the nation."

Later, King would reflect on one omission in Johnson's address: "In his eloquent 'We Shall Overcome' speech," King wrote, "[the president] paused to mention that one person, James Reeb, had already died in the struggle. Somehow the president forgot to mention Jimmie Lee Jackson, who died first. The parents and sister of Jimmie received no flowers from the president."

Students with whom King spoke noticed the slight. "Not that they felt that the death of James Reeb was less than tragic," he explained, "but because they felt that the failure to mention Jimmie Jackson only reinforced the impression that to white America the life of a Negro is insignificant and meaningless."

King terms the president's pending voting rights legislation "a good strong bill." It will send federal registration officials to six states in the South—Alabama, Mississippi, Georgia, Louisiana, Virginia, and South Carolina. Those officials will have the power to put African Americans on the election books wherever discriminatory practices and devices have prevented them from registering and voting. Local officials engaging in such discriminatory practices will be subject to criminal prosecution.

Data showing that fewer than half the voting population is registered or voted in a general election in a particular state or voting district with a literacy test will be considered evidence of discrimination. Federal registrars will then be dispatched to register those previously denied the right to vote. The only requirement will be to fill out a form stating name, age, and place of residence.

Early passage of the bill seems likely. The only strong opposition comes from congressmen and senators representing states in the South. Senator Allen Ellender, a Democrat from Louisiana, threatens to hold up the legislation. He vows to "filibuster against it as long as God gives me breath."

Alabama's Democratic senator John Sparkman uses the occasion to criticize the outsiders who have come to his state. "Qualified citizens of Selma and Dallas County, Negro and white, are [already] being given the opportunity to register," he asserts. He adds that the people of Alabama overwhelmingly do not like the Civil Rights Act of 1964, but they "obey because it is the law." Dr. King and his lieutenants should do the same—obey the court orders that ban them from marching, he says.

King, however, has no intention of stopping the marches. "We must keep the issue alive and the urgency of it before the nation," he says. SNCC's Jim Forman agrees, though he takes issue with King's assessment of Johnson's speech, calling the president's "We Shall Overcome" reference "a tinkling empty symbol" that "spoiled a good song."

Joseph Smitherman, Selma's mayor, also reacts to Johnson's

invocation of the hymn. "It was like you'd been struck by a dagger in your heart," he says.

• • •

The issue remains before the nation on Tuesday, March 16. In Montgomery, whip- and club-wielding possemen on horseback attack six hundred white and black demonstrators, many of them students, participating in a street sit-down organized by SNCC. Eight people are hospitalized. Law enforcement officials later apologize for the attack, claiming that orders on how to disperse the crowd were misunderstood.

A second demonstration is held after this debacle. One thousand blacks, most from Alabama State College, march to the Capitol building with a petition calling for a biracial commission on civil rights and adherence to current civil rights laws. Governor Wallace refuses to accept the petition.

At the same time the demonstrations are taking place in Montgomery, two marches are attempted in Selma. Sheriff Clark halts the first group of three to four hundred people. Public Safety Director Baker stops the second wave.

As Selma continues to show what Dr. King called "its true colors," eight hundred mourners fill All Souls Church in Washington, D.C., for the funeral of James Reeb. Marie Reeb sits in the front pew with her oldest child, thirteen-year-old John, described by one reporter as "a lanky boy with brown hair and apple cheeks." James Reeb's parents sit beside them. Sitting across the aisle are Vice President Humphrey, U.S. Senator Ted Kennedy and his wife, and Lee White, a personal representative of President Johnson.

Unitarian Universalist president Rev. Greeley and Howard University vice president Dr. William Stuart Nelson deliver eulogies. "James Reeb went to Selma for the same reason he came to All Souls," Rev. Duncan Howlett says of his colleague and friend. "Because he felt by doing so he could help suffering men in their need. He was impatient with rules, customs, and tradition. His heart told him what was right and by this standard he judged everything. . . . His death brought new life to the civil rights movement. He has shown the Negro again . . . that white men are willing to die for his cause . . . recognizing that it is not his alone, but ours together."

At the end of the service, all rise, link arms, and sing "We Shall Overcome."

Two days later, Boston's Arlington Street Church says farewell to the slain minister. Those gathered together with the Reeb family at the Unitarian church he attended include blacks and whites, religious leaders of all faiths, Mayor John F. Collins, and Senator Leverett Saltonstall. John Sullivan of AFSC delivers an unusual eulogy that offers both praise for his colleague and criticism of the city.

Borrowing lines from the nineteenth-century historian and poet W. E. H. Lecky, Sullivan says: "James Reeb was one of the unusual few who could touch the latent strings and could hear the faint voices from afar. He saw in people not only the disadvantage they may have suffered . . . but the potential and hope that lay in them and the precious opportunities they had or must discover."

The Quaker leader remembers his colleague as direct, law-abiding, intelligent, good, and fearless. That fearlessness not only led him to Selma, but moved him to confront the city about its housing code violations. He quotes Reeb's last log entry about the fire chief's threat, "If you are wrong, I will murder you."

Sullivan concludes by imagining what Reeb would say if he were present on this day:

There is a killer in the dark and racist streets of the South. But there is a killer in the North, too, one which strikes Negro and white in the bright light of day, every day, and the killer's name is non-involvement; it is apathy and lack of interest; it is self-concern. This is the killer James Reeb was stalking, and when he found him he was going to wrap him around with righteousness and justice and love.

Marie Reeb sits between her parents and Senator Saltonstall. Soon she and her children will move to Wyoming. There, in the petrified forest by the Shirley Basin, they will scatter his ashes.

Some years later Orloff Miller will tell Marie that before he ever met her husband he picked up a petrified log in this very area. For some reason he has kept it all these years. It is one more connection he feels to the friend he watched die. Would the Reeb family like it?

They would.

CHAPTER EIGHT

"WE HAVE A NEW SONG TO SING . . ."

March 21, 1965

Walter Dobyne intends to make it all the way to Montgomery this time. The eighteen-year-old student who was arrested in Marion in February and teargassed in Selma on Bloody Sunday now stands with some 3,600 other would-be marchers outside Brown Chapel. This time they will not be defying a court order when they embark upon the five-day, fifty-four-mile journey. Four days ago, Judge Johnson issued an injunction permitting the march.

In his decision, Judge Johnson blasted Jim Clark, finding that the sheriff, along with his deputies and possemen, had engaged in "an almost continuous pattern of conduct . . . of harassment, intimidation, coercion, threatening conduct, and, sometimes, brutal mistreatment." To prevent a recurrence of the brutality on the Edmund Pettus Bridge and to ensure safe passage through inhospitable counties, the judge ordered both the state of Alabama and the federal government to provide marchers with protection. One thousand U.S soldiers have been called to Selma. Army helicopters fly overhead.

After promising to call in the state's National Guard, Governor Wallace changed his mind and passed the buck. "I intend to call on the president of the United States to provide sufficient officers to guarantee the safety and welfare of citizens in and around the route," he said. "The federal government has created this matter, they can help protect them."

An angry President Johnson then nationalized the Guard, mobilizing 2,500 troops. "Now why in the hell didn't you stand up like a man and say what you were going to do to begin with?" he asked the governor.

Despite the presence of the soldiers, a safe march is not assured. The majority of white Alabamans remain sympathetic to Governor Wallace and Sheriff Clark and hostile to the movement and Dr. King. Just hours before the march is to leave Selma, five time bombs are discovered in Birmingham. Two are found at black churches, one at a high school, one at the home of a civil rights lawyer, and one at the former home of Dr. King's brother.

Birmingham is not on the route. The marchers will, however, pass through one of the most violent and racist areas in the country, Lowndes County. Verbal, if not physical, assaults are assured.

Even if the marchers are not harmed, they will endure cold, damp weather. Sleeping and bathroom accommodations will be modest at best for five days. So why is Dobyne, who is not even old enough to vote, so committed to this cause? Engaged originally by the words of Dr. King and Rev. Abernathy, he explains that his "eyes were opened" by the death of Jimmie Lee Jackson and Bloody Sunday. Before those traumatic events, he was blind to such hatred because he had always had white friends.

George Baker, the white college student from Illinois, is also committed. As he arrives at the church to help organize the departure, he sees "people, people, and more people." These include civil rights figures, clergy of all faiths, labor leaders, politicians, and the faithful foot soldiers of the movement. Among those faithful are the two young girls from Selma, Sheyann Webb and Rachel West; sixteen-year-old Johnny Flowers from Perry County; Viola Liuzzo, a white thirty-nine-year-old mother of five who has driven from Detroit; and Jimmie Lee Jackson's grandfather, Cager Lee, who will walk the first mile and then turn back.

Judge Johnson would not permit the march to proceed until he received a detailed plan from SCLC. The court-approved itinerary allows all participants to walk the seven-mile leg to the first campsite this Sunday. On Monday and Tuesday, however, only three hundred will be allowed to march through Lowndes County because the highway narrows to two lanes and a larger crowd could disrupt traffic. On Wednesday, when the highway widens to four lanes, people may again join the procession to Montgomery. The participants must reach the state capital by 4 p.m. on Thursday.

Provisions have been made to ferry supplies and portable bathrooms to the preselected roadside campsites. The Medical Committee for Human Rights has volunteered to set up and staff mobile hospitals. Other volunteers will prepare and serve meals.

The march is scheduled to begin at 10 a.m., but Dr. King does not arrive until 11. He then holds a mass meeting in the church. About two hours later, the crowd departs for Montgomery.

"Lining the people up gave me the feeling of organizing a wagon train to go west," Baker will write.

Dr. King is joined in the front ranks by Dr. Ralph Bunche, John Lewis, Rosa Parks, A. Philip Randolph, Albert Turner, Amelia Boynton, Rev. F. D. Reese, Rabbi Abraham Heschel, Episcopal bishop Richard Millard, Cager Lee, and others. Two American flags and a United Nations flag lead the way. Several cars full of newsmen precede the procession.

As the marchers exit Selma, Sheriff Clark declares, "I'm glad to get rid of the ones who are leaving, but I wish they'd come back and get the rest of them." His sentiment is echoed by Mayor Smitherman: "I will be glad to get these people out of town— but I am afraid some of them will come back."

The *Selma Times-Journal* describes the "them" referred to by Clark and Smitherman: "Priests, nuns, ministers and rabbis walked. Beatnik types were there. So were white women, Negro civil rights leaders, a Negro pushing his baby in a stroller. Some were well-dressed, some wore Levis. Some sang freedom songs, some carried placards."

Several local clerical leaders remain at home, opposed to the march. Catholic archbishop Thomas Toolen of Mobile says he respects Dr. King, but claims "he is trying to divide our people." The demonstrations, he adds, "are not helping anything at all." King and the priests and nuns and other "crusaders" from out of state should go home and let Alabamans solve their own problems. "There are certainly things that need correcting," the archbishop concedes, "but with the sane help of our people, they will be corrected in time." He does not offer a timetable.

Rev. W. Kenneth Goodson, bishop of the Methodist church in the Birmingham area, agrees with his Catholic brother and urges all members of his faith to stay home. "I see this march as doing a great disservice to the cause of human freedom and delaying still further the struggle for reconciliation that surely awaits all who call Alabama home," he says.

Like Archbishop Toolen and some southern politicians who consider themselves "moderate," Rev. Goodson does not voice opposition to the extension of voting rights to African Americans. Rather, he objects to outsiders telling Alabamans how and when they should extend those rights. Ministers and laypersons who have come to Alabama should, he says, "return to their homes where I am sure there is ample responsibility and opportunities for Christian witness and service."*

After helping line up the marchers, Baker drives Rev. James Bevel's car to the first campsite. "I left just before [the march] started and got out over the bridge and parked," he recalls. "White people all along the highway. Army uniforms never looked so great and wonderful and protective."

The protection is necessary. The white people along the highway spew profanities. Cars with "I Hate Niggers" written on their sides follow the marchers. King receives death threats.

Years later, Andrew Young will share a secret about how he tried to keep Dr. King as safe as possible during protests and marches. "Martin always wore the good preacher blue suit," he tells the makers of the documentary *Eyes on the Prize*, "and I figured since we couldn't stop him from marching, we just kind of had to believe it was true when white folks said we all look alike. So everybody that was about Martin's size and had on a blue suit, I put in the front of the line with him."

---

*The news stories quoting Archbishop Toolen and Rev. Goodson, along with an Associated Press article headlined SNCC LIES, SAYS RABBI FROM NORTH, were compiled and then distributed by the Selma and Dallas County Chamber of Commerce, which also opposed the march.

By evening the marchers reach what Baker calls "the promised land." Canaan is actually a farm owned by the Hall family. "Everyone is tired, happy, joyous, and contented," writes Baker. Dinner is spaghetti, pork and beans, and coffee.

It is estimated that as many as eight thousand people marched at some time on Sunday. Knowing that only three hundred may continue once they reach Lowndes County midday Monday, most participants return to Selma before bedtime in cars and buses provided by the organizers. Those who remain sleep on cots or in sleeping bags in two tents, one for men, one for women. King, already suffering a blister that makes him wonder if he will be able to complete the march, stays in a pink and white heated house trailer. National Guardsmen protect the camp, as do volunteer security guards from SNCC and other organizations.

The temperature is about thirty degrees when the marchers break camp early the next morning. They reach Lowndes County shortly after noon. By this time Dobyne has moved as close to the front of the line as possible to make sure he is in the select three hundred allowed to stay on the road. So, too, have Johnny Flowers and five other young men from Uniontown. Dobyne survives the cut, but Marion's Albert Turner tells those from Uniontown to get out of the line.

Because the people of Uniontown have not been as active in the movement as those from Marion and other towns in Perry County, Turner does not want anyone from there to continue today. Relatively more comfortable than Marion residents in the early 1960s, Uniontown blacks were largely reluctant to join early efforts for voting rights. Black businesses were able to succeed there, and the incessant protests in Marion and elsewhere were viewed by some as a threat to a more tolerable status quo in Uniontown.

These Uniontown teenagers, however, are not concerned with this history; they want to march. And they think they have earned their stripes. Flowers notes that he marched on Bloody Sunday and was gassed. Eighteen-year-old Charles White, whom Flowers calls "kind of our leader," tells Turner they aren't leaving. When Turner, too, refuses to back down, White tells his friends to sit down.

"So we boycotted," recalls Flowers. Hearing the commotion, Andrew Young intervenes and tells Turner to let the young men march. That this dispute is resolved in part by eager teens applying a nonviolent tactic speaks to how ubiquitous and embedded the philosophy of nonviolence has become.

In the end, about 280 black marchers are joined by twenty whites. This mix does not satisfy everyone. When the march reaches the point when only three hundred may continue as dictated by the injunction, one African American asks, "Why can't all the white people go back?"

Andrew Young replies: "We must have at least a small group of white people because, finally, the white people are our protection. Besides, this is not just a Negro movement. We are dramatizing all of America's problems."

The population of Lowndes County is more than 80 percent black, but whites hold all the power. As in other counties throughout the South, the blacks in Lowndes suffered greatly when Jim Crow laws were enacted. There were more than five thousand registered African American voters in the county at the turn of the twentieth century, but constitutional disenfranchisement through poll taxes and literacy tests drove that number down to a mere fifty-seven in just six years.

The voter registration efforts of SCLC and SNCC in the Black Belt are beginning to pay dividends. In early March, for

the first time in many years, four African Americans attempted
to register in Lowndes. Within weeks, two had won the right to
vote. And shortly before the march, about two dozen residents
had—with help from SCLC and the Episcopal Society for Cultural and Racial Unity—formed the Lowndes County Christian
Movement for Human Rights.

When the three hundred marchers enter Lowndes County,
King leads them in singing "We Shall Overcome." A small
plane buzzes ominously overhead. Soon it drops leaflets created
by White Citizens' Action Inc. of Tuscaloosa. Claiming that
"[an] unemployed agitator ceases to agitate," the material calls
on whites to engage in "selective hiring, firing, buying, [and]
selling," enforcing economic repercussions upon blacks for their
participation in the movement.

As they continue their journey, the marchers also see a bill-
board sponsored by the Citizens Council of Louisiana Inc.
showing "Martin Luther King at Communist training school."
(The photograph was actually taken at the interracial Highlander Folk School in Tennessee, a center for movement training
and social justice programs.) Ned Touchstone, secretary of the
Citizens Council, says his group plans to put up more than eight
hundred of these billboards across the country.

There are hecklers, too. "At about every intersection you
passed, there would be a handful of whites out cussing, calling
us 'niggers' and stuff, 'go back to Africa' and stuff, and every
day you put up with that," remembers Dobyne. "The National
Guard were posted at each street and made sure whites didn't
get close, but you had all that verbal abuse the whole distance."

There are hopeful signs as well in Lowndes. "Along the road
are Negroes who watch. Some smile and wave," writes Baker.

Such interest does not escape SNCC's Stokely Carmichael,

who opposes the march but is trying "to make a positive out of a negative." He ventures off the road to collect names and addresses of blacks who have turned out to see the marchers pass by. "Listen, we're going to stay in Lowndes County, we're not going to pass through," he tells them. Unsatisfied with the symbolic power and media potential of the march, Carmichael focuses on recruitment for black political engagement that will later bring about the Black Panther Party.

As the march makes its way to Montgomery, President Johnson is reported to be following its progress. Leaders in the Senate say that if a voting rights bill is not passed by April 15 they will work through their Easter break. Harry Truman also weighs in. As president in 1948, he signed an order committing the United States to integrating its military, but the current march is "silly," he says. "They can't accomplish a darned thing," he explains. "All they want is to attract attention."

The second day's campsite is on land owned by Rosie Steele, a seventy-eight-year-old black woman. Conditions are far from comfortable. Red ants plague the marchers. A light rain turns into a heavy downpour.

Dr. King does not spend this second night on the road. He flies to Cleveland to accept an award. He plans to return before the march reaches Montgomery.

On Tuesday, March 23, the third day of the march, John Lewis, Albert Turner, and others lead the procession. The rain continues. Wet clothes and shoes cannot be escaped, nor can chafed skin and blisters. Some shoes fall apart and are repaired with cellophane. The evening's campsite is all mud.

Led by Andrew Young, the marchers leave early Wednesday morning on a sixteen-mile leg that will bring them to the outskirts of Montgomery. They exit Lowndes County a few hours later. Back on a four-lane road, they are joined by more and more people.

King returns before noon with his wife and Ralph Abernathy. Surveying the crowd, he announces, "We have a new song to sing. We *have* overcome."

Dr. Quentin Young of Chicago, one of the founders of Medical Committee for Human Rights, is in the crowd. He has spent the last three days tending to "battlefield wounds." To get a "sense of who is in the movement," he tries to march with as many different people as possible. On this day his companion is a middle-aged white woman who has come because of her religious beliefs.

After passing a group of local white hecklers, the woman laments, "Why don't these people understand that they've lost their battle? We're all God's children, and we should settle this."

"True," says Young, who is white and has led many integration efforts within his profession and his city and will soon become King's personal physician.

One hundred yards later the doctor feels the need to offer a more thoughtful response to the woman. "That's not a simple request you're making of these folks," he tells her. "The black population has been the object of slavery, of rape. Children born of these illicit cohabitations were sold; their own children were sold off as slaves. You're asking a great deal when you ask them to accept racial equality, because if they do, they plead guilty automatically to all the crimes."

George Baker marches the entire distance on day four, serving as a marshal who keeps everyone in line. He notes that by evening, "[the] line is *very* long. Can't see the end of it." An estimated five thousand people approach that night's destination, the City of St. Jude, a Catholic institution on a thirty-six-acre campus four miles from the Alabama State Capitol. Here they will spend the final night of the march on a baseball field turned campground.

"Negroes who watch, wave and cheer," Baker will write. "Have the feeling of the Allied Armies when they march through Paris and people cheer them."

A few hours later, the nineteen-year-old volunteer is among those in charge of security for a free evening of entertainment arranged by singer and activist Harry Belafonte. An estimated thirty thousand people attend the "Stars of Freedom Concert" featuring Sammy Davis Jr., Mahalia Jackson, Dick Gregory, Joan Baez, Leonard Bernstein, Nina Simone, Nichols and May, Peter, Paul & Mary, Pete Seeger, Odetta, Ossie Davis, Ruby Dee, Ella Fitzgerald, Tony Bennett, Chad Mitchell, Nipsey Russell, and others. The makeshift stage sits on top of coffins donated by black funeral homes.*

Worn down like so many on the journey, Baker has neither the time nor energy to enjoy the performances. He is dealing with "mobs of people" trying to get as close to the stars as possible. Some faint. He fears the stage is overloaded and will collapse.

I have blisters on my feet which cause me to limp. For three hours I try to control crowd. Almost have nervous breakdown, take tranquilizers. When show starts I stumble away in state of shock. I sit in a car away from stage,

---

*Two weeks later, Davis will host "Broadway Answers Selma," a benefit revue at New York's Majestic Theater featuring Barbra Streisand, John Gielgud, and dozens of additional celebrities. The event raises $150,000, which the Anti-Defamation League of B'nai Brith distributes to the Reeb and Jackson families, and to SCLC, SNCC, and CORE for voter registration drives.

oblivious of songs. Have had stomach cramps all evening from lack of food. Saliva in mouth is like whipped cream from lack of water. Am hoarse from yelling all day. No water—no water—stumble to First Aid station and demand water, get it, is sweet, very sweet. Performance is over. Cramps get worse as I walk, so I stop every 20 feet to rest. Find sleeping bag and stumble into gym and crawl into oblivion.

Baker makes no reference to Dr. King, who is cheered when he takes the stage and says, "This is the greatest march on any capitol that there has ever been in the South. This will go down in history as one of the greatest developments in the civil rights movement."

King does not sleep at the campground, but returns the next morning to lead the march to the Capitol. Security is so tight that army guards initially deny his car entry to St. Jude. Then a Montgomery policeman recognizes him and tells a sentry, "You danged fool. This is the man. Let him through."

There is tension as everyone assembles for the last leg of the journey. Orange vests are to be handed out to the three hundred who marched all the way and will now follow directly behind King. Other dignitaries, however, want the vests and want to march at the front. If they knew that King just received another death threat, they might not be so eager.

Some fifteen thousand people finally exit the St. Jude gate towards the Capitol. Army helicopters and military airplanes fly overhead. A light rain falls.

Four miles away, the state of Alabama is ready. Governor Wallace is in his office, which looks out over the site of the rally that will soon take place. He has no plans to interact with the marchers. Because female state employees have been given the day off to protect them from potential harm, legislative business is at a standstill.

The *Selma Times-Journal* describes the scene:

> The old capital of the Confederacy looked like an occupied military zone. Hundreds of battle-ready National Guardsmen and Army regulars, carbines slung from their shoulders, patrolled broad Dexter Avenue leading to the gleaming white Capitol. Soldiers were stationed atop the buildings. Military police, their green helmets gleaming, stood guard around the Capitol itself. One of the MP's standing at the end of a driveway was a Negro.
>
> A plywood covering lay over the big bronze star on the marble portico where Jefferson Davis took the oath as president of the Confederacy. Wallace stood on the star when he was sworn in—the only governor known to have done so. . . . An aide to the governor said the portico was covered only to protect the marble, but an unidentified state trooper said it was covered to prevent King from standing on the historic star.

Too exhausted to march, George Baker drives Viola Liuzzo's car to the Capitol. He is accompanied by another volunteer, nineteen-year-old Leroy Moton. Moton, who is black, will later recall that a few years earlier, when he was working in an all-white restaurant in Selma, "my boss told me if I ever got involved with 'that nigger [Martin Luther] King mess,' he'd kick my behind through my nose."

Walter Dobyne is exhilarated, not exhausted. "I tell you what, I never really thought about the weather or being tired or anything," he will say nearly fifty years later. "It was the mission to make it all the way, and I was so proud to be in that three hundred that had the opportunity to go all the way. The conditions never really bothered me. I never really focused on them. To arrive there, it was a great accomplishment and we were proud to take part in it."

"To me, there was never a march like this one before and hasn't been one since," John Lewis adds. "It was a sense of community moving there. And as you walked, you saw people coming, waving, bringing you food or bringing you something to drink. You saw the power of the most powerful country on the face of the earth."

The crowd, which includes Rev. Orloff Miller and Rev. Joseph Ellwanger, swells to at least twenty-five thousand. There are so many people that those in the back do not arrive at the Capitol until an hour after those in the front. Eight-lane Dexter Avenue is jammed, and the throng extends for several blocks.

Amelia Boynton later remembered those final steps:

> White hecklers, together with secret sympathizers and well-wishers were among those who watched us. . . . A young white woman, very pretty and intelligent looking, stood in the doorway of an office building. Seeing the integrated group passing seemed to enrage her, and she screamed vile things. . . . She held her nose, turned her back to the street, and hoisted her dress.

A flatbed truck serves as the stage for speakers and performers. Odetta, Oscar Brand, Joan Baez, Len Chandler, and Leon Bibb all sing before the speeches begin. The rally is broadcast live to the nation until Mary Travers of the folk trio Peter, Paul & Mary kisses Harry Belafonte on the cheek. White viewers angered by the interracial kiss telephone the networks, and CBS temporarily switches back to its regular afternoon programming.

Albert Turner is among the civil rights leaders who speak. "I look worse than anybody else on this stage. That's because I marched fifty miles," he says. After reading the Perry County voting statistics, he says. "We are not satisfied." The crowd cheers.

Dr. King now addresses "all the freedom-loving people who have assembled" in Montgomery. "We are not about to turn around," he tells them. "We are on the move now." He praises nonviolent resistance and details how Selma "generated the massive power to turn the whole nation to a new course." Noting that the campaign in Alabama has been focused on the right to vote, he calls for a "march on ballot boxes."

He then responds to the newspaper editorialists, politicians, and others who have called for SCLC and SNCC to leave and let Alabama return to normalcy. Normalcy, he says, resulted in the murder of Jimmie Lee Jackson, Bloody Sunday, and the beating of James Reeb. King concludes what is now known as his "Our God Is Marching On" speech with a verse from "The Battle Hymn of the Republic."

"The real victory wasn't the fact that we went to Montgomery and had that rally," Sheyann Webb later reflects. "The real triumph had been on March seventh at the bridge and at the church afterwards when we turned a brutal beating into a nonviolent victory."

Among those at the rally is Morris Dees, a white twenty-nine-year-old lawyer and businessman from Montgomery. Dees attended segregated schools as a youth; his first law client was a Klansman accused of attacking Freedom Riders in 1962. In recent years, however, he has become more sympathetic to the civil rights movement. He did not march, but did drive participants back and forth from Selma. Now he and his colleague Millard Fuller have come to hear King speak, ignoring city officials who have been encouraging white people to stay away lest it seem anyone was "interested in what black people were doing."

Shortly after the speeches start, Dees is approached by his uncle James. "He loved me like a son, but the stories of my recent civil rights activities had not sat well with him," Dees remembered. "He looked at me and Millard coldly. 'I know all about you,' he snarled. 'You're nothing but a bunch of nigger lovers.'"

James Dees opens his coat to reveal a .38 pistol in his belt. "I oughta take this gun and kill both of you on the spot," he tells his nephew.

Years later, after founding the Southern Poverty Law Center to fight discrimination and intolerance, Dees wonders if his uncle might have been planning to kill Dr. King if he could have gotten close enough. "In these changing times," he decides, "Uncle James probably just wanted to take a stand for his way of life, the old Southern way of doing things. It was more than he could stomach to see black people so close to the seat of power in Montgomery."

In his speech, King invokes others who have fallen in addition to Jackson and Reeb. The three civil rights workers in the Mississippi field—James Chaney, Andrew Goodman, and Michael Schwerner. The four little girls in the Birmingham church—Denise McNair, Addie Mae Collins, Cynthia Wesley, and Carol Robertson. The NAACP's Mississippi field secretary gunned down in his own driveway—Medgar Evers. And William Moore, a white postal worker and CORE member from Baltimore murdered in 1963 in rural Alabama as he marched by himself to protest segregation. By evening's end another name will be added to this list.

Viola Liuzzo—a part-time college student and NAACP member in Detroit—took leave of her husband and five children and drove to Selma to help with the march. Assigned to the transportation committee, she shuttled participants from campsites to Selma and neighboring counties. She was also able to march on the first and final days, when she loaned her Oldsmobile to George Baker and Leroy Moton.

When the speeches in Montgomery end and the crowd disperses, Liuzzo and Moton drive marchers back to Selma. As they shuttle between the two cities, they are harassed on the road and at gas stations by whites furious at the sight of a black man with a white woman. One car pushes their bumper, almost sending them off the road.

At about 7:30 p.m., they leave Selma on their second return trip to Montgomery. They are on the narrow, two-lane stretch of U.S. 80 running through Lowndes County when they notice two or three cars following them. One car tries to force them off the road, then passes.

At least one other car still follows. Alarmed, Liuzzo hits the accelerator. The car stays on her tail. Afraid, she starts singing "We Shall Overcome."

The car, a Chevy Impala, pulls alongside Liuzzo's Oldsmobile. The men inside the Impala fire their pistols. Liuzzo is hit in the head and slumps into the door.

Moton, who has not been hit, puts a foot on the brake and tries to steer from the passenger seat. The Oldsmobile swerves off the road and into a field, where it hits a fence. Fearing more shots, Moton pulls Liuzzo away from the window. She shows no signs of life. It will soon be determined that she died instantly.

A few minutes later a car stops. A white man gets out and heads toward the Oldsmobile. Moton, covered in Liuzzo's blood, pretends to be dead. The man shines a flashlight into the car, then leaves. In shock, Moton passes out for almost half an hour.

When he awakens, Moton climbs to the roadside. He flags a truck that, by chance, is carrying marchers back from Montgomery. He is rushed to Selma, where ministers who were in the truck hide him until the FBI can be called in to protect him. By the end of the evening, he is being held in protective custody in the Selma County Jail.

After the shooting, thirty-one-year-old Gary Thomas Rowe calls the FBI. An informant since 1960, "Tommy" Rowe is a Klansman with a history of violence. The unemployed, divorced father of four tells his handlers that he was in the Impala with three other men, whom he names. Those men fired shots at the white woman and black man, but Rowe explains that he only pretended to fire.

Within twelve hours of the shooting, Rowe and three fellow Klansmen from the Birmingham area—forty-one-year-old William Eaton, a retired steelworker; forty-two-year-old Eugene Thomas, a U.S. Steel employee; and twenty-one-year-old Collie Wilkins, a self-employed mechanic recently convicted for possession of an unregistered shotgun—are arrested for Liuzzo's murder. Rowe, who is not publicly identified as an informant, receives the same treatment as the others. The government does not want to blow his cover. Nor does it want to have to explain how an FBI operative allowed a murder to take place in his presence.

Briefed by J. Edgar Hoover, President Johnson addresses the nation on television and radio. He calls Liuzzo's death "a tragedy and horrible stain on our American society." Praising the quick work of the FBI, he promises to bring those arrested to trial. "Mrs. Liuzzo went to Alabama to serve the struggles for justice," says the president. "She was murdered by the enemies of justice who for decades have used the rope and the gun and the tar and the feathers to terrorize their neighbors."

Comparing the "terrorists of the Ku Klux Klan" to the "terrorists in North Vietnam," Johnson declares war. He promises that as soon as voting rights legislation is passed, he will submit legislation to "bring the activities of the Klan under effective control of the law."

Robert Shelton, imperial wizard of the Ku Klux Klan, pushes back. He says he deplores the murders, but insists that the four Klansmen charged are "not connected in any way" to them. He claims that the killings of Liuzzo and Reeb are part of a "trumped-up Communist plot to destroy the right wing of America." Without offering evidence, the Wizard suggests that the minister was a suitable candidate for martyrdom because he was already dying of cancer. "How are we to know that this was not another created incident?" he asks.

Over the next week, movement leaders pay tribute to Liuzzo while keeping pressure on Alabama's state government to extend civil rights. Five days after the murder, Dr. King, John Lewis, Roy Wilkins, and James Farmer attend a funeral mass for Liuzzo in Detroit. Lewis, who met the victim in Selma, calls her a "freedom fighter." Vice President Humphrey also visits the family.

That same day, SCLC field secretary Willie Bolden preaches to five hundred blacks and whites gathered at an African American church just four hundred yards from where Liuzzo was murdered. "The cost for freedom just might be another life," he tells them.

After the service three hearses and a pickup truck head a procession of fifty cars to Montgomery. The lead vehicles carry ten empty coffins, one for each person killed during the civil rights struggle in Alabama, including the often forgotten thirteen-year-old Virgil Ware Jr. In 1963, Ware was riding on the handlebars of a bike when white teenagers returning from a segregationist rally shot him to death. The coffins are placed on a marble walk outside the Capitol.

The Capitol is also the site of an eighty-five-minute meeting between Governor Wallace and sixteen civil rights leaders. Rev. Ellwanger is the only white person in the group, which is headed by Rev. Joseph Lowery, one of the founders of SCLC. They bring with them the petition they had tried to present to the governor five days earlier, after the conclusion of the march from Selma, only to be told Wallace was "out."

The petition calls for removal of the poll tax, an end to brutality, opening voter registration at more convenient hours, and better employment opportunities for blacks in state government and the private sector. Wallace makes no promises.

One week later a federal grand jury indicts Eaton, Wilkins, and Thomas for conspiring to pursue and assault civil rights marchers. As they are not charged with murder, the maximum penalty they face for these violations is ten years in prison.

The grand jury does not indict Rowe. A federal spokesman explains that charges against Rowe will probably be dropped, but offers no reason. Within a week, the charges are dropped and rumors circulate that Rowe must be an informer.

When a state grand jury hands down indictments for murder against Eaton, Wilkins, and Thomas on April 21, Rowe again escapes charges. This time, however, there is an explanation. After Rowe—wearing a gun in a hip holster and escorted by FBI agents—testifies before the grand jury, the press confirms that he was working undercover.

The state of Alabama decides to try the Klansmen separately. Wilkins goes on trial during the first week in May. The jury is all white. So is the gallery in the old Lowndes County Court-house.

Moton and Rowe are the prosecution's star witnesses. Rowe testifies that on the morning of the shooting, his FBI handlers gave him permission to ride in Thomas's Impala. After driving around Montgomery, the four men headed to Selma. At dinner in the Silver Moon Café, Thomas introduced Rowe to Elmer Cook and the others charged with killing Reeb. On parting, Cook said, "Well, God bless you, boys. Go do your job. I already did mine."

Wilkins's attorney, Matt Murphy, himself a Klansman, tries to put Liuzzo, Moton, and Rowe on trial. He suggests that Liuzzo and Moton had a sexual relationship and that Rowe fired his gun at Liuzzo. Of the six defense witnesses, five are called to cast doubt on Rowe's honesty and reputation.

Murphy's sixty-seven-minute closing argument—more than three times longer than his entire defense presentation—is a hate-filled diatribe against integration and the U.S. government. He says he is proud to be a white supremacist. He calls Liuzzo a "nigger lover" who came South in search of "black meat." He calls Moton a "nigger" who "hasn't got any courage or morals or decency." He questions what Moton did to Liuzzo during the half hour that he was supposedly passed out after the shoot-ing. He argues that even though a toxicologist for the state said there was no evidence of sperm or semen in Liuzzo's body, that doesn't prove she didn't have sexual relations with Moton. He calls Rowe a "liar and a perjurer" and compares him to Judas

Iscariot because he betrayed the Klan for money. He adds that Rowe's testimony is not corroborated by the FBI's identification of the murder weapon and bullets.

Although Murphy needs no help in developing a theory to assassinate Liuzzo's character, he has an ally at the highest level of government. Within days of the shooting, J. Edgar Hoover had ordered an investigation into Liuzzo's background. Soon, he told President Johnson that Liuzzo had needle marks on her arms. He also said that Liuzzo had been attacked because the Klansmen saw "this colored man . . . snuggling up pretty close to this white woman . . . it had all the appearances of a necking party."

After Johnson ignored the slurs, Hoover leaked the information—none of which proved to be true—to draw attention away from his informant. "The press was starting to ask why Rowe had done nothing to prevent the shooting," historian Gary May would explain years later. "Hoover created a more alluring subject for media attention."

Syndicated columnist Inez Robb is not fooled, and pushes the FBI to explain its actions in the Liuzzo case. "What sorely troubles me, if we accept the prosecution's account of the slaying, is the moral aspect of Rowe's presence in the car," she writes. "Under what kind of secret orders did Rowe work? Was he expected to join in crime, strictly observe, or try to prevent murder?"

In his closing argument, prosecutor Arthur Gamble makes the case for convicting Wilkins, while acknowledging that neither he nor the jury endorses the reasons for Liuzzo's trip to Selma. "But, gentlemen, she was here," he tells them, "and she had a right to be here on our highways without being shot down in the middle of the night."

After deliberating for two days, the jury tells the judge it is hopelessly deadlocked. A mistrial is declared. Jurors then reveal that they had voted 10–2 in favor of conviction. Alabama's attorney general, Richmond Flowers, promises a new trial in September. Federal civil rights charges are also pending.

It is unclear what impact the Liuzzo case will have on the next high-profile civil rights murder trial in Alabama. In April, a grand jury in Selma indicted Elmer Cook. William Hoggle, and Namon O'Neal "Duck" Hoggle for the murder of James Reeb. When the trial in state court begins in December, a jury of their peers can determine if, as Cook allegedly told Rowe in the Silver Moon, the three men did their job.

CHAPTER NINE

"HE HAD TO DIE FOR SOMETHING . . ."

March 21, 1965

As the march from Selma to Montgomery began, Cager Lee reflected on his grandson's death. "Yes it was worth the boy dying," he told reporters. "He was my daughter's onliest son, but she understands. . . . He was a sweet boy. Not pushy. Not rowdy. He took me to church every Sunday. He worked hard. But he had to die for something, and thank God it was this."

If the deaths of Jimmie Lee Jackson, James Reeb, Viola Liuzzo, and others who have fallen in the struggle for civil rights are to change America, three things must happen over the months that follow Lee's remarks. Congress must pass a voting rights bill. Those who have been disenfranchised must register to vote. And newly registered men and women, along with those previously registered, must go to the polls and elect candidates who can effect change.

The bill, sponsored by U.S. Senate majority leader Mike

Mansfield, a Democrat from Montana, and minority leader Everett Dirksen, a Republican from Illinois, is introduced on March 17, two days after President Johnson's address to the nation. On April 9, it is reported out of the Senate Judiciary Committee. Two weeks later, the full Senate begins debate on the legislation. By this time, another sixty-four senators have signed on as cosponsors.

On May 26, the Senate passes the bill by a vote of 77–19. The nay votes are all cast by southern senators, seventeen Democrats and two Republicans. President Johnson calls the result "triumphant evidence of this nation's resolve that every citizen must and shall be able to march to a polling place and vote without fear or prejudice or obstruction."

Attention now turns to the House of Representatives. The recently ratified Twenty-Fourth Amendment bans poll taxes as a condition for voting in federal elections. Senate liberals failed in their attempt to incorporate a provision in the bill that would extend this ban to state and local elections. Fearing a court might rule the entire bill unconstitutional if poll taxes are applied beyond the federal level, Attorney General Katzenbach and Senator Dirksen argue against the extension. Nevertheless, the House version bans state and local poll taxes.

Despite the current difference between the House and Senate versions, supporters are confident a compromise will soon be reached. Anticipating passage before the summer, SCLC, SNCC, and other organizations launch previously planned lobbying and registration initiatives. In a speech at UCLA on April 27, Dr. King announces the creation of SCOPE (Summer Community Organization and Political Education Project).

Inspired by the Mississippi Freedom Summer, SCOPE recruits five hundred white college students to help activists register African American voters in six southern states. SCLC's Rev. Hosea Williams heads the effort, which runs from mid-June until the end of August. Albert Turner, Willie Bolden, and James Orange are among those in leadership positions.

As with the Freedom Summer, the work is dangerous. In Wilcox County, Alabama, whites shoot at cars carrying SCOPE volunteers. In Sussex County, Virginia, volunteers are run off the road and threatened by a man with a shotgun. In Luverne, Alabama, whites beat SCOPE workers and local students attempting to integrate a restaurant. And in Americus, Georgia, John Lewis and others are jailed while attempting to integrate churches.

Because it takes Congress longer than anticipated to pass the voting rights bill, SCOPE's goal of registering 400,000 blacks is not immediately reached. Still, by the end of the ten-week program, almost 50,000 blacks have been added to the voting rolls. Thousands more have attended political education classes. King thanks the participants: "We were part of a history-making enterprise which has gripped us all in its infinite garment of destiny,[breaking] much new ground and [laying] a solid foundation upon which we will continue to build for years to come."

While SCOPE volunteers work in Alabama and other states, SNCC focuses much attention on Lowndes County, just as Stokely Carmichael promised. Between the end of March and the end of June, about five hundred blacks try to register. Half are successful.

When passage of the bill appears imminent, the Lowndes registrar eliminates the literacy test and extends office hours. He is not altruistic. If enough blacks register, the county may be able to avoid an influx of federal registrars mandated by the pending legislation. The Klan and other whites in the area are not conciliatory. They continue to terrorize activists and stymie efforts at integration or the empowerment of blacks.

One of the volunteers working with SNCC is a twenty-six-year-old Episcopal seminarian from New Hampshire. Jonathan Daniels, a former Harvard undergraduate, answered Dr. King's call to come to Selma after Bloody Sunday. He stayed for several weeks, returned north to take exams in May, and then came back to Alabama in July. He has been tutoring students and helping people register.

A few weeks after his return, he and members of SNCC are among twenty-nine people arrested while picketing a whites-only store in Fort Deposit, Alabama. They are jailed in Hayneville, seat of Lowndes County. When released six days later, Daniels and a small group of blacks and whites attempt to enter a nearby store that serves black people. Tom Coleman, an armed special deputy, blocks their entrance.

Coleman aims his shotgun at a black teenage girl. Daniels pushes the girl out of the way. He is shot and dies instantly. The deputy also wounds Father Richard Morrisroe, a Roman Catholic priest.

Although the deputy claims he acted in self-defense because he thought Daniels had a knife, a grand jury indicts him for manslaughter. The indictment does not satisfy Richmond Flowers, the state's attorney general, who thinks murder charges are in order. Flowers takes over the case because he fears local prosecutors do not want a guilty verdict.

The judge shows no sympathy to the prosecution. He refuses to delay the trial until Father Morrisroe is well enough to testify, then removes Flowers from the case. An all-white jury takes only two hours to find Coleman not guilty.

Prospective jurors are chosen from state voting rolls. If blacks win the right to vote and their names are added to these rolls, they will finally have a voice on juries that impact their lives.

On August 3, by a vote of 328–74, the U.S. House of Representatives passes the Voting Rights Act of 1965 (VRA), or as it is officially titled, "An act to enforce the fifteenth amendment to the Constitution of the United States, and for other purposes." On August 4, the U.S. Senate passes the jointly agreed upon measure, 79–18.

The final bill is similar to the one introduced almost five months earlier. Literacy tests and other means used to deny blacks the right to vote will be struck down. Federal registrars will be sent to counties and states that discriminate against black applicants. A state or county is deemed to be guilty of discrimination if it has a literacy test and less than half of its voting-age population was registered or voted in the 1964 presidential election. Alabama, Mississippi, Louisiana, Georgia, South Carolina, and Virginia qualify, as do more than twenty-five counties in North Carolina.

Passage of the Voting Rights Act took longer than expected because of the differing approaches to the elimination of state and local poll taxes. When the House and Senate failed to reconcile their differences, Attorney General Katzenbach proposed a compromise: The bill would not categorically eliminate such poll taxes. Instead, it would declare that state and local poll taxes are unconstitutional and instruct the Department of Justice to sue states where those measures are in effect. Liberals did not like the compromise but agreed to it in late July after Dr. King gave it his blessing.

On August 6, 1965, Luci Baines Johnson asks her father: "Why are we going up to the halls of Congress? Why aren't we just signing it here in the East Room?"

"We're going up to the halls of Congress because the Congress will never look the same again as a result of the courageous decisions that these men and women are making," the president replies. "Some who are here today will not be here again because they dared to support the Voting Rights Act. And some who will be coming would never have had the opportunity but for this act."

A few minutes later, the president enters the Capitol Rotunda and speaks to a standing-room-only crowd that includes members of Congress, his cabinet, Supreme Court justices, and invited guests, including Dr. Martin Luther King Jr., John Lewis, Roy Wilkins, James Forman, Rosa Parks, and Vivian Malone, who became the first black student to enroll at the University of Alabama two years earlier despite Governor Wallace's personal effort to block her from entering.

In a somber voice, President Johnson tells those present and millions watching on television that the bill he is about to sign "is a triumph for freedom as huge as any victory won on any battlefield." Calling the right to vote "the most powerful instrument ever devised by man for breaking down injustice," he adds: "Today we strike away the last major shackle of those fierce and ancient bonds [of slavery]. Today the Negro story and the American story fuse and blend."

Johnson also issues several challenges. Leaders must "teach people their rights and responsibilities and lead them to exercise their right to vote." African Americans must register and vote: "You must learn so your choice advances your interest and the

interest of the nation." And the country "must move now toward a different battlefield . . . granting every American Negro
freedom to enter the mainstream of American life."

Following his address, Johnson and the assembled gather in
the President's Room near the floor of the Senate. Here, 104
years earlier, Abraham Lincoln signed an order freeing slaves
impressed into Civil War service by the Confederacy. As he
signs the Voting Rights Act, President Johnson presents com-
memorative pens to senators, congresspersons, and others.

Luci Baines Johnson later asks her father why he gave the
first pen to Vice President Humphrey and the second pen to
Senator Dirksen instead of a civil rights leader. "I didn't have to
convince one of the great civil rights leaders to be for that legislation. They were already for it," the president explains. "But
because of Everett Dirksen's decision to support this law and
bring his supporters with him, the great civil rights leaders and
I have a law, not just a bill. That's why Senator Dirksen got the
pen. He deserved it."

Dr. King calls the president's speech "eloquent and persuasive" and says the law will help remove "all the obstacles to the
right to vote." Republican senator Strom Thurmond of South
Carolina refuses to attend the ceremony and offers a different
perspective. He accuses "the president and his friend Martin
Luther King [of] celebrating another step in the disintegration
of the United States Constitution."

The federal government wastes no time in trying to bring
the vote to an estimated two million unregistered blacks. On
the same day Johnson signs the bill, the Justice Department files
a lawsuit challenging the constitutionality of the Mississippi poll
tax. Similar suits are filed the following week in Alabama, Virginia, and Texas.

Three days after the signing, the government sends examiners to nine counties in the Deep South to begin registering voters. Far more counties warrant federal intervention, but the Justice Department hopes they will voluntarily change their discriminatory policies. Four of the nine counties are in Alabama. They include Dallas County—where, over the last six months, local officials rejected the applications of twenty-four blacks with college degrees—and Lowndes County, where less than 4 percent of eligible blacks are registered.

The attorney general says there are over five million blacks of voting age in the eleven states of the Old Confederacy. If they all register and vote, he continues, "I think a good many politicians in the South will rethink some of their positions."

Among those five million is an eighty-two-year-old man whom local registrars have turned away multiple times. On August 20, 1965, six months after his grandson was shot by a state trooper, Cager Lee returns to the Perry County clerk's office. This time, with the help of federal registrars, he is successful.

With many local, state, and federal races scheduled for 1966, the *Los Angeles Times*' Jack Nelson speculates whether "the new voting rights act could shake loose the white man's stranglehold on politics in the Black Belt . . . and revolutionize Southern politics." He notes: "Negroes already are being groomed by civil rights organizations to run for local offices and state legislative posts and some are certain to be elected."

Senator Thurmond and Governor Wallace are among the "staunch segregationists" who might see "their political careers curtailed by a large Negro electorate."

During the summer and fall of 1965, the number of blacks who register increases dramatically in counties to which the Johnson administration sends federal registrars. But those registrars are sent to only twenty-two of the hundreds of counties covered by the legislation and to only six of the Black Belt's twenty-plus counties. Pressed by civil rights leaders, Katzenbach says that many of the counties without these registrars are complying voluntarily.

Literacy tests may be gone, but intimidation remains. The Southern Regional Council, a not-for-profit organization created to end racial violence and promote equality, documents 122 incidents of "reprisal and violence" against blacks who try to register during the act's first six months.

Undeterred, SCLC and SNCC intensify registration efforts as the 1966 elections approach. In Alabama, voters must register by March to cast ballots in the May primaries. SCLC focuses on those areas with large numbers of potential black voters—the Black Belt and the state's bigger cities. After federal registrars come to Montgomery in the fall, eight thousand men and women are registered within a month. Fifteen thousand register in the Birmingham area in January after the registrars arrive.

By March 1966, there are more than 235,000 black voters on the rolls in Alabama, about twice as many as before passage of the act. They make up 30 percent of the state's population and 16 percent of the electorate. That latter percentage might have been larger, but white Alabamans launched their own registration efforts and added 110,000 new voters to the rolls.

Throughout the South, the Democratic Party reigns supreme. Republicans have been out of favor since the days of Abraham Lincoln. SCLC believes that newly registered blacks can make a difference by voting for fellow blacks slated by the Democrats or white Democrats sympathetic to their cause. In Black Belt counties with populations that are overwhelmingly

African American, the Democrats slate about seventy-five black candidates for local office.

After passage of the VRA, the Democratic Party in Alabama increases its filing fee for candidates to five hundred dollars. This discourages some economically strapped blacks from running for office and emboldens SNCC and the Lowndes County Freedom Organization (LCFO) to devise an alternative strategy. They create a new political party to run its own slate of black candidates for county sheriff, coroner, tax assessor, and the board of education.

Prospects for success appear good. Of the county's 15,417 residents, 81 percent are black. In 1964, 5,122 blacks were eligible to vote, and none were registered. Now 2,500 blacks are registered, only 200 fewer than the number of whites who are registered.

Required by law to produce an emblem for the new party, SNCC and LCFO choose a black panther. LCFO's African American leader John Hulett explains that, like the panther, Lowndes County blacks have been pushed into a corner and will come out "fighting for life or death."

The newly christened Black Panther Party plans to hold its nominating convention on primary day, May 3. Local whites threaten to disrupt the event, but the county's sheriff refuses to provide security for the convention. Carmichael's response, a sign of the movement's splintering, emphasizes a growing preference for self-defense over nonviolence. "That's okay, baby," he says. "We're gonna bring our guns and we're gonna have our meeting uninterrupted."

Hearing this, the Justice Department warns Hulett to tell his members "not to start any trouble." Hulett replies: "We don't intend to. We are within our rights. We will come armed. You tell the crackers not to start any trouble, because if they start something, we're going to finish it."

Nine hundred blacks attend the convention. Whites do not interfere. Still, as SNCC's monthly newspaper the *Movement* reports, the blacks in Lowndes County "have no illusion that whites will turn over their power peacefully. Already a $1,000 reward has been offered for the person who kills the first Negro sheriff."

The VRA does not revolutionize southern politics overnight, but the results of the 1966 primaries and general elections offer African Americans hope. In the Black Belt's Macon County, home of the Tuskegee Institute, thirty-two-year-old Lucius Amerson wins the Democratic nomination for sheriff. After prevailing in the general election in November, he becomes the first black sheriff in the South since Reconstruction, and President Johnson invites him to the White House. Macon County also elects a black tax collector and black county commissioner.

In Dallas County, both candidates for sheriff are white, but the votes of African Americans decide the election. Before the VRA, fewer than 1,000 blacks were registered to vote in the county. By May 1966, that number has swelled to 10,300, only 2,200 fewer than the number of registered whites. Backed by newly enfranchised blacks, Wilson Baker defeats incumbent sheriff Jim Clark in the primary for the Democratic nomination. When Clark runs as an independent in the general election, Baker beats him again.

Despite their emerging clout, blacks recognize that the old guard will continue attempts to suppress the vote. The Dallas County Democratic Executive Committee—populated by members of the segregationist White Citizens Council—tries to exclude primary votes cast in black precincts, citing technical errors. Baker wins only after a federal judge rules that the ballots are valid.

The African American vote does not decide the Alabama governor's race. State law forbids the governor from succeeding himself, so George Wallace slates his wife to run in his place. Surrogate Lurleen Wallace prevails in the May primary, beating two former governors, a congressman, and the moderate Richmond Flowers. "The choice of Mrs. George Wallace as the Democratic candidate for governor proves that the [Democratic] Party in Alabama is still fully in the hands of racists," writes the *Movement*.

Mrs. Wallace wins in November, as do the Democratic candidates for all seven county office positions in Lowndes County. African Americans opine that the Black Panther Party nominees lost there because white landowners threatened their black sharecroppers with eviction if they did not vote for white candidates.

"The new Southern Negro vote will have a marked effect on candidates and government—but not by controlling or dominating elections," the *New York Times'* Tom Wicker concludes, surveying the election results. "This 15 percent of the electorate is not likely to be ignored or slighted again, either in elections or by state government. In the long run that may be more important than the fate of specific candidates."

In the twelve months following passage of the VRA, the percentage of registered blacks rises from 30 percent of those eligible to 46 percent. "We are firmly convinced," says the NAACP's executive director, Roy Wilkins, "that the continuing increase in Negro registration will bring about a wholesome regeneration and liberalization of southern politics."

That regeneration and liberalization begins to take root in the years that follow. In 1970, the LCFO's party merges with Alabama's Democratic Party. Black candidates from 1966 run again for county offices and win. Hulett is elected sheriff. That same year civil rights attorney Fred Gray and state NAACP president Thomas Reed become the first blacks elected to the Alabama Legislature since Reconstruction. Before the decade is over, blacks are elected to key posts in Perry County, including sheriff. They also win seats on the Perry County Commission and Board of Education.

Does the election of these black officials make a difference? In 1968, a black man tells Macon County's Sheriff Amerson that he was terrorized by a white state trooper and a local white police chief after being arrested for disorderly conduct. The man claims he was beaten and that one officer made him dance by shooting at his feet.

"The whole eyes of the black community were going to see whether this black sheriff was a defunct placeholder or whether he was going to really do his job," Amerson's son Anthony later said.

The sheriff ordered the two white officers arrested. "It made everybody have respect," Anthony Amerson said. "It was unheard-of."

CHAPTER TEN

"A MOST UNUSUAL
OCCURRENCE . . ."

December 7, 1965

*I**f it should appear from the evidence or testimony that the victim was friendly with, or social with, or consorted with or treated as equals, or lived in the same quarters with Negroes, or in his conduct or relations considered Negroes as good as whites, or sympathized with their efforts to gain equality with whites, should such conduct or activity make the victim a low person to such an extent that it would bias or prejudice your favor of the defendant?*

Given the fact that those prosecuting James Reeb's alleged attackers in Selma feel it necessary to ask this question of prospective jurors, few who sympathize with "the victim" expect a guilty verdict. Still, as the proceedings begin, some of those sympathizers see a sliver of hope that defendants Elmer Cook, Namon O'Neal "Duck" Hoggle, and William "Stanley" Hoggle will be held accountable.

The hopeful point to two verdicts in Alabama just a few days earlier. On December 3, a federal jury in Montgomery found Klansmen Wilkins, Thomas, and Eaton guilty of violating the civil rights of Viola Liuzzo. Assistant U.S. attorney general John Doar prosecuted this case in Judge Frank Johnson's court. It followed the state court trial in May that had resulted in a hung jury and a second trial in state court in October that had resulted in acquittal.

One day earlier, an all-white state court jury in Anniston, a city in northeast Alabama, had convicted white supremacist Hubert Strange of the July murder of black factory worker Willie Brewster Jr. Strange shot Brewster after attending a National States' Rights Party rally. The verdict marked the first time in the civil rights era that a white person was found guilty of murdering a black person in Alabama.

Just four years earlier, Anniston had made headlines for a very different reason. A mob there burned a bus carrying Freedom Riders. Now, however, the murder of Brewster had so outraged white civic leaders that they had offered a twenty-thousand-dollar reward for the apprehension and conviction of the killer.

The eyewitness testimony of the two ministers beaten alongside Reeb on March 9—Clark Olsen and Orloff Miller—will be critical to the prosecution's case in Selma. Edgar Stripling, who worked near the scene of the attack, has also come forward and identified the defendants as the attackers. Nevertheless, just a few weeks before the trial, prosecutor Blanchard McLeod told the *New York Times*, "I have a very weak case." Because Olsen had run after being hit and Miller had been crouching to avoid further attack, their ability to identify the suspects was compromised, McLeod explained. And while Stripling claimed to have had a clear view of the beating, the defense would be certain to challenge his sanity. "We have a man that had been in an asylum eight years previously," said the prosecutor.

Asked by the *Times* why he sought indictments if the case was so shaky, McLeod replied with a question of his own: "If I hadn't indicted them, what would you newspaper people have said?"

The fifty-three-year-old prosecutor's personal history, as well as his words, suggest he is less than enthusiastic about trying the case. A friend and colleague of Selma's segregationist sheriff, Jim Clark, McLeod has been an active member of the White Citizens Council. Along with Sheriff Clark and others, he has been a defendant in lawsuits brought by local blacks and by the U.S. Department of Justice seeking enforcement of civil rights laws. And five years to the day before Reeb's beating, he deputized hundreds of citizens to break up anticipated sit-ins at Alabama State College. "We must meet force with force," he told them. "The days of passive resistance are over."

Aware of this history, the FBI, in an internal memorandum, deems McLeod an "adamant segregationist," adding: "It cannot be anticipated from the attitude which he has displayed that he has any intention of forcefully and aggressively prosecuting the case."

The "newspaper people" and the FBI aren't the only ones with their eyes on McLeod and Selma. The Unitarians, devastated by the loss of one of their ministers, have engaged Daniel Bickford, a prominent Boston lawyer, to monitor the trial. He will be joined by Rev. Walter Roy Jones Jr., chairman of the church's Commission on Religion and Race. Jones will later write about his arrival from Virginia:

Selma is getting ready for Christmas. The pervasive shabbiness of Broad Street is partly concealed, partly accented by the bright decorations which, especially at night give an air of commercial gaiety. . . . On the surface little tension is visible. Negros can be seen patronizing Broad Street stores alongside whites, despite a partial boycott. Dolls for Negro girls grace the windows of the five-and-ten-cent store, alongside white dolls. There seems to be full freedom of movement for Negro shoppers. Although it takes a while to penetrate, however, the tension is there.

The Dallas County Courthouse is the center of that tension, having seen its share of confrontations over the preceding year. After attempting to register at the building in late January, Annie Lee Cooper punched Sheriff Clark when he poked her with his cattle prod. On February 1, Dr. King and others were arrested on the courthouse steps after refusing to stop a protest. Two weeks later, Clark lost his temper and punched SCLC's Rev. Vivian, bloodying his face but not silencing his grievances. On March 6, angry whites cursed Rev. Joseph Ellwanger and the CWCA at the conclusion of the march in support of voting rights for blacks. And on March 15, four days after Reeb's death, 3,500 mourners gathered in front of the courthouse for a thirty-minute vigil.

In April, the grand jury meeting at the courthouse heard Olsen and other witnesses describe the attack on Reeb. On a break, the minister from Berkeley struck up a conversation with a local merchant, who asked why he was in town. Hearing Olsen's explanation, the merchant promptly condemned the assailants for "violating the code of southern hospitality." Olsen was dumbfounded. "I thought to myself, *Jesus Christ, is that what you call it? They murdered somebody!*" he later recalled.

Before deciding whether or not to indict those who had been arrested, the all-white, all-male grand jury received instructions from Circuit Court judge James J. Hare, the same judge who had previously banned meetings of three or more SCLC, SNCC, or DCVL members. The judge took this opportunity to spend forty minutes expressing his thoughts on everything from outside agitators to the intelligence of blacks.

"Many self-anointed saints took it upon themselves to come here and help us solve our problems," he said. "But integration will solve no social problems." Hare explained that the blacks in Selma were descended from two African tribes, the Ebo and the Angol, and that the IQs of these tribesmen did not exceed 65. As far as intelligence went, these people were the same as "white riff-raff and river rats."

Following Judge Hare's speech, the Selma grand jury indicted Cook and the Hoggles after four hours of deliberation. It did not charge the fourth man who had been arrested, R. B. Kelley. He was thought to be cooperating with the prosecutors and was expected to be called as a witness when the trial began in December.

On Tuesday, December 7, front-page headlines in most American cities proclaim that the chairman of the Federal Reserve Board has called inflation a threat, that NASA's Gemini 7 astronauts are enjoying a smooth ride in space, and that North Vietnam's president, Ho Chi Minh, has listed his terms for peace on U.S. television. In Selma that day, the local *Times-Journal* focuses on the Reeb murder trial.

Senior circuit court judge L. S. Moore, described by local moderates as "a straight shooter who'll allow no nonsense," enters the walnut-paneled courtroom at 9:15 a.m., climbs a few steps up to his seat, and calls for order. "It took me some time to figure out who the judge was," recalled Daniel Bickford, "as he wore no robe and entered the room without introduction. He carried what appeared to be the docket books. No one stood when he entered the courtroom. There was no indication that he was anything other than a clerk."

The lack of formality extends to crowd control. There are no law enforcement officials or court officers present to check those wishing to enter. The courtroom, with a seating capacity of about 350, is soon overflowing with potential witnesses and jurors and onlookers. About one hundred African Americans have come to watch. They sit, as always, in a section separate from their white counterparts.

Judge Moore begins the day by swearing in potential witnesses. Defense attorney Joe Pilcher explains that most of the seventy-five-plus witnesses on his list are prepared to testify to the good character of his clients. The prosecution's list, including Olsen, Miller, and Stripling, numbers about a dozen. All witnesses, except the character witnesses, will be forbidden from attending the trial until they take the stand. This will reduce the possibility of a conspiracy in which everyone says the same thing.

Having sworn in the witnesses, the judge addresses the potential jurors. About 110 have been summoned. Newspapers will report that thirteen of these were black, but Jones will insist he saw only four men of color.

Whatever the precise number, it is not surprising that so few are African American. In a 1954 court action, the Selma Circuit Court clerk's office admitted to excluding blacks from the jury rolls. While that office now maintains that it has addressed the problem, "No Negro has sat as a juror in a civil or criminal case involving white litigants in the memory of anyone in the Selma courthouse," the *New York Times* reports.

Several potential jurors are excused after revealing that they are friends with the defendants, have a preconceived opinion of the case, oppose capital punishment, or could not convict based on circumstantial evidence. Then Judge Moore reads that lengthy question designed to ferret out those who might be unable to convict because victim Reeb's "conduct or activity" made him "a low person."

State attorney general Flowers has ordered the prosecution to make this inquiry, and another judge has ruled that it could be addressed to each prospective juror privately. McLeod, however, chooses to let Judge Moore ask it to everyone at the same time. "I am sure that experience must show that it is difficult to give a 'yes' answer in front of 350 other persons," Bickford wrote, second-guessing this approach. "Would it not have been better to propound the question individually so that a prospective juror would not have to become a volunteer on exposing his prejudice?"

Three on the panel do rise to admit that Reeb's conduct would influence their deliberations. One, a railroad employee, says: "I am sick of civil rights. I've been sleeping civil rights. I have a fixed opinion." After acknowledging he cannot be impartial, the man is dismissed by the judge.

A second prospective juror, a farmer, says: "I am prejudiced against a man who came down here from Boston when he should have been preaching up there." And a third, a city employee, says: "I feel Reeb didn't belong down here." Both men, however, say they could be impartial, and the judge chooses not to dismiss them. The prosecution uses two of its allotted challenges to keep them off the jury.

Elmer Cook, forty-two, manages a novelty company. Duck Hoggle, thirty-one, is an auto mechanic. Stanley Hoggle, thirty-seven, is a salesman. The three defendants will be judged by a jury of their peers. The all-white, all-male panel includes a mail carrier, insurance agent, auto sales manager, salesman, an electric company manager, a grocery manager, a business owner, a logger, a truck driver, and a cigar store employee.

In their opening statements to the jury, each side outlines its case and offers a surprise. After a short speech in which he says the prosecution will prove that the defendants "did the killing," McLeod announces that he is turning the trial over to his colleague Virgis Ashworth, a former Speaker of the Alabama House of Representatives. Due to a recent stroke, he explains, he is under doctor's orders to refrain from trying a case until January. Ashworth seems to share McLeod's view of civil rights, and has long been aligned with John Patterson, the segregationist governor of Alabama who served from 1959 to 1963 and was succeeded by George Wallace.

Following McLeod's opening statement, defense attorney Pilcher raises eyebrows when he offers two seemingly contradictory defenses. First, he says, several witnesses will testify that the defendants were elsewhere when the attack occurred. Duck Hoggle was in a restaurant, while his brother and Cook were at their respective businesses.

But, Pilcher continues, even if the evidence demonstrates the defendants attacked Reeb, the three should not be convicted of murder because something happened subsequent to the beating that further harmed the victim. "Leading doctors from the University Hospital in Birmingham will testify that the wounds of James Reeb were not the same when he arrived there as when he was diagnosed here [in Selma]." Somehow, he says, they had been "altered." Why? The court will have to wait to hear his explanation.

The *Boston Globe* characterizes this altered-wounds defense as a "bizarre twist." Pilcher, however, is no stranger to twists. Defending two of those accused of the 16th Street Baptist Church bombing that killed the four young Birmingham girls in 1963, he argued that the Montgomery Improvement Association, a civil rights group composed of black ministers and community leaders, committed the act to win sympathy and donations from the North.

Pilcher then offers a second, equally bizarre twist. "You are all aware of the racial overtones and national attention focused on this courtroom," he tells the jury. This is a civil rights case, he argues, "because the basic rights of these men are involved," referring to the *defendants*. He urges the jurors not to be influenced by what they have read in an "unfriendly press," but when he goes on to attack those who "shout about civil rights, but have no concern for the rights of others," Ashworth objects. Judge Moore sustains the objection.

Clark Olsen will be the first witness for the prosecution. After the attack in March, he returned to his church duties in Berkeley. Later in the spring, he led a student group on a tour of Russia—the tour that he and Reeb and Miller had discussed over dinner just minutes before their fateful walk. He frequently thinks about Reeb and considers the minister a martyr. "He didn't know he was going to be killed, but he knew he was going into the face of great danger," he explains. "His life was sacrificed in a just cause. Attacked by people who hated what he stood for makes him a martyr, as was Jimmie Lee Jackson."

As terrible as all the events in Selma and elsewhere in the South have been, Olsen finds some solace in the passage of the Voting Rights Act. He realizes, too, that he himself is part of history. This realization will become even clearer a few years later when the minister takes his daughter to see a documentary on Dr. King. The film shows King's announcement at Brown Chapel that he has just learned that three ministers have been beaten. Watching this in the darkened theater, Olsen whispered to his daughter, "That was me."

In the witness box, Olsen describes leaving Walker's Café with Reeb and Miller at about 7:30 p.m. As the three ministers neared the Silver Moon Café, they heard men yelling at them in threatening tones. "Four or five men came after us from across the street," Olsen testifies. "They shouted at us. We continued walking, going twelve or fifteen feet before they reached us. One carried a stick or a pipe—an object of some length."

Reeb was hit on the side of the head, Olsen continues. "Miller crouched down with his hand over his head to keep from being hit. I ran rather than fall to the pavement. One man came after me. I ran a few steps to the street. The man hit me there a few times and my glasses fell off. I had an especially good view of the man attacking me. I turned to face him. I raised my arms to protect myself and saw him as he hit me. After a few seconds he stopped his attack on me and left the scene. I turned and saw two or three men kicking Reverend Reeb and Reverend Miller."

Ashworth: Do you think you could recognize the man who attacked you? If he were present, do you think you could recognize him?
Olsen: Yes.
Ashworth: Is he in this courtroom? Is he present?

"The minister arose," Edward McGrath wrote for *Globe* readers. "He scanned the packed room. Silence enveloped the courtroom as Rev. Mr. Olsen stared at defendant Cook, pointed, and said, 'He's next to the lady in the red dress.' Cook returned the stare. The defendant, dressed in a neat business suit, showed no emotion." The lady in red is Pilcher's secretary.

Ashworth then asks Olsen if he recognizes the other two defendants. The minister says they resemble the other attackers in build, height, age, and even facial characteristic. However, he says, "I cannot positively identify them."

Olsen describes how he and Miller helped Reeb walk to the SCLC office, the trip to the Burwell Infirmary, and the events that prolonged the ninety-mile drive to Birmingham.

Is it possible that Reeb's wounds had been, as the defense has suggested, "altered?" No, says Olsen. He was with Reeb the entire time—from the attack to arrival in Birmingham—except when X-rays were taken at the infirmary. Nothing happened to aggravate the wound.

On cross-examination Pilcher wastes no time trying to discredit Olsen's character and account of the attack. The defendants' attorney tries to link the minister to causes that would apparently label him as an agitator and repel the jury.

Pilcher: Are you a pacifist?

Olsen: No, I'm not.

Pilcher: Are you a member of the National Committee for a Sane Nuclear Policy?

Olsen: No.

Pilcher: Why did you come to Selma?

Olsen: I heard news reports of those supporting the voting rights and felt I wanted to come to lend my presence to this effort as an individual.

Pilcher: Was this an organized effort?

Olsen: No, not as far as my involvement was concerned.

As this line of questioning has nothing to do with the matter at hand, Ashworth finally has had enough. "I know what he's trying to do," says the prosecutor. Judge Moore sustains his objection.

Pilcher turns to Olsen's identification of Cook, trying to point out inconsistencies between the minister's prior statements to the police and FBI and his testimony in court. The attorney also notes that Olsen's vision may have been faulty because his glasses were knocked off during the attack. Olsen, however, maintains that he is certain that it was Cook who had hit him.

As the first day of the trial ends, the prosecution is sanguine. McLeod, still in the courtroom to observe, confesses that he was surprised by Olsen's ability to identify Cook as his attacker. "I respected his conscientious approach," he says of the clergyman. "He had never seen the defendants—at least not since the attack, and was not sure he would recognize them. Now our case is considerably strengthened."

The next day's proceedings seem to solidify the case against Cook and, to some extent, the Hoggle brothers. Olsen's testimony concludes with his acknowledgment under cross-examination that he does not think the man who attacked him, Elmer Cook, struck Reeb. While this might appear to hurt the prosecution's case, Alabama law makes it clear that a participant in an attack that ends in murder can be convicted of the crime even if he did not actually strike the fatal blow. Before beginning its deliberations, the jury will be instructed to follow that law.

Rev. Miller takes the stand, and his testimony brings what McGrath calls "the second bombshell of the trial." Asked if he can identify any of the attackers, Miller rises in the witness stand, looks around the courtroom, and then points to Cook. "He was

in the lead that night," the minister says. "The other two defendants resemble others in that group," he adds soon after. "I
believe I saw the other two that day, but I could not be positive."

On cross-examination, Pilcher asks Miller to demonstrate
the position he took to protect himself. Miller leaves the witness
stand and kneels before the jury box. As the twelve jurors stand,
he covers his head with his hands. "You had little time to see the
attack?" Pilcher asks. "I looked directly at the men as they came
across the street," Miller counters. When Pilcher suggests that it
had been dark outside, Miller says it was not fully dark yet, and
the streetlights were on.

Pilcher: Did you see the instrument that hit the de-
ceased?
Miller: I did not.
Pilcher: You got a glancing look at the lead man?
Miller: I got a good look.

Attempting to establish that the attack was not the cause of
Reeb's death, Pilcher interrogates Miller about the ambulance
trip. "It was brought up that the injured man was not lying on
his stomach, that there was no emergency equipment, such as
oxygen tanks and respirators, to keep the circulatory passages
open," Daniel Bickford will later write. "The stretcher did not
fit the ambulance and had to be kept up against the side by
him. Miller said that it had a tendency to roll." Miller also says
that Reeb was unconscious and in obvious pain, but that he did
nothing for the injured man, because he knew of nothing to do.

Although both Olsen and Miller have testified that the Hoggle brothers resemble two of the other attackers, the prosecution
will need more to link them to the crime scene. Pilcher has

already promised to produce witnesses that place the two men (as well as Cook) elsewhere and apart from one another. The state calls its next witness, Ouida Larson.

Described by one reporter as "an attractive blonde," Larson is a waitress at the Silver Moon. Cook and the Hoggles were in the cafe "sometime between 6:30 and 8 p.m." on the night of the attack, she tells the court. She remembers serving them coffee. She also remembers that it was a typically quiet night and that she did not learn of the attack until the next day.

Larson's testimony is hardly dispositive, but it suggests the three defendants were together near where the beating occurred, around the time it occurred. Can anyone link the Hoggles directly to Cook during the attack? Blanchard McLeod had previously said that the prosecution's next witness, forty-eight-year-old Edgar Stripling, observed "part of the scuffle." Before Stripling can tell the jury what he saw, however, he will have to overcome the defense's attempt to disqualify him as incompetent based on his history of mental illness.

Stripling, described by the Associated Press as a "small, swarthy man who said he served beer and swept the floor at the Silver Moon Café," enters the witness box wearing a black T-shirt. "His right hand trembled. He frowned at the judge. He had some difficulty speaking and told the judge he suffered from rheumatoid arthritis."

Under Alabama law, "persons who have not the use of reason, as idiots, lunatics during lunacy, and children who do not understand the nature of an oath, are incompetent witnesses." Judge Moore asks Stripling a few questions to determine whether he can distinguish between truth and fantasy, then sends him out of the courtroom.

Pilcher calls witnesses to prove Stripling is incompetent.

Wilson Baker testifies that he observed Stripling carrying on a conversation with a cup and saucer and shadowboxing with parking meters. Peter Lackeos, owner of the Silver Moon and a longtime friend of Stripling, testifies that Stripling previously told him of fights that occurred at the café when he (Lackeos) was absent. Lackeos says he is certain those fights never took place.

Then Dr. P. Caldwell DeBardeleben, an internist, takes the stand and reads at length from Stripling's Veterans Administration medical records. These indicate that on Stripling's last visit in 1959, he was deemed a residual schizophrenic. Certain forms of that illness make it impossible to distinguish fact from fantasy, the doctor says, though he adds that he has never met or examined Stripling.

"The State made no attempt to medically qualify [Stripling], nor did it object to the testimony of a general practitioner," Bickford writes, noting that the medical records being used to evaluate the potential witness were six years old. "There was certainly no testimony that this witness did not understand the oath at the time it was being administered."

Still, Judge Moore disqualifies Stripling. "I realize that it is a serious thing to determine whether a man is competent to testify," he explains. "I am not God. Mr. Stripling might be able to tell the truth or he might not, I do not know. But I feel it would not be right to lay this witness before the jury in the face of his medical record and ask them to take credence in what he has to say."

The remainder of the second day is devoted to medical testimony. Dr. Dinkins details his treatment of Reeb at Burwell, the decision to send the victim to Birmingham, and the mishaps that slowed down the trip. On cross-examination, he acknowledges that the ambulance was not equipped with respiratory tubes or oxygen to keep a patient's air passages open. He also says that he did not instruct the ministers on how to care for Reeb during the ride.

Was this lack of equipment and care responsible for Reeb's death? None of the five doctors who testify next—either in court or through sworn deposition—is prepared to say that. Dr. Stanley Graham, a neurosurgeon who saw Reeb in the operating room in Birmingham, comes closest to supporting the defendants' theory. He states that proper treatment on the ride from Selma might have saved the minister's life. Reeb contracted pneumonia because of food particles lodged in his windpipe, a situation that might have been avoided, he says. In addition, the delay in making the trip "seriously impaired" the chance of survival.

In contrast, Dr. James Argires, a Birmingham neurosurgeon who performed emergency surgery on Reeb, says he believes the minister died due to irreversible brain damage. The severe head injury would have led to death in any patient, he testifies. Dr. Thomas Allen, who performed a tracheostomy on Reeb, agrees.

In addition to Olsen, Miller, and Stripling, the prosecution has identified two other men who witnessed the attack: R. B. Kelley and Billy Dowd Edwards. Each is called to testify as the trial continues into its third day. Neither makes it to the witness stand.

Kelley, a thirty-year-old Selma television repairman, was arrested for the attack on Reeb along with the three defendants. Like them, he still faces federal conspiracy charges for his role in the murder. Because of these pending charges, he refuses to testify in the state trial, citing his constitutional right against self-incrimination. Ashworth argues that he should be allowed to interrogate Kelley, who could choose whether or not to invoke his Fifth Amendment privilege on a question-by-question basis. Judge Moore disagrees and dismisses Kelley.

Edwards, the prosecution's next witness, is not in the courtroom. Indeed, he is not even in Alabama. Currently working as a mechanic in Greenville, Mississippi, he lived in Selma at the time of the attack and is alleged to have witnessed the beating. Apologizing to the judge for the witness's absence, Ashworth says: "He told me he was [coming] at midnight last night."

The court recesses for forty-five minutes to give the missing witness time to arrive or for Ashworth to track him down. Back in session, the prosecutor says he called Edwards's employer in Mississippi. Apparently Edwards reported for work and has no intention of coming to testify. "The state has made every effort to have him in court," Ashworth tells the judge. "I doubt if we would ever be able to get him here. He is out of the jurisdiction of this court."

The prosecutor pauses for a moment before announcing, "We have presented all the witnesses available. The state rests."

In 2000, a CNN film crew doing a story on the events in Selma found Edwards (who is now deceased, as is Kelley) in Mississippi. "He would not talk to us on camera," said CNN's Bernard Shaw. "But off camera, he said he would have been a hostile witness at the trial, unwilling to say under oath what he saw that night. What's more, he said the Klan would have killed him if he had gone to Selma to testify."

Pilcher immediately asks for dismissal of the charges against the Hoggle brothers. "The record is completely devoid of evidence," he argues. "Witnesses could not positively identify these defendants. The two ministers, Rev. Olsen and Rev. Miller, tried to be honest and conscientious witnesses, and by being honest and conscientious they could not identify them." Conceding that there is enough evidence against Cook to continue, Pilcher does not move to dismiss the charges against him.

Judge Moore denies the motion. "I'm going to leave with this jury the question of whether they were present." The Hoggle brothers are still on trial.

If the prosecution's case ends with a whimper, the defense begins with a bang. After telling the jury that the defendants were not present at the assault, that there were intervening events that led to Reeb's death, and that another man was the true killer, Pilcher calls Wilson Baker back to the stand and asks about civil rights demonstrations that preceded the attack on Reeb and his companions. When Ashworth objects to this line of questioning, Judge Moore asks Pilcher what he is attempting to prove.

Pilcher says he will show that civil rights workers who said they had aided Reeb when he was injured had instead "willfully" let him die because "it was to the advantage of certain civil rights movements to have a martyr." This audacious accusation—apparently directed at Olsen and Miller—echoes Pilcher's defense in the Birmingham church bombing trial.

The judge allows Baker to state that there was considerable tension in Selma on the day of the attack. He is not allowed to testify what caused that tension. Pilcher, however, suggests that Dr. King and other out-of-town agitators like Reeb, Olsen, and Miller were responsible.

Pilcher calls five witnesses, all of whom are white, to establish that the defendants were elsewhere when the beatings took place. George Hamm, a retired Baptist minister currently working as a janitor in a local factory, says that he went into the Silver Moon between 7 and 7:30 p.m. to make a phone call. As he looked outside, he saw an assault taking place and observed someone who appeared to drop to his knees. He couldn't identify the attackers because "they just flushed out like birds." Hamm did not intervene or come to the aid of those attacked. Rather, he went to the Coffee Pot Café. There he saw Edgar Vardaman standing at the counter.

Vardaman, the next witness, says that he and Duck Hoggle were in the Coffee Pot when Hamm entered and mentioned the attack. Hamm did not testify that he saw Hoggle; Vardaman says Hoggle was making a telephone call at the time. "I can't see how he could have got across the street," he says.

Vardaman does not testify that he saw Cook in the Coffee Pot. He did, however, see him earlier—wearing a dark suit. Since Olsen and Miller have each said the lead man, Cook, was wearing a light suit, Pilcher is trying to cast doubt on the ministers' identification.

Under cross-examination, Vardaman admits that he and Duck Hoggle are business partners. The witness is not asked about another important relationship: he is the brother of juror Harry Vardaman. When informed of this later, Ashworth says he was unaware, as McLeod had been the one to question potential jurors before handing over the case to him.

"The State should have known of the relationship prior to the time the jury was selected, because the defense had listed their prospective witnesses and had them sequestered," Bickford observes. "The prosecution should have moved for a mistrial because of the relationship between the witness and the juror. It would be difficult for a juror to disbelieve his brother's own testimony."

Frances Bowden, the Coffee Pot's manager, confirms Vardaman's testimony when she takes the stand. She, too, saw Duck Hoggle in the café at about the same time the attack took place.

Then she and Vardaman went out for dinner at the nearby Bamboo Club.

Vardaman and Bowden have supplied an alibi for one of the defendants, but what of the other two, Cook and Stanley Hoggle? Paul Woodson, one of the owners of the Bamboo Club, says he saw all three of the accused in the establishment between 8 and 9 p.m. Under cross-examination, however, he testifies that he cannot remember anyone else present that night, including Vardaman and Bowden, whom he knows.

Pilcher calls Lewis Foreman next. Foreman, another owner of the club, recalls seeing Cook at the club that night. When questioned by Ashworth, however, he says that unlike Woodson, he did not see the Hoggle brothers. Like Woodson, he cannot remember anyone else who was at the Bamboo Club.

Whether the combined, seemingly inconsistent accounts of these witnesses has successfully established alibis for the defendants will be up to the jury. Pilcher now moves to his second line of defense. He calls J. South to demonstrate that Reeb's trip from Selma to Birmingham took far longer than necessary. The implication is that his companions wanted him to die and become a movement martyr.

South, who works as a bread man, says that while stopped at Buchanan's Service Station in Selma, he saw the ambulance pass by. Because the vehicle was heading in the direction of South's home, he decided to follow it. He continued even after the vehicle turned around and parked at the radio station.

Although Olsen, Miller, and Dinkins all testified that the ambulance had a flat tire, South saw nothing wrong with the vehicle. He was still outside the radio station when the second ambulance arrived. It had a broken turn signal, which he repaired, he testifies.

South drove back to Buchanan's, picked up proprietor Charles Buchanan, and returned to the radio station. The second ambulance was still there. Thirty to fifty minutes passed until that ambulance departed. No one attended to Reeb during that interlude, says South.

Jurors will have to decide if they believe that the ambulance carrying the unconscious minister proceeded out of Selma and then turned around and traveled back to town even though there was nothing wrong with it and that, after the second ambulance arrived, for no apparent reason (other than to allow Reeb's nonfatal wounds to become fatal), it did not depart for the hospital in Birmingham for at least half an hour. This is the defense's account of events.

Pilcher calls one more witness before resting his case. Paul Boddiford, an auto repairman, states that after noting the post-march gathering at Brown Chapel, he had gone to the Silver Moon. He drank beer there between 6:30 and about 7 p.m., and then went outside. He remained there until about 8 p.m., except for a brief trip to get a bottle of wine. During this ninety-minute period, he saw nothing unusual and no attack.

Floyd Grooms was among those with whom he was standing outside the café, says Boddiford. While there Grooms told him he had been involved in a fight with civil rights workers and said that he had tried to tip over a station wagon. He has not seen Grooms since that night.

It is not yet noon on the fourth day of the trial. Judge Moore instructs the prosecution to make its closing argument before lunch. In his brief remarks, Ashworth says he isn't "sticking up" for those in the civil rights movement, but reminds the jurors of their duty to render a just verdict.

After lunch, Pilcher stresses the fact that no one has definitively identified the Hoggle brothers as attackers. He also notes that no one has identified Cook as the assailant who struck the blow to Reeb's head. The attorney also returns to his point that Reeb's injuries were altered between Selma and Birmingham and that his treatment during that period was "grossly negligent. . . . They put this man in an ambulance like a sack of potatoes."

Finally, Pilcher argues that the wounds Reeb suffered—no matter who delivered them—should not have been fatal. Rather, he was "knowingly and deliberately" allowed to die by those who had said they were seeking medical care for him. He was the "martyr" the civil rights movement wanted and needed.

In his rebuttal, Ashworth responds to the "negligent treatment" defense. "The law of the state of Alabama is that if a dangerous blow is made, whoever makes the blow cannot expect medical treatment to reach down and pick him out of his guilt."

The judge instructs the jury that it can find each and every defendant guilty of first-degree or second-degree manslaughter or first- or second-degree murder. "He also instructed that it was not necessary to identify the defendant who struck the blow," observed Bickford, "that it was only necessary to find that one or all of the defendants were part of a group that contained an individual who struck the fatal blow."

The case goes to the jury at 2:54 p.m. At 3:58 p.m. Sheriff Clark, wearing his "NEVER" button, goes into the jury room for five minutes. He gives no reason for this unusual entry into an area that is traditionally off-limits to all.

At 4:31 p.m.—after ninety-seven minutes of deliberation—the panel returns to the courtroom. Judge Moore asks foreman William Vaughan, owner of a local oil company, if the jury has reached a verdict. Voice quivering, hands shaking, Vaughan says, "We have." As the largely white audience in the courtroom watches, he declares William Stanley Hoggle and Namon O'Neal Hoggle "not guilty."

"He left the big question mark until last," wrote Edward McGrath. "Evidence against the Hoggle brothers was thin, but Elmer L. Cook had been identified by Rev. Orloff F. Miller and Rev. Clark Olsen as among the attackers." When Vaughan and the jury exonerate Cook with another "not guilty" verdict, most of the white spectators applaud. "Negroes in a body, groaned, rose in their seats, and broke for the doors," McGrath reports, but Sheriff Clark, with two deputies at his side, rushed toward the blacks and ordered them back to their seats. They complied.

"Your verdict is in form," Judge Moore tells the jury. "The court accepts it. The defendants may depart."

The Hoggle brothers' father, tears in his eyes, kisses his son Stanley. Cook smiles as his wife joins him. White onlookers congratulate all three men. Prosecutor Ashworth and defense attorney Pilcher shake hands.

As the crowd thins out, reporters seek out all the parties. "No comment," says Cook. But a moment later he says, "I'm happy of course."

Stanley Hoggle refuses comment. When his father is asked for a reaction, Hoggle says, "Don't tell 'em nothing, Pa."

Ashworth says he is "not surprised" by the verdict. "The jury considered the evidence and this was their decision." Pilcher remarks that, given the evidence, there could be no verdict other than not guilty.

A Justice Department attorney who monitored the trial refuses comment. The three defendants and R. B. Kelley still face the possibility of trial in federal court for conspiring to violate Rev. Reeb's civil rights. They have been arrested and charged, but have not yet been indicted by a grand jury.

Describing a verdict in just ninety-seven minutes as "a most unusual occurrence," Bickford analyzes the outcome. "There was no real defense offered for the defendant Cook," he writes, "except that during the day he was wearing a dark suit, as opposed to what Mr. Miller and Mr. Olsen said was a light suit. The defense's own witnesses clearly put Elmer Cook at the scene and the State's witnesses made him one of the attackers. The Judge instructed that this was enough to convict."

None of the jurors has ever publicly discussed the decision. In 2013, one surviving juror continued to maintain his silence. "What happened in the jury room will stay in the jury room," he said before hanging up the telephone on his interviewer. A second juror confessed that after forty-eight years his memory of the trial and the deliberations were hazy. "I wouldn't swear to it on a Bible, but I seem to recall that the victim didn't die from getting hit," he said. "I think he choked on his own vomit." While one of the five doctors who testified suggested that Reeb caught pneumonia because of food particles stuck in his throat, there was no evidence suggesting that this was the cause of death.

After the trial, Rev. Frederick Douglass Reese, the African American who has led voting rights efforts in Dallas County, says, "I feel all that should have been done to get sufficient facts and witnesses was not done on the part of the prosecution."

Richmond Flowers agrees. He suggests the verdict reflects "failure or refusal of the citizens of our state to face their responsibilities as public officials and jurors." The UPI reports that Flowers "says he waged a long fight to see prejudiced jurors disqualified, and that testimony vital to the trial was never used because prosecutors did not follow his orders." The prosecution tried to "sweep it under the rug," the state attorney general says.

Flowers says he is shocked by the prosecution's refusal to

follow his order to ask Judge Moore for a written ruling concerning the state's ability to challenge prospective jurors on the grounds of prejudice, the failure to call as a witness a toxicologist who was prepared to testify unequivocally that the blow Reeb received would have killed him regardless of any medical help he might have received, and the failure to call on FBI informant Tommy Rowe, who had testified in the Liuzzo murder trial that Elmer Cook had told him, "Go do your job. I already did mine."*

Dr. Dana McLean Greeley, founder and president of the Unitarian Universalist Association, provides the church's response. The verdict suggests that "there is little protection under Southern justice from the violence perpetrated upon members of minority groups and upon persons attempting to assist those minority groups to secure their legitimate rights," he says.

"Of course revenge is not what anyone seeks," he adds. "Jim Reeb is dead, and his ministry and life are now part of history."

Like Reeb, Jimmie Lee Jackson is also dead and a part of history. But while those who allegedly attacked the minister were brought to trial, the man who admits to shooting Jackson will not be prosecuted. Both state and federal grand juries have refused to indict James Bonard Fowler. The Alabama trooper will remain free from further scrutiny until he opens his mouth forty years later.

---

*Later, it is also revealed that one of the jurors was a Klansman who had been with members of the American Nazi Party when one of them assaulted Dr. King in Birmingham in 1963.

CHAPTER ELEVEN

"HE'S GONNA HAVE TO GO TO JAIL . . ."

April 2005

District Attorney Michael Jackson begins his investigation on the street, appealing to passersby for information. He quickly learns that there are more than a few people in Marion who know something about the night Jimmie Lee Jackson was shot. There is the man who has a small shop on a side street near the Perry County Courthouse. The woman on the sidewalk heading to an appointment. And several other older black townspeople who either remember February 18, 1965, or know someone who does. The DA starts writing down names.

Jimmie Lee's younger sister is among those mentioned. Jackson's grandfather Cager Lee and mother, Viola, have passed away, but Emma Jean is said to live in the area. An investigator from the DA's office eventually locates her, as well as Jimmie Lee's daughter Cordelia Heard Billingsley, who was four when her father died.

Emma Jean is happy to learn that the prosecutor is trying to bring the man who killed her brother to justice. Cordelia will later say that for years people shared "bits and pieces of how it was" the night her father was shot. Now she hopes to "find out exactly what really happened."

After the shooting, the FBI interviewed Emma Jean and others who were in the church, on the street, and in the café. Witness statements taken by agents while memories were fresh and Jimmie Lee Jackson was still alive would be invaluable. The district attorney asks for the FBI case file. Those records no longer exist, the bureau tells him. They were either lost or destroyed. And so the legwork continues.

As Jackson interviews family members and witnesses, the victim comes into focus for him: "Jimmie Lee Jackson was a young guy who didn't ever think first of himself," he says. "He was committed. That's different from today, when you have a lot of apathy among young people. During the civil rights movement, people that were thirty or younger, they just seemed to be very active. Back then Jimmie Lee had to worry about the things we worry about today like paying bills, but that didn't distract him from the bigger cause. You have to admire him for that."

Not everyone regarded Jimmie Lee so highly. "To this day, there are two big opposite views about who Jimmie Lee Jackson was," the prosecutor observes. "And they are divided purely along racial lines. . . . From the white perspective, he was a troublemaker—basically, a criminal."

Dredging up the past angers many in the white community, and not just those who say Fowler was simply doing his duty when he shot Jimmie Lee. Though moderate and progressive whites say they are appalled and embarrassed by the injustice and violence inflicted on blacks during the civil rights era, many feel the cities and towns of today's New South are unfairly cast in a bad light when the world is reminded of the sins of the Old South.

Michael Jackson pays little attention to those who oppose the investigation. "I think it helps heal the country when you have justice being done," he explains. "You don't do it for a vengeful reason. You do it for justice, because you don't want to think that because of somebody's race or ethnicity or religion, they can get away with killing people. If nothing is done, it dehumanizes a whole race, a culture."

Born in 1963, the prosecutor understands that he would not be where he is without the sacrifices of Jimmie Lee Jackson and others who fought for voting rights. After passage of the VRA, his father became the first African American chairman of the Sumter County Commission, a short distance west of Selma. Jackson moved from Alabama to Decatur, Georgia, as a child, then returned to his home state after earning his law degree from Florida State University. Raised to believe in the importance of public service, he joined the office of the district attorney in Marion, but soon moved to Selma, where he eventually became a municipal judge. In 2004, he became the first African American to be elected district attorney in the state's Fourth Judicial Circuit, which includes both cities.

As a boy, Michael read how Jimmie Lee's death inspired the march from Selma to Montgomery. After moving to Marion in 1990, he heard little talk of the shooting. When he was sworn in as district attorney early in 2005, he did not think about looking into the forty-year-old case. State and federal grand juries had heard the evidence and refused to indict the trooper, who until publication of the *Anniston Star* article was known only by his last name. "I figured this Fowler guy was dead," Jackson says.

Everything changed on March 6, 2005, when the *Star* published its story about James Bonard Fowler, who was very much alive and very quotable. Editor at large John Fleming began:

James Bonard Fowler is a man given to frankness and simplistic statements. Conversations with him tend toward the folksy. He mingles odd yarns from his native rural south Alabama with a sprinkling of short, declarative sentences. He'll mangle grammar now and then, hurl a curse word at some distant persona and ask abrasively for whatever alcoholic beverage might be available. His is a sort of controlled rudeness and overbearing, tools he seems to want to use to convince the listener he fits the seldom-used definition of the word Mean: destitute of moral dignity or elevation; ignoble, small-minded. All of this, however, is a façade belying an enormous complexity and intelligence. Talk to him long and hard and you begin to see bolts of brilliance punching through his 71-year-old redneck manner. Bonard Fowler, you might say, hides his intelligence well.

Fowler's account of the shooting is similar to the account in the affidavit he gave his supervisors on the night of the shooting. He tells Fleming that he and other troopers arrived in Marion from Montgomery around 9 or 9:30 p.m. By that time there had already been widespread chaos, including looting, he says. (There is no record of any such looting in FBI files or newspaper accounts from the day.) Al Lingo, head of the state troopers, then sent him and about ten other troopers to Mack's, "where there were reports of people throwing bottles at passing cars."

When the troopers arrived, they were hit with bottles and

bricks thrown from the second-floor balcony of the café. "We headed up the stairs," Fowler tells Fleming:

> I might have been the first one. I don't know. We went inside, the juke box was blaring and it was pretty crowded. We told them that this has got to stop. There might have been a few billy clubs swung. And out of the corner of my eye I saw a state trooper and I saw an elderly black lady. She hit him upside the head with an old timey coke bottle. There were several people on this state trooper. They were men and women on him, clinging to him, swinging at him. I think one state trooper was down. I was going to their assistance when I realized someone was pulling my pistol out of my holster. And the pistol was out of my holster and I reached down and grabbed it around the cylinder and he had the handle of the pistol and I had the pistol and at that time I was very strong and I remember swinging him around with my elbows and arms right like that, and he was right there, and my hand was on the trigger then and I pulled the trigger.

That "someone pulling the pistol" was Jimmie Lee Jackson, says Fowler. "Jimmie Lee Jackson was not murdered. He was trying to kill me and I have no doubt in my mind that, under the emotional situation at the time, that if he would have gotten complete control of my pistol that he would have killed me or shot me. That's why my conscience is clear."

The former trooper "rails against police who beat prisoners, saying that it is unforgivable what Los Angeles police officers did to Rodney King." He also objects to being called a racist, insisting that he has great respect for Nelson Mandela and Colin

Powell. As a youth in rural Geneva County, Alabama, he was close to his black neighbors. "Ms. Bessie Swear had a crowd of youngins. I slept at her house a million nights," he tells Fleming.

Those blacks "always fared better when they stayed in their place," he claims, but the blacks in Selma and Marion in 1965 were different. "[They] were incited to riot, to loot" by outside agitators like Martin Luther King.

Fowler was not reprimanded after shooting Jackson. In fact, he was soon promoted. "No one from the DA's office in Perry County contacted him about the Jimmie Lee Jackson case," Fleming writes, "nor did his superiors at the Alabama Department of Public Safety want to know more. U.S. Attorney General Nicholas Katzenbach's men at the Department of Justice also seemed strangely absent."

Fleming's ability to find and report an important story dates back to his childhood in Alabama. He grew up working for his mother Karol Fleming's paper, the *Geneva County Reaper*. After attending the University of Alabama and the Columbia School of Journalism, he spent about five years reporting from sub-Saharan Africa. He then returned to the South, where the *Star*'s progressive publisher, Brandt "Brandy" Ayers, hired him as editorial page editor. About seven years later, he became the paper's editor at large.

At the same time, he joined two other crusading journalists, Jerry Mitchell and Hank Klibanoff, to found the Civil Rights Cold Case Project, whose goal is "to reveal the long-neglected truth behind unsolved civil rights murders, and to facilitate reconciliation and healing." The interview with Fowler grew out of his research into Jimmie Lee Jackson's death for the project.

Why does Fowler talk with the reporter? "Fowler wants his side of the story to be told and does not fear indictment,"

Fleming explains. "I don't think legally I could get convicted for murder now no matter how much politics they got," says Fowler, "'cause after forty years they ain't no telling how many people is dead."

By mid-2006, Jackson has learned all too well how many witnesses have died or cannot be found. "I had a lot of witnesses, but I just didn't feel I had the exact amount that I needed to go forward with the grand jury," he will say later. The governor of Alabama offers a five-thousand-dollar reward for information leading to an arrest and conviction in the case, but no one emerges holding the proverbial smoking gun.

Jackson is frustrated. "You get a belief in your head as a prosecutor about a situation," he says. "Somebody gets killed, or somebody does something really bad, and so you get a picture, you get a story in your head about what happened. But if you can't prove that, if you don't have evidence, then you know, it's like having a dream, it's just not going to do you any good. The dream can seem so real, you can even wish the dream was a reality, but you have to have good evidence."

Then the prosecutor speaks with Vera Booker, the registered nurse who was the night supervisor at Good Samaritan Hospital in Selma when Jimmie Lee Jackson was admitted. She tells him what she told the FBI in 1965. Jimmie Lee Jackson was in acute pain when brought in on an ambulance stretcher. He said he had been shot by a state trooper when a riot broke out between troopers and the people in Mack's Café. He had been trying to help his grandfather and mother when he was shot. The riot was started by a state trooper who said Jackson had thrown a bottle. Jackson said he could not identify the state trooper who made the accusation and shot him. He also said that he did not throw a bottle or try to hit anyone.

Convinced Nurse Booker is "the final piece to the puzzle," the district attorney tells his assistant prosecutors, Vernetta Perkins and Jimmy Thomas, "We have enough to go to a grand jury."

Grand juries do not deliver verdicts of guilty or not guilty. They only determine whether the prosecutor has presented enough evidence to warrant an indictment. Jackson's newfound confidence stems from the fact that Jimmie Lee is on record stating that he did not provoke the shooting by throwing anything or hitting anyone. This contradicts Fowler's version that he acted in self-defense.

But isn't Booker's recitation of Jimmie Lee Jackson's words hearsay? Since Jimmie Lee is dead and unavailable for cross-examination by the defense, wouldn't a judge disallow Booker from testifying as to what Jackson said?

The district attorney is well aware of the rules that deny introduction of hearsay, which is defined as an out-of-court statement introduced to prove the truth of the matter asserted therein. But he also knows there are exceptions to those rules, circumstances under which the person who made the statement is presumed to have been telling the truth. Dying declarations—statements made under a belief of certain or impending death, when the statement concerns the causes or circumstances of that impending death—are one such exception. Jackson knows that a competent defense attorney will argue that Jimmie Lee was not certain that he was going to die, but he believes he has a good chance of persuading the judge that in those early hours after the shooting, both the patient and many at the hospital thought death was indeed impending.

State senator Hank Sanders, one of the first black legislators to pressure Jackson to launch an investigation, is among those pleased with the decision to bring the case to the grand jury. "Justice was never brought about," Sanders says of his reaction to the *Star* interview with Fowler. "I shouldn't wait for someone else to do something. I have a duty to do something. I thought it was a long shot, but even if it was a long shot we would be doing an injustice by not trying. . . . You see, it was one thing when it was a Klansman doing this sort of thing. It was another thing when it was a state trooper."

In 2007, Michael Jackson takes his case to the grand jury in Marion. He presents them with a range of evidence, from old newspaper articles to testimony from witnesses he and his fellow prosecutors found over the course of the new investigation, including Vera Booker, whose account of her conversation with the dying Jimmie Lee the district attorney will later describe as "key."

Though the proceedings are closed to the public, the media is able to report that Jackson did not call on any witnesses who actually saw the shooting at Mack's Café. "You don't put on your whole case for the grand jury," the prosecutor explains by way of confirmation. He felt that Booker's appearance, along with the past statements of others, provided enough evidence to win an indictment. "Half the battle in a prosecution like this is identifying who killed the person," Jackson says. "Fowler never denied that he shot Jimmie Lee Jackson. So, once that identification has been made, you're just trying to show he wasn't justified in the killing."*

---

*Fowler did not testify before the grand jury; suspects rarely do. In one high-profile exception, however, police officer Darren Wilson appeared before a grand

On May 9, 2007, the grand jury takes only two hours to indict Fowler on charges of first-degree and second-degree murder. First-degree murder is an intentional killing that is willful and premeditated. Second-degree murder is nonpremeditated. A trial court will hear all the evidence and determine which charge, if either, applies to the trooper's actions.

Fowler's attorney, George Beck, tells the press: "I think somebody is trying to rewrite history, and I don't think it's fair to this trooper." Beck, a former deputy attorney general of Alabama who successfully prosecuted Klansmen for the 16th Street Baptist Church bombing in Birmingham nearly a decade and a half after it occurred, will be a formidable adversary. "I think that we have to be real careful in discriminating between those acts of intentional violence as opposed to the trooper who's trying to protect the public, who may be trying to act on orders of his supervisor," he says. "I just don't think that every civil rights injury and killing means that something was done illegally."

The indictment draws praise from the African American community. Grand jury witness Willie Martin, who marched the night Jackson was shot, draws a distinction between 2007 and 1965, when "they kept it smothered down. We didn't have nobody to represent us back then." If not for the election of a black district attorney, "it would still have been swept under the rug," agrees Cordelia Heard Billingsley, Jimmie Lee's daughter. "I feel like, if my father was living, a lot of things could be different in my life," she tells a reporter from National Public Radio. "I mean, he [Fowler] took a lot from me—my father. I think about it often."

---

jury investigating the 2014 shooting of Michael Brown in Ferguson, Missouri. That grand jury eventually declined to bring charges against Wilson.

Trying Fowler will "give the wound a little more healing," says Emma Jean Jackson. "As the passage of time goes on the wound heals. It's never gone. . . . There's a season for everything, and this is the season for the healing."

John Lewis, now a congressman from Georgia, also issues a statement: "It was the killing of Jimmie Lee Jackson that provoked the march from Selma to Montgomery," he says. "It was his death and his blood that gave us the Voting Rights Act of 1965. This indictment will lead to closure. It will lead to healing. It will lead to reconciliation."

Accompanied by Beck, Fowler surrenders to authorities the day after the grand jury indicts him and posts a $250,000 property bond. Fowler says he is a farmer. "You must understand this, he is not a man of means," says Beck. He adds that his client suffers from diabetes and possible exposure to Agent Orange.

That information seems aimed at potential jurors who might think that an old man of modest means and in ill health should not be prosecuted after so many years. Beck also says he will move for a dismissal of the case because so much time has elapsed and so many witnesses are no longer alive or available.

On the same day that Fowler posts bond, the *Star*'s Fleming reports that the trooper was fired in September 1968. Although state employment records do not reveal the reason, the dismissal coincides with a report that Fowler beat up his supervisor after a disagreement over sick pay.

Fleming will later report more details of Fowler's past: After being fired from the state troopers, he enlisted in the military to avenge his brother's death in Vietnam. "He later worked with military prosecutors to expose a murder-for-hire plot in Southeast Asia. He raised a family in Thailand and in Alabama, and for about five years in the early 1990s, he was in a Thai prison cell after being arrested for heroin trafficking."

Less than a month after the indictment, the case takes another interesting turn thanks to Fleming. The newspaper has discovered the files that the FBI said no longer existed in a collection of documents donated to the Film and Media Archive at Washington University in St. Louis by the producers of the civil rights documentary *Eyes on the Prize*. They contain statements from Jimmie Lee Jackson, Nurse Booker, state troopers, other law enforcement officials, FBI agents, participants in the Marion march, witnesses to events in Mack's Café, and others. Many names are redacted in the copies the *Star* provides to both the prosecution and the defense, but the district attorney will later obtain a copy that is free of most redactions.

The autopsy report is also in the files, and a forensic pathologist who has seen the report believes that "poor medical treatment and a mistake by the attending physician helped lead to [Jackson's] death." Dr. Kris Sperry, the chief medical officer of the Georgia Bureau of Investigation, notes that Jackson had four holes in his bowels as a result of the shooting. The autopsy, Sperry tells the *Star*, suggests that the doctor did not properly close the holes. "In my opinion, had the holes been closed, this would have been a survivable injury."

Echoing one of the arguments used by the defense in the James Reeb murder trial, attorney Beck asserts that his client's actions did not cause Jackson to die. "This report shows there was a botched medical procedure that led to the man's death."

The district attorney counters: "If he wouldn't have been

shot, he wouldn't have been in the hospital. What he died of, infection, whatever, it doesn't change the fact that he was killed for no reason."

Dr. Sperry agrees. "It's a tough defense to use, really. I mean, if he hadn't been shot, he wouldn't have been in the hospital, right? The shooting precipitated the event."

By the time Fowler is formally arraigned on murder charges in July, his attorneys have filed several motions before Circuit Court Judge Tommy Jones in Marion. In their motion to dismiss, they argue that Fowler cannot receive a fair trial because too many potential defense witnesses have died since the shooting. These deceased witnesses include state troopers and others present in Mack's Café, Governor George Wallace, Sheriff Jim Clark, and Chief of Police T. O. Harris. In their motion for a change of venue, they argue Fowler cannot get a fair trial in Marion because of all the pretrial publicity.

One year later, the parties are still at odds over the defense's claim that the state took too long to indict Fowler. At the beginning of June 2008, Judge Jones gives Jackson thirty days to produce a list of "all persons presently known to the district attorney's office to have personal knowledge of any facts relevant to this prosecution, but who were unknown to the State prior to January 15, 2005 and a copy of all written and recorded materials reciting or memorializing any of these facts communicated to the State since January 15, 2005." In other words: What did the district attorney's office know and when did it know it? Could the case have been brought years earlier when more witnesses were available?

On the day the deadline is to expire, Jackson presents the judge with a document titled "District Attorney Michael W. Jackson's brief notes on Grand Jury testimony on Jimmie Lee

Jackson's death investigation and other newly discovered evidence." The list contains the names of six individuals and includes a brief description of their testimony.

Two and a half months later, Judge Jones issues a ruling:

The State of Alabama is ordered to provide to [Fowler] any and all statements in its possession of any and all witnesses the State intends to call at the trial of this case, and is further ordered to provide the defendant a witness list of possible witnesses the State intends to call at the trial of this case, together with a summary of the testimony of the witnesses.

The order appears contrary to established judicial rules in Alabama, but Jones points to extraordinary circumstances: "I want the record to be very clear that [the above order] was precipitated by the lack of response from the district attorney's office in response to my order. I had given the district attorney's office a full 30 days in my order to respond to my request for an in camera inspection. And on the 30th day I was given a one-page summary of six witnesses and a magazine article or a newspaper article."

Jackson finds the order "outrageous." Under Alabama's rules of criminal procedure, the state cannot be compelled to provide the defense with a summary of the testimony of its proposed witnesses. The district attorney had brought a copy of those rules to the court and cited the relevant portions to the judge. He files an appeal asking the Alabama Court of Criminal Appeals for a writ of mandamus ordering Judge Jones to follow the rules and change his order.

Because Judge Jones delays the trial until the appeals court rules, Beck says the district attorney filed his appeal to forestall the case because it is weak "and he's embarrassed by it."

"I see George Beck has started the spinning," Jackson responds. "I'm more than ready to go to trial. . . . George knows we have a very strong case. We have witnesses. We have photographs. We have all kinds of evidence. He can't spin all of that, and he knows it won't change the fact that his client killed Jimmie Lee Jackson."

On January 9, 2009, the Alabama Court of Criminal Appeals denies Jackson's appeal. He quickly petitions the Alabama State Supreme Court, which rules in the state's favor on September 4, affirming—after fifteen months of motions, orders, briefs, and appeals—that Jackson does not have to disclose the testimony of his witnesses.

With the motion finally resolved, trial preparation can begin. Plea bargaining goes nowhere. Fowler's attorneys say he will plead guilty to a lesser charge if he does not have to serve any time in jail—probation only. Jackson refuses. "Fowler had lived all this time after 1965, where he was out and about, living his life," the prosecutor explains. "I just felt like he needed to spend some time behind bars before he died, to realize what he had done. The seriousness of what he had done. And also, just for the justice situation."

Judge Jones sets the trial for November 29, 2010. Jackson is under the impression that the defense and perhaps Judge Jones—whom he is seeking to recuse because of comments made concerning the writ of mandamus—are waiting to see the results of the November 2 election for district attorney before starting a trial. "They were all looking to see whether I won reelection. I suspect if I lost the election, the case would have probably disappeared in Never-Never Land."

After Jackson is reelected, Judge Jones phones the DA and Beck. Is there any possibility of settling the matter, he asks? "Well, he's gonna have to go to jail," says the prosecutor. Beck says he is willing to talk about this.

The judge hangs up and the two lawyers begin negotiating. "We did come to an agreement after a couple days," Jackson remembers, "but then over the weekend they tried to back out, saying Fowler wasn't going to take it. Then the judge tried to ask me whether we could make it less jail time than what we had agreed on. They were trying to act like they were gonna pull back, hoping I would budge and give in even more. Finally I said, 'No. We're just gonna go to trial.'"

On November 15, 2010, Fowler pleads guilty to misdemeanor manslaughter and agrees to serve six months in jail. Beck says his client is in poor health and he is worried he couldn't get a fair trial in Marion. "He wants to put it behind him," the defense attorney adds. "It puts to rest a long chapter of civil rights history here in Perry County."

Members of Jimmie Lee Jackson's family who are in the courtroom hear Fowler apologize for the shooting while insisting that he acted in self-defense. "I was coming over here to save lives. I didn't mean to take lives. I wish I could redo it," he says.

Reaction to the plea bargain is mixed. "The Jimmie Lee Jackson case is perhaps the most significant of all the civil rights cold cases," says Richard Cohen, president of the Southern Poverty Law Center. "The more important verdict in the case was rendered by the thousands of people who marched from Selma to Montgomery in the name of voting rights in response to Jackson's killing."

"One thing we've never experienced in the South is anything close to a truth and reconciliation commission," John Fleming writes in the *Star.* "What happened today was a moment of that experience." He calls the resolution "an appropriate end."

Not everyone agrees. Perry County commissioner Albert Turner Jr., the son of the late civil rights figure, calls the brevity of the sentence "a slap in the face of the people of this county." And state senator Sanders will later say he does not think the district attorney "put enough effort and resources into it. I think that's why it ended up with a six-month jail sentence."

"We try not to be hateful. It's very, very difficult," says Jimmie Lee's cousin, Florence Lauderdale. "But we don't feel that justice was served because here you have this man [Fowler] who has lived his whole life outside. He has done everything pretty much he wanted to do without any limitations. Jimmie had nothing. He's dead. He can't say I have a son over here who's doing this and doing great things, you know. . . . [Fowler] may have gotten by, but he didn't get away because God is going to judge him, because He knows the heart, even all those little secret things that we hide from everybody else. He knows."

District Attorney Jackson defends his actions and the plea bargain. "Time was starting to run out," he argues. "We wanted to make sure justice was done before he died." Fowler was seventy-seven and supposedly in ill health, he explains. He could have died before the motions for a new judge and a change of venue were resolved.

There was also the possibility of a hung jury if the case went to trial. This was not like other civil rights murder cases that had been revived after many years. The shooting of Medgar Evers and the 16th Street Baptist Church bombing cases, for example, involved well-planned, premeditated acts. In Fowler's case, a jury would have to determine whether he acted in self-defense in what all agreed was a chaotic scene.

Don Cochran, who helped prosecute one of the church bombers in 2002 and is now a professor at Cumberland School of Law at Samford University in Birmingham, adds that there are dangers in trying cold cases. "In a lot of these cases, it would have been difficult to try them even two weeks after they happened, especially in a self-defense case. Your witnesses, a lot of them, are just gone."

Michael Jackson says his office achieved its three goals in the case. "Fowler admitted his guilt, he apologized to the family for what he had done, and he served some time." He adds: "We feel the family showed more mercy than he did to Jimmie Lee Jackson."

Later, the district attorney will explain that he discussed the plea bargain in advance with the Jackson family. "Obviously everybody would like to have had him serve more time, but I got their approval." Unfortunately, the manner in which Fowler apologized—he did not look at the family—"left a bitter taste in the family's mouth," says Jackson.

"No matter what happened," he reflects, "there was gonna be hollerin' and screamin'" about the plea bargain from some in both the white and black communities. "I was very happy, but also relieved, that he didn't die before we finished all this."

Jimmie Lee Jackson's daughter also reflects on the outcome, forty-five years after her father's death. "This is supposed to be closure," Billingsley says, "but there will never be closure."

CHAPTER TWELVE

"A DAGGER INTO THE HEART . . ."

June 25, 2013

Willie Nell Avery does not like what she is seeing. Ever since the Voting Rights Act was passed in 1965, blacks in Alabama and the rest of the South have become a political force. In Perry County, where she still lives, African Americans hold most elected and appointed offices. She is now the voter registrar in the very community that denied her the right to vote for so many years. Today, however, the gains of the last half century are in danger of being lost.

This time it is not the state troopers in Marion who pose the threat. It is the United States Supreme Court in Washington, which has just issued what Avery calls a "ridiculous, devastating" decision in *Shelby County v. Holder*.

The case originates in April 2010 when Shelby County, Alabama, some seventy miles northeast of Marion, files suit in federal court asking that Section 5 of the Voting Rights Act of 1965 be declared unconstitutional. Section 5 mandates that certain jurisdictions obtain "preclearance" from the U.S. attorney general or a federal district court in Washington, D.C., for all voting changes before initiating them. If, for example, a state or county wants to require voter ID cards or limit early voting, it has to demonstrate in advance that the change has neither a discriminatory purpose nor discriminatory effect. The county asserts that Congress exceeded its constitutional authority when, in 2006, it reauthorized Section 5 for another twenty-five years.

Which states and counties are subject to preclearance? Section 4(b) of the act presents a formula covering jurisdictions that, as of November 1964, November 1968, or November 1972, maintained a prohibited "test or device" as a condition of registering to vote or voting and had a voting-age population of which less than 50 percent either were registered to vote or actually voted in that year's presidential election. Most of these jurisdictions, including Shelby County, are in the South and Southwest.

In 2011 a federal district court denies Shelby County's challenge to the reauthorization of Section 5, and in 2012, a U.S. Court of Appeals also rules against the county. But on June 25, 2013, the Supreme Court holds that Section 4 of the Voting Rights Act, which establishes the formula that determines which jurisdictions must comply with Section 5, is unconstitutional and can no longer be used. The discrimination that existed in the past has abated so the formula is no longer timely, says a 5–4 majority. Chief Justice John Roberts writes, "We issue no holding on Section 5 itself, only on the coverage formula. Congress may draft another formula based on current conditions."

As legal analyst Jeffrey Toobin explains, the decision "basically gives a green light to these nine southern states and a handful of other jurisdictions to change the law any way they want and basically say to the Justice Department, 'Catch me if you can.'"

The white power structure in the South applauds the decision. "I'm just not aware of any discrimination of that kind," says U.S. Senator Jeff Sessions of Alabama. "And if it happens I have no doubt that the Alabama attorney general would prosecute it or the U.S. Department of Justice will." Shelby County Attorney Frank Ellis Jr. adds: "The justices correctly acknowledged that the covered jurisdictions should no longer be punished by the federal government for conditions that existed over forty years ago. The South is an altogether different place than it was in 1965."

"In my judgment the Court errs egregiously by overriding Congress' decision," Justice Ruth Bader Ginsburg writes in a fiery dissent. "The Court's opinion can hardly be described as an exemplar of restrained and moderate decision making. Quite the opposite. Hubris is a fit word for today's demolition of the VRA. . . . One would expect more from an opinion striking at the heart of the nation's signal piece of civil rights legislation."

Those who fought for voting rights agree with Ginsburg and Avery. John Lewis calls the decision "a dagger into the heart." Speaking of the Supreme Court justices, he says: "These men never stood in unmovable lines. They were never denied the right to participate in the democratic process. They were never beaten, jailed, run off their farms, or fired from their jobs. No one they knew died simply trying to register to vote. They are not the victims of gerrymandering or contemporary unjust schemes to maneuver them out of their constitutional rights."

After the decision, many of the nine states previously covered by Section 5 move swiftly to institute restrictive voting regulations that previously would have required federal approval before going into effect. Legislators in several Republican-controlled states in the North and South argue that even if voter ID laws present some hardship, they are necessary to prevent fraud at the polls. But instances of such fraud are rare. A study conducted by News21, a journalism project at Arizona State University, finds just twenty-eight cases of voter fraud conviction since 2000.

Texas reinstitutes photo ID rules that a federal court had rejected as too "stringent" before the *Shelby* decision. When the U.S. Supreme Court upholds the Texas law in October 2014, Justice Ginsburg again dissents. The decision "risks denying the right to vote to hundreds of thousands of eligible voters," she writes, the vast majority of them African Americans and Hispanics.

These new voter rules—no longer subject to preclearance by the federal government because of the *Shelby* decision—make a difference in the Lone Star State. After the election in November, investigative reporter Brad Friedman notes: "A decrease of some 271,000 total voters this year is one of several, at least anecdotal early indicators that suggest the Texas GOP's strategy of suppressing the vote this year with polling place Photo ID restrictions seems to have worked."

Alabama, the battleground for voting rights five decades ago, also changes its laws. Voters can no longer present utility bills or Social Security cards to prove their identity. Photo ID cards are now required, as is proof of citizenship

Alabama is at the center of another debate concerning the provisions of the Voting Rights Act. In November 2014, the U.S. Supreme Court hears arguments in a case brought by Democratic and African American officials from the state. The suit charges that the Republican-controlled state legislature enacted a redistricting plan based on race and that the plan has diluted the electoral power of minorities.

By packing African Americans into certain newly drawn

districts, the plan changes Alabama's political landscape. The last white Democrat representing a majority-white district in the Alabama Senate is defeated because the black voters who supported him are no longer in his district. Each of the twenty-six majority-white districts in the state is now represented by a white Republican state senator. Each of the eight majority-black districts is now represented by a Democrat, seven of whom are African American.

"The lawmakers said they had no choice, that many of the districts had lost residents and, they believed, the Voting Rights Act required them to keep the percentage of black voters in each district the same as before," explains a *New York Times* editorial critical of the redistricting and skeptical of the legal argument. The irony is not lost that the same partisans who successfully persuaded the Supreme Court to dilute the Voting Rights Act in 2013 are now arguing that their redistricting decisions are mandated by the very legislation they sought to eliminate.

What would Dr. Martin Luther King Jr. and President Lyndon Baines Johnson say about the present state of affairs? Of course, they are no longer here to comment or to effect great social change. Nor are civil rights leaders Hosea Williams, James Bevel, Fannie Lou Hamer, Albert Turner, Lucy Foster, and James Orange. Antagonists like Governor George Wallace and Mayor Joseph Smitherman, each of whom softened their stance on segregation in later years, are also gone. So, too, is Sheriff Jim Clark, who spent time in prison after being convicted of attempting to smuggle three tons of marijuana from Colombia. Marie Reeb, who remarried after her husband's murder, still lives in Wyoming but does not give interviews.

But many of those who were involved in the events in Marion and Selma fifty years ago—events that shaped a movement and changed a nation—are willing to share their views about the Supreme Court's 2013 decision that so diminished the Voting Rights Act they fought for.

"The weakening of the Voting Rights Act is a tragic undoing of the sterling, sacrificial work carried out by the thousands of persons who marched, went to jail, suffered bodily injury, and even gave their lives—such as Jimmie Lee Jackson, Rev. James Reeb, Viola Liuzzo, and Jonathan Daniels—to ensure the right to vote for every adult in the United States," says **Rev. Joseph Ellwanger**, who led the march of Concerned White Citizens of Alabama in 1965 and is still fighting for human rights today. "Sadly, counties and states around the country, even states that were not listed in the Voting Rights Act as states required to get approval for changes in voting practices, took the Supreme Court decision to mean that states could place barriers in front of voters with impunity."

Florence Lauderdale, Jimmie Lee Jackson's cousin, is now a "semiretired" teacher and school psychologist living in Marion. "I do believe that voting rights have been undermined," she says. "And not just by the white populace, but by blacks, too. And I say that because we are not fully taking advantage of the opportunities afforded to us by the people who lost their lives and who made the movement."

"I was crushed by the action of the Supreme Court," says **George Baker**, the young volunteer and diarist beaten in Marion, now a retired teacher and mental health counselor doing volunteer political work for the Working Families Party. "It seemed so heartless, politically motivated, and antidemocratic. It seemed supremely unfair to repudiate the efforts of so many who sacrificed so much."

Rev. C. T. Vivian, Dr. King's lieutenant, now in his

nineties, is still active in the movement and frustrated by the
Shelby ruling. "Anybody on the Supreme Court knows what the
Voting Rights Act did," he says. "The Court knew its decision
would destroy what we had worked for."

"The Supreme Court was full of shit," says **Walter Dobyne**,
one of the select three hundred who marched the entire route
from Selma to Montgomery in 1965. "They weren't brought up
in Alabama or Mississippi. They didn't know how white folks
treated blacks and what they did to prevent blacks from voting.
If they knew the story and what blacks had to do to get the right
to vote, they wouldn't have done it."

"Hundreds and even thousands of Americans risked their
lives to bring about the end of practices which had prevented
people from registering to vote across the South," reflects **Rev.
Clark Olsen**, who continues to educate young people about the
events of 1965 through the Sojourn to the Past Project. "Now
the Supreme Court has decided to allow the reestablishment of
a variety of restrictions on voting. These decisions—by both the
Supreme Court and various state authorities—must be reversed.
Following the 'arc of justice' to full citizen participation should
be our primary goal."

Rev. Orloff Miller, who along with Olsen was beaten by
those who murdered his friend, remained with the Unitarian
Church, and is today a minister emeritus living in Germany.
"The U.S. Supreme Court's 2013 decision to weaken the Voting
Rights Act of 1965 is a self-indictment of that Court," he says.
"It demonstrates the utter contempt the majority of that Court
has for those citizens, black and white, who were martyred in
the long struggle for civil rights in America."

As education disparities and mass incarceration continue to
disproportionately affect African American youth, the further

erosion of voting rights portends deeper disengagement and marginalization. Whether today's activists can succeed in restoring the protections of the Voting Rights Act may depend on how well they can emulate their forebears. The architects and bricklayers of the civil rights struggle—and of the Alabama epicenter for the voting rights campaign, in particular—were painstaking and unrelenting in building their movement. That movement's model of strategic nonviolent organizing is relevant today, as is its media savvy, embrace of music, and commitment to activist training.

At first glance, Jimmie Lee Jackson and James Reeb appear to have been almost polar opposites. One was a twenty-six-year-old black woodcutter from the rural South with a high school education. The other was a thirty-eight-year-old white minister from the urban North with a degree from an Ivy League school.

But the two men had much in common. Each was a spiritual being. Each was committed to family. Each was also committed to ending racial discrimination and improving the lot of African Americans. And, sadly, each was killed by hostile whites in Alabama after marching for voting rights.

Jimmie Lee and James never met each other, yet their lives and deaths are forever linked. Their names are printed together in books, spoken together in speeches, and engraved together on the black granite table of Maya Lin's Civil Rights Memorial in Montgomery, Alabama. The memorial, which sits on a plaza in front of the Southern Poverty Law Center, pays tribute to all who gave their lives in the struggle between 1954 and 1968. On the evening before its dedication on November 5, 1989, more than six hundred family members of those martyrs gathered in the Montgomery Civic Center to honor the fallen. Jimmie Lee Jackson's family was present, as was the family of James Reeb.

Rev. Joseph Lowery of the Southern Christian Leadership Conference spoke to the assembled, calling those who died "a cloud of witnesses" and issuing several challenges to the living. "We must lay aside the weight of our retreat from activism. We have grown movement lazy. We have to be activists again," he said. "Don't let the assault from without make us fall victim to the faults from within. We've always been a people of hope."

Thousands of people from around the country attended the dedication the following day. "Most of those who made the movement weren't the famous; they were the faceless," Julian Bond, an early organizer of the Student Nonviolent Coordinating Committee who would go on to become chairman of the NAACP, told the crowd. "They weren't the noted; they were the nameless—the marchers with tired feet, the protestors beaten back by billy clubs and fire hoses, the unknown women and men who risked job and home and life."

The movement, Bond continued, has much to teach us: "As the old Freedom Song reminds us, 'Ain't but one thing we did wrong; stayed in segregation a day too long. Ain't but one thing we did right; that's the day we started to fight!'"

ACKNOWLEDGMENTS

This book would not have been possible without the contributions of countless individuals and institutions.

We started our journey in Alabama. In Montgomery, we received invaluable assistance and support from the Southern Poverty Law Center, its founder Morris Dees, and its president Richard Cohen. They are good friends and always offer excellent counsel. Outreach Director Lecia Brooks was also most helpful.

In Selma, we interviewed District Attorney Michael Jackson and Rev. F. D. Reese. And in Marion, thanks to the efforts of Robert Turner, Sr., Mary Cosby Moore, and Elijah Rollins, we gathered at Lottie's Café to speak with several friends and family members of Jimmie Lee Jackson, and others who participated in the voting rights movement fifty years ago. These included: Willie Nell Avery, Johnnie McAlpine, Mattie S. Atkins, James W. Oakes, Florence Lauderdale, Preston and Dorothy Hornbuckle, and the Cureton family.

Other movement participants also consented to lengthy interviews. Rev. Orloff Miller and Rev. Clark Olsen relived the night they were beaten with James Reeb. Rev. C. T. Vivian recounted his iconic encounter with the infamous Sheriff Jim Clark. Walter Dobyne shared recollections of life in Marion, Bloody Sunday, and the successful march to Montgomery. Rev. Joseph Ellwanger explained how the Concerned White Citizens of Alabama marched to show their support for those denied

the right to vote. Ron Engel detailed his friendship with James
Reeb. And George Baker, who took leave from college to volunteer in Selma, shared his memories and the diary he kept
during February and March of 1965.

Reporters Richard Valeriani, Al Benn, and John Fleming
provided valuable information and directed us to others. Lila
Quintero Weaver, author of *Darkroom: A Memoir in Black and
White*, supplied us with footage of Marion circa 1965. Several
archivists and librarians were also extremely helpful: Chris
Pepus of Washington University; Donald Davis of the American Friends Service Committee; Kevin Ray of University of
Alabama; Alexis Burson and Dilnesa Eshete of DePaul University; Ethan Vesely-Flad of Fellowship of Reconciliation; Andrea
Abernathy of Marion College; and the whole team at the Wis-
consin Historical Society Library Archives.

The Unitarian Universalist Association provided guidance and
photographs. Special thanks to John Hurley and Michael McGlone.

Our irreplaceable agent Gail Hochman believed in this project
from Day One, as did our superb editor Ron Hogan. The book is
better for the contributions they made. The whole team at Regan
Arts was also invaluable, including Judith Regan, Emi Battaglia,
Tracy Brickman, Richard Ljoenes, and Lynne Ciccaglione.

Thanks also to early readers Jim Fiffer and Rob Fiffer, tape
transcribers Emily Heppard and Francesca Miroballi, and others who contributed in a variety of ways: Elaine Fiffer, Diana
Gourguechon, Elodie Mailliet Storm, Denise Morse, Robert
Dorsett, Susie Mazaheri, Penny Weaver, Sen. Hank Sanders,
and Julian Bond.

Finally, the most special of thanks to our spouses, Sharon and
Nora. Without their counsel, support, and understanding this
important story could not have been told.

NOTES

Epigraphs

vii   John Lewis, "It was the killing of Jimmie Lee Jackson": Fleming, John. "The Death of Jimmie Lee Jackson." *Anniston Star.* Anniston, AL: 6 Mar. 2005: Web. 21 Sept. 2014.

vii   Gustav Niebuhr, "Dr. King's murder": Niebuhr, Gustav. "Religion Journal; Remembering a Martyr in This Season of Hope." *New York Times* 8 May 2000: Web. 23 Sept. 2013.

Prologue

xiii   "I don't remember how many times I pulled the trigger": Fleming, "The Death of Jimmie Lee Jackson", *op. cit.*

xv   Potential jurors: Jackson, Michael. Personal Interview. 18 Aug. 2014.

xv   Fowler's remarks: Fleming, "The Death of Jimmie Lee Jackson", *op. cit.*

xvi   "I can't emphasize enough": Jackson, Michael. Personal Interview. 18 Aug. 2014.

xvii   "If one word could describe Perry County": *Perry County Chamber of Commerce.* Web. 6 Sept. 2014.

xvii   Jimmy Wilson death sentence and clemency: Dudziak, Mary L. *Cold War Civil Rights: Race and the Image of American Democracy.* Princeton, NJ: Princeton University Press, 2011. 3-5. Web. 13 Nov. 2014.

xviii   DA Jackson on the street: Jackson, Michael. Personal Interview. 25 Oct. 2013.

Chapter One: "I Was Half Dead Anyway"

1   Willie Nell Avery observing arrival of state troopers: Avery, Willie Nell. Personal Interview. 25 Oct. 2013.

2 "Something strange is happening:" *Ibid.*

3 "Look, it's going to be rough tonight": *Ibid.*

3 Avery on how she could "keep fighting and keep pushing," her childhood, and becoming an activist: *Ibid.*

4 Percentages of blacks and whites registered to vote in Perry County: *Civil Rights Movement Veterans.* Tougaloo College. Web. 17 Sept. 2014.

4 Imbalance in voter registration and political power: *Encyclopedia of Alabama.* Alabama Humanities Foundation, Auburn University, The University of Alabama, and Alabama State Department of Education. Web. 25 Nov. 2014.

4 "Democrats feared losing local and state offices": *Ibid.*

4 Black disenfranchisement in Mississippi, South Carolina, Louisiana, and North Carolina: *Ibid.*

5 They proposed requirements: *Ibid.*

5 "a movement going on": Avery, Willie Nell. Personal Interview. 25 Oct. 2013.

5 "When the six months was up": *Ibid.*

5 "Whenever they were open": *Ibid.*

6 "I think they knew my walk . . . And it just went on and on": *Ibid.*

6 would be asked questions such as: *1965 Alabama Literacy Test.* Ferris State University Jim Crow Museum of Racist Memorabilia.

6 registrars often capped the number: *Civil Rights Movement Veterans, op. cit.*

6 "We pooled our little resources": Avery, Willie Nell. Personal Interview. 25 Oct. 2013.

6 "any act or practice": *Open Jurist.* 335 F. 2d 153–United States v. B Mayton. United States Court of Appeals Fifth Circuit. 23 July 1964. Web. 7 Sept. 2014.

7 "When Dr. King came to Marion": Dobyne, Walter. Personal Interview. 22 Oct. 2013.

7 "They had this pact": *Ibid.*

7 "He didn't want to wave at you anymore": *Ibid.*

7 accounted for 51 per cent of the population: *Civil Rights Movement Veterans, op. cit.*

7 Nicknamed the Queen City: *Welcome to Selma, Alabama.* City of Selma. Web. 23 Nov. 2014.

8 A major Confederate manufacturing center: *Ibid.*

10 "they could protect black children": Nash, Diane. Interview with Blackside, Inc. *Eyes on the Prize: American's Civil Rights Years*

(1954–1965). Washington University Libraries, Film and Media Archive, Henry Hampton Collection. 1985. Film.

11   LBJ couldn't get the southern votes: Carson, Clayborne. "1965: A Decisive Turning Point in the Long Struggle for Voting Rights." *The Crisis* July/Aug. 2005: 16–20. Print.

12   "the valley filled" and "Political reform is as necessary": *Ibid.*

12   "We wanted to raise the issue" and "We were using Selma": *Civil Rights Movement Veterans, op. cit.*

12   "There are more Negroes in jail with me": Carson, Clayborne, *op. cit.*

13   "Five of us went in and sat down": Dobyne, Walter. Personal Interview. 22 Oct. 2013.

13   "Sing one more song": Herbers, John. "Negroes Step Up Drive in Alabama; 1,000 More Seized." *New York Times* 4 Feb. 1965: Web. 24 Sept. 2014.

13   "Sing another song": *Ibid.*

13   "We have a saying that you don't mess": Evans, Susan M., ed. *Do What The Spirit Says Do: An Oral History of the Civil Rights Struggle in Perry County, Alabama.* Atlanta: Together For Hope Press, 2012. Print.

14   "In the nonviolent movement": Lawson, James. Interview with Blackside, Inc. *Eyes on the Prize: American's Civil Rights Years (1954–1965).* Washington University Libraries, Film and Media Archive, Henry Hampton Collection. 1985. Film.

14   "the parents came to the meeting": Avery, Willie Nell. Personal Interview. 25 Oct. 2013.

14   "It was terrible": *Ibid.*

14   "It was plain cornmeal": *Ibid.*

15   four hundred teens stood outside the courthouse: Herbers, John. "Dr. King Leads 2,800 in 3 Alabama Vote Marches." *New York Times* 16 Feb. 1965: Web. 24 Sept. 2014.

15   "There was no violence and there were no arrests": *Ibid.*

15   "125 Negroes" and "Chief of Police was taking names": FBI memorandum. SA Archibald L. Riley, Marion, AL: 18 Feb. 1965. Mobile 44-1226.

15   "going to send a letter": *Ibid.*

15   Thirty minutes later: *Ibid.*

16   "a new crew": *Ibid.*

16   Baker has only been in Alabama for two days: Baker, George. Personal Interview. 8 Oct. 2013.

16 "Was listening to someone talk" and "As it turned out C. T. Vivian led 60 people to courthouse": Baker, *Diary of George Baker, op. cit.*

16 "all in helmets and carrying billy clubs", "They were very pleasant", "a little colder": *Ibid.*

18 "6:58 Started singing in church": FBI memorandum. SA Archibald L. Riley, *op. cit.*

18 "7:10 Crowds have been going in and singing loud": *Ibid.*

18 "I was very moved by the emotion present": Baker, *Diary of George Baker, op. cit.*

19 "7:13 about 300 were in church at this time": FBI memorandum. SA Archibald L. Riley, *op. cit.*

19 At 7:36 Riley observes three cars: *Ibid.*

19 "8:19: About 400 in church": *Ibid.*

19 "stop scratching when you ain't itching": Rieder, Jonathan. *The Word of the Lord Is Upon Me: The Righteous Performance of Martin Luther King, Jr.* Cambridge, MA: Belknap Press, 2008. Web. 5 Oct. 2014.

20 Clark and Cooper on courthouse steps: "Annie Lee Cooper, Civil Rights Legend, Dies." *Selma-Times Journal* 24 Nov. 2010: Web. 1 Dec. 2014.

20 Sheriff Clark has also recruited Klansmen: Newton, Michael. *The Encyclopedia of American Law Enforcement.* New York: Checkmark Books, 2007. Web. 4 Deb 2014.

20 "Don't you have enough trouble" and "Things got a little too quiet": Herbers, John. "Negroes Beaten in Alabama Riot; Troopers Battle Marchers in Marion—Dr. King Asks for Federal Protection." *New York Times* 19 Feb. 1965: Web. 1 Oct. 2014.

20 hoping for the opportunity to harm or even kill Vivian: *Ibid.*

21 "His society, his culture allowed bullies": *Ibid.*

21 "What do you tell your wife at night?": *Ibid.*

21 Exchange between Vivian and Clark at courthouse steps: Cotton, Henry. "A Snapshot of a Living Legend: Dr. C.T. Vivian." Online video clip. *YouTube.* YouTube, 9 Mar. 2014. Web. 5 Nov. 2014.

22 "When I started that day, I had no idea what I was gonna say": Vivian, Cordy Tindell. Personal Interview. 21 Aug. 2014.

22 "When you're being beaten up, you don't think about that": *Ibid.*

23 "I'm gonna lay this trowel down": Turner, Robert. Personal Interview. 25 Oct. 2013.

23 "Our arguing was this: He said politics, and I said economics": *Ibid.*

23 Big Al tells those assembled at Zion United: Baker, *Diary of George Baker, op. cit.*

23   "We gonna be peaceful, and we don't want nobody starting no riot": Atkins, Mattie Mae. Personal Interview. 25 Oct. 2013.

23   "If we were to get beaten": *Ibid.*

Chapter Two: "I Got Him . . ."

24   "helmeted police with billy clubs": Baker, *Diary of George Baker, op. cit.*

24   the organizers tell Baker that he is not to march: *Ibid.*

25   "You are hereby ordered to disperse" and "unlawful assembly": Herbers, John. "2 Inquiries Open on Racial Clash in Alabama Town." *New York Times* 20 Feb. 1965: Web 4 Nov. 2014.

25   "they planned to put on a show that night": FBI memorandum. SA Archibald L. Riley, *op. cit.*

25   "would not take the initiative, but would back local officials up": Harris, T.O. "Written Statement to FBI 20 Feb. 1965." *T.O. Harris Papers.* Civil Rights in Marion, Alabama Collection. University of Alabama. 3. Print.

25   "their presence was an indication that something was planned" and "prevent it being spread over too large an area to control": FBI memorandum. SA Archibald L. Riley, *op. cit.*

25   "May we pray before we go back?" and "opening a bloody wound": *Violence in the Night in Marion, Alabama, February 18, 1965.* Birmingham, AL: Inter-Citizens Committee, Inc. 5. 1965.

25   "They drug me off and carried me to jail, beating me all the way": *Ibid.*

26   "What's your name, nigger?" and "I'll blow your f—in' brains out": Bolden, Willie. "Reflections on Georgia Politics." Interview with Bob Short. Richard B. Russell Library for Political Research and Studies, University of Georgia Libraries, and Young Harris College. 2009. Web. 13 Sept. 2014.

26   "upset my negroes, my niggers": *Ibid.*

26   "Are you an outsider?": Slaughter, John. *New Battles Over Dixie: The Campaign for a New South.* Dix Hills, NY: General Hall, Inc., 1992. 139. Print.

26   "they have surrounded me and are hitting me all over": Baker, *Diary of George Baker, op. cit.*

26   "They started taking me to jail": *Ibid.*

27   "I received a blow on my head from behind": *Ibid.*

27   Baker is put into a cell with Dobynes: *Ibid.*

27 "Troopers put rest back in church midst loud yelling and scream-ing": FBI memorandum. SA Archibald L. Riley, *op. cit.*

27 "We weren't going to have anybody come into the church and beat folks about the head": Slaughter, *op. cit.*

27 "If you get by one, the next one will get you" and "After we busted a couple of heads": *Ibid.*

28 struck across the head from behind with a nightstick: *Violence in the Night in Marion, Alabama, February 18, 1965, op. cit.*

28 "We don't have doctors for people like you": Valeriani, Richard. Personal Interview. 31 Oct. 2013.

28 punched in the face "five or six times": FBI memorandum. SA Ar-chibald L. Riley, *op. cit.*

28 After a long wait, Turner asks the troopers: Slaughter, *op. cit.*

28 C. T. Vivian, who has also sped off in a car: Vivian, Cordy Tindell. Personal Interview. 21 Aug. 2014.

30 "Who you have there?", "He's a pretty good boy", "I was badly hurt": *Violence in the Night in Marion, Alabama, February 18, 1965, op. cit.*

31 "I was not arrested or charged with anything, but just beaten and left on the highway": *Ibid.*

31 "I don't know why he hit me": *Ibid.*

31 "I fell down into a deep ravine", "Several times I had to hide": *Ibid.*

31 "It appeared to me that the front of the Negro line made a surge" and "since they were in custody I didn't watch them": FBI memo-randum. SA Archibald L. Riley, *op. cit.*

31 "push (the protestors) back toward Zion Methodist Church": *Ibid.*

32 The press sees and experiences something far different: Herbers, "Negroes Beaten", *op. cit.*

32 "Troopers armed with billy-clubs" and "Then came the attack on newsmen": Lynch. John. "A Bloody Night in Marion, Ala." *The Knickerbocker News* 19 Feb 1965. 1. Web. 28 Sept. 2014.

33 "the Negro race does not have a monopoly on injustice": Harris, T.O. "Law Enforcement and Race Relations: Speech at University of Alabama May 1966." *T.O. Harris Papers.* Civil Rights in Marion, Alabama Collection. University of Alabama. 1. Print.

33 "go up and down the scale": *Ibid.*, 1–2.

33 "the cultured, educated, well dressed": *Ibid.*, 2.

34 "to stop the night-time march": *Ibid.*, 5.

34 seventy-five to a hundred protestors: *Ibid.*, 4.

34 (footnote) "We were both fired because we wanted to register to vote": *Violence in the Night in Marion, Alabama, February 18, 1965, op. cit.*, 7.

34 "Goddamn, this is old Cager": *Ibid.,* 15.

35 "A large group of Negroes" and "Instead, they went into the café": FBI memorandum. SA Archibald L. Riley, *op. cit.*

36 "I went in and saw a trooper" and "The bottle apparently had been thrown": *Ibid.*

36 "The Negro had a hold of Corporal Fowler's gun": *Ibid.*

36 "I saw a tall black Negro": *Ibid.*

36 "eleven stitches were required": *Ibid.*

36 "Two colored males began beating": *Ibid.*

37 "One of the Negroes hit Corp. Fowler": *Ibid.*

37 "I and three other officers went inside", "My assailant, being taller", and "My assailant, fell backwards": *Ibid.*

38 "Jimmie took me out": *Violence in the Night in Marion, Alabama, February 18, 1965, op. cit.,* 15.

38 "Jimmie did not have anything in hand that I could see": FBI memorandum. SA Archibald L. Riley, *op. cit.*

38 "I picked up one bottle" and "As I threw": *Ibid.*

38 "Jackson picked up a bottle" and "More troopers came in": *Ibid.*

39 "A state trooper hit Jimmie Lee Jackson" and "The trooper that shot": *Ibid.*

39 Jeff Moore provided a similar account: *Ibid.*

39 "All I know is that white men came into the café", "They had Jimmie", and "I have not given up yet": *Violence in the Night in Marion, Alabama, February 18, 1965, op. cit.,* 16.

39 The FBI interviewed Jimmie Lee Jackson: FBI memorandum. SA Archibald L. Riley, *op. cit.*

41 A warrant was issued February 18, 1965: *Ibid.*

Chapter Three: "We Are Going to See the Governor!"

42 "I didn't hit anyone": *Violence in the Night in Marion, Alabama, February 18, 1965, op. cit.,* 10.

42 "a Negro run out of the café": FBI memorandum. SA Archibald L. Riley, *op. cit.*

42 "the Negro (is) lying on the sidewalk": *Ibid.*

43 Dobyne has heard about the attack: Dobyne, Walter. Personal Interview. 22 Oct. 2013.

43 "When Jimmie Lee came in": *Ibid.*

43 cleans Jackson's bullet wound and sedates him: FBI memorandum. SA Archibald L. Riley, *op. cit.*

44 "was in pain and praying": *Ibid.*

44 "I've been shot": *Ibid.*

44 "I tried to kill that black bastard": *Ibid.*

44 "I tried to kill the son-of-a-bitch": *Ibid.*

44 "very critical condition" and "His insides are torn up": *Ibid.*

44 registered nurse Vera Booker, files a report: *Ibid.*

45 performs an exploratory laparotomy: Dinkins, William. Interview with Blackside, Inc. *Eyes on the Prize: American's Civil Rights Years (1954–1965).* Washington University Libraries, Film and Media Archive, Henry Hampton Collection. 1979. Film.

45 "outside integration leaders from Selma", "We're sorry that someone was struck", "Of course we can't have that": Herbers, "Negroes Beaten", *op. cit.*

46 "Now we have come to the happiest way of life": Owsley, Frank Lawrence, Jr., John Craig Stewart, and Gordon T. Chappell. *Know Alabama: An Elementary History.* Montgomery: Viewpoint Publications, Inc., 1970. Print.

46 "The things that happened in these years caused bad feelings": *Ibid.*

46 "What happened in Marion last night": "The Marion Massacre." *Alabama Journal.* Montgomery: 19 Feb. 1965. 4. Print.

47 "This situation can only encourage chaos": Fleming, "The Death of Jimmie Lee Jackson", *op. cit.*

47 "observed no police brutality": FBI memorandum for the Attorney General. 19 Feb. 1965. 44-17669-161.

47 "most dangerous and effective Negro leader in the country": Christensen, Jen. "FBI tracked King's every move." *CNN: Black in America.* 29 Dec. 2008. Web. 24 Oct. 2014.

47 a packet of secretly recorded tapes: Corn, David. "The Dark Side of 'I Have a Dream': The FBI's War on Martin Luther King." *Mother Jones.* 28 Aug. 2013. Web. 24 Oct. 2014.

47 "struck on the head by a bottle and severely cut": FBI memorandum. John Doar, Acting Assistant Attorney General, Civil Rights Division: 19 Feb. 1965. Mobile 44-1226. DJ 144-3-NEW.

48 Doar now requests an investigation: *Ibid.*

48 "refused interviews with troopers": FBI memorandum. Clyde Tolson, Associate Director: 19 Feb. 1965. 44-17669.

48–49 "It was my responsibility", "I knew everybody had stuff": Slaughter, *New Battles Over Dixie, op. cit.,* 140.

49 "there was no TV coverage": *Ibid.,* 136.

49 "Three generations of one Negro family", "with broken scalps and bruises": Herbers, "Negroes Beaten", *op. cit.*

50 "Voting is what all this is about": Herbers, John. "Selma Negros Tell of Attack." *New York Times* 22 Feb. 1965: 12. Web. 9 Oct. 2014.

50 Those who pick cotton: Lauderdale, Florence. Personal Interview. 4 Sept. 2014.

50 Family members today say: *Ibid.*

50 "You can see straight through the whole house": *Ibid.*

50 Jackson tended a family garden: *Ibid.*

51 "He was a real quiet": Turner, Robert Sr. Personal Interview. 25 Oct. 2013.

51 "He was kind, gentle": Oakes, James W. Personal Interview. 25 Oct. 2013.

51 "He went to register, but everyone went", "It's an honor": Lauderdale, Florence. Personal Interview. Personal Interview. 4 Sept. 2014.

52 "While we did not always see eye to eye": "Telegram from Martin Luther King, Jr. to Betty al-Shabazz." *Stanford University Martin Luther King, Jr. Research and Education Institute.* Web. 3 Oct. 2014.

52 "If I can't live in the house as a human being": Haygood, Ryan Paul. "Malcolm's Contribution to Black Voting Rights." *The Black Commentator.* Web. 3 Oct. 2014.

53 "that an alternative philosophy awaited them": *Ibid.*

53 "maybe the biggest yet": Baker, *Diary of George Baker, op. cit.*

53 "FREEDOM DAY", "I never saw such poor living conditions", "The people I was trying to get": *Ibid.*

53 "a marked increase in the number of hostile-looking white men": Herbers, John. "Dr. King, Back in Alabama, Calls for March on Capitol to Push Voting Drive." *New York Times* 23 Feb. 1965. 16. Web. 4 Dec. 2014.

54 King calls the edict "clearly unconstitutional": *Ibid.*

54 "he seems to be in very good spirits": *Ibid.*

54 "We are going to have a motorcade": *Ibid.*

55 "Sister, don't you think this is a high price to pay for freedom?": Dunne, Colleen. "Q&A with Sr. Barbara Lum." *Global Sisters Report: A project of National Catholic Reporter.* Web. 29 Oct. 2014.

55 "physically able to be interviewed": FBI Memorandum. SA Allison A. Catlin and SA Paul R. Keiser, Selma, AL: 26 Feb. 1965. 44-1226.

55 An autopsy performed: "Wounded Negro Dies in Alabama; He Said Trooper Shot Him–Statement by Assailant Reported by Prosecutor." *New York Times* 27 Feb. 1965. Web. 30 Sept. 2014.

56 "I believe they wanted him to die": Fager, Charles E. *Selma 1965: The March that Changed the South*. New York: Charles Scribner's Sons, 1974. 82. Print.

56 "Nobody needs martyrs": Vivian, Cordy Tindell. Personal Interview. 21 Aug. 2014.

56 "was struck several times": "Wounded Negro Dies in Alabama", *op. cit.*

56 "I tell you the death of that man is pushing me": *Ibid.*

56 Earlier in the day: Halberstam, David. *The Children*. New York: Fawcett Books, 1998. 508. Print.

57 Foster originally proposed: Avery, Willie Nell. Personal Interview. 22 Aug. 2014; Garrow, David. *Bearing the Cross: Martin Luther King, Jr., and the Southern Christian Leadership Conference*. New York: Harper Collins, 2004. 394. Print.

57 "The Selma to Montgomery march was prompted", "A man of African heritage": Vaughn, Wally G. and Mattie Campbell Davis. *The Selma Campaign, 1963–1965: The Decisive Battle of the Civil Rights Movement*. Dover, MA: Majority Press, 2006. 13–14. Print.

58 "I must go see the king": Fager, *The March that Changed the South, op. cit.*, 83.

59 "The boy who was shot", "A march on Montgomery is being planned": Baker, *Diary of George Baker, op. cit.*

59–60 "FREEDOM DAY", "We didn't have a permit to parade": *Ibid.*

60 "Last week John Lewis was in Marion", "I got stopped", "This act very likely saved me": *Ibid.*

60 "This was a Christian funeral": Reed, Roy. "Alabama Victim Called a Martyr." *New York Times* 4 Mar. 1965. Web. 20 Sept. 2014.

61 "As the service began", "He has just gone home": *Ibid.*

61 "We are gathered": *Ibid.*

62 "We pray for the policemen of this town": *Ibid.*

62 King's eulogy: *Ibid.*

63 "We are going to see the governor!": *Ibid.*

Chapter Four: "You and the Two Girls Are Next . . ."

65 "the moment they thought of registering": Ellwanger, Joseph. Personal Interview. 21 Oct. 2013.

65   not "conducive to the orderly flow": "Massive Disorder Averted Here When Officers Intervene." *The Selma Times-Journal.* 7 Mar. 1965. Archived at Klann-Moren, Nancy. "March 6, 1965, Selma, Alabama, 48 Years Ago, today." *Nancy Klann-Moren, Author and Artist.* Web. 18 Oct. 2013.

65   "Negroes should not be permitted to make this senseless march": *Ibid.*

65   "We shall plan to march": *Ibid.*

65–66 "One is to go back and get a court order": *Ibid.*

66   "Why don't you stay in your own town": Ellwanger, Joseph. Personal Interview. 21 Oct. 2013.

66   "We're not simply pointing the finger at Selma": *Ibid.*

66   He sends a telegram to Ellwanger: Freeland, Gregory. "Lutherans and the Southern Civil Rights Movement." *Journal of Lutheran Ethics* 6.11 (2006): Web.

66   King, Martin Luther, Jr. "Letter from a Birmingham Jail." 6 Apr. 1963. Archived at *African Studies Center, University of Pennsylvania.* Web. 19 Oct. 2013.

67   "had the locks on the doors of the church changed": Collins, Donald E. *When the Church Bells Rang Racist: The Methodist Church and the Civil Rights Movement in Alabama.* Macon, GA: Mercer University Press, 1998. 107. Print.

67   "asked him not to use the words 'love' or 'brotherhood' ": *Ibid.*

67–68 "any priest or sister in the diocese who marched": Dunne, *op. cit.*

68   "a good man caught in his time": *Ibid.*

68   "because I wanted to be in the hospital", "felt very precarious": *Ibid.*

68   "talked about the movement but were very fearful of physical violence": *Ibid.*

68   fear keeps "scores if not hundreds" of supporters from participating: Ellwanger, Joseph. Personal Interview. 21 Oct. 2013.

68   "Since Jim Clark was in charge there": *Ibid.*

69   "That shows you how committed she is": *Ibid.*

69   "It was very much Jim Crow": *Ibid.*

69   After attending seminary: *Ibid.*

69   Ellwanger in seminary, BCHR, and first brush with white supremacists: *Ibid.*

70   "I was still reading the account of this event": *Ibid.*

70   "I hope that is not what I think it was": *Ibid.*

70   The horror hit Ellwanger's congregation, "shock, disbelief, and then a reaction of anger", "I can honestly say": *Ibid.*

70–71 "But to show what the Jim Crow culture really fostered", "because a couple of them were stupid enough": *Ibid.*

71   The anger of the black community, "I am reading this scripture
today": *Ibid.*

71   "It was interesting that there were three or four white clergy": *Ibid.*

72   "The photographer escaped": "Massive Disorder Averted", *op. cit.*

72   "When the taunts came": *Ibid.*

72   "lead Selma into dignity": May, Gary. *Bending Toward Justice: The
Voting Rights Act and the Transformation of American Democracy.* New
York: Basic Books, 2013. 40. Print.

72   Clark will castigate Baker: Clark, James. Interview with Blackside,
Inc. *Eyes on the Prize: American's Civil Rights Years (1954–1965).*
Washington University Libraries, Film and Media Archive, Henry
Hampton Collection. 1985. Film.

72   "Baker was a good and smart man": Fager, Chuck. "The Clash
of the Titans." *Independent Quaker Journalism, Commentary & More.*
11 Jan. 2012. Web. 25 Oct. 2014.

74   "outsmarted and outmaneuvered": *Ibid.*

74   "Selma, fortunately for us, was not Albany": *Ibid.*

74   "Damn the Kingdom's come": Morrison-Reed, Mark D. *The
Selma Awakening: How the Civil Rights Movement Tested and Changed
Unitarian Universalism.* Boston: Skinner House Books, 2014. 98.
Print.

74   "Tension over tomorrow's activities": Baker, George. Personal Interview. 8 Oct. 2013.

75   "We expect a lot of tear gas": *Ibid.*

75   King floats the idea: Garrow, *Bearing the Cross, op. cit.,* 396–397.

75   Baker wants to peaceably arrest the protesters: *Ibid.,* 397.

76   King "reluctantly" gave approval: *Ibid.,* 396–397.

76   "We have to do something": Slaughter, John. *New Battles Over
Dixie, op. cit.,* 141.

76   "Well, Hosea, if y'all are fool enough": *Ibid.*

76   "Hosea lost": Baker, George. Personal Interview. 8 Oct. 2013.

76–77 "crying, 'cause I had fought on the wrong side": "The Rev. Hosea Williams, 74, leaders of civil-rights marches, figure in politics,
service dies after long service." *The Baltimore Sun* 17 Nov. 2000.
Web. 13 Dec. 2014.

77   "my wild man, my Castro": Branch, Taylor. *Pillar of Fire: America in
the King Years, 1963–65.* New York: Simon & Schuster, 1998. 124.
Print.

77 "we strongly believe that the objectives": Lewis, John, with Michael D'Orso. *Walking with the Wind: A Memoir of the Movement.* New York: Mariner Books, 1999. 330. Print.

77 when SCLC came to Selma after SNCC had already been on the ground for two years: *Civil Rights Movement Veterans, op. cit.*

77 "If we can't sit at the table": *Eyes on the Prize: American's Civil Rights Years (1954–1965).* Blackside, Inc. Washington University Libraries, Film and Media Archive, Henry Hampton Collection. 1985. Film.

78 "I just felt during the period, it was too much": *Ibid.*

78 "In the nonviolent movement": *Ibid.*

78 "The whole point was walking from Selma to Montgomery": *Ibid.*

78 "They told us what to expect": Dobyne, Walter. Personal Interview. 22 Oct. 2013.

79 "We really thought half of us were going to get thrown in the river": Slaughter, John. *New Battles Over Dixie, op. cit.,* 141.

79 As John Lewis will later write: Lewis, *Walking with the Wind, op. cit.,* 338.

80 "dead still", "There, facing us": *Ibid.*

80 Armed with clubs and bats and bullwhips: *Ibid.,* 339.

80 "Can you swim?": *Ibid.*

80 Cloud gets on his bullhorn: "Massive Disorder Averted", *op. cit.*

80–81 "Troopers forward", "The troopers stormed": "Massive Disorder Averted", *op. cit.*

81 Dobyne recalls: Dobyne, Walter. Personal Interview. 22 Oct. 2013.

82 "That was a horrible day": Avery, Willie Nell. Personal Interview. 25 Oct. 2013.

82 "We parked a block away": Baker, *Diary of George Baker, op. cit.*

82 "We witnessed possemen on horseback", "It turned out to be Mrs. Boynton": *Ibid.*

83 Baker orders the sheriff, "Everything will be all right": "The Central Points." *Time Magazine* 19 Mar. 1965. Web. 5 Oct. 2014.

83 Dobyne remembers: Dobyne, Walter. Personal Interview. 22 Oct. 2013.

83 "I think both sides were shooting": *Ibid.*

83 "Thirty minutes after the marchers' encounter": "Massive Disorder Averted", *op. cit.*

83 "Negroes lay on the floors and chairs, many weeping and moaning": Reed, Roy. "Alabama Police Use Gas and Clubs to Rout Negroes." *New York Times* 8 Mar. 1965. Web. 4 Oct. 2014.

84 "I don't know how President Johnson can send troops to Vietnam": *Ibid.*

84 Reese feels triumphant despite the attack: "Interviewing a Living Legend: Rev. Frederick D. Reese." *Civil Rights Pilgrimage.* University of Wisconsin—Eau Claire. Web. 17 Oct. 2014.

84 "I fought in World War II, and I once was captured": Reed, Roy. "Alabama Police Use Gas", *op. cit.*

84 The tune is familiar, but the words are new: Webb, Sheyann, and Rachel West Nelson, as told to Frank Sikora. *Selma, Lord, Selma: Girlhood Memories of the Civil-Rights Days.* Tuscaloosa: University of Alabama Press, 1980. 105–106. Print.

85 "And everybody's singing now": *Ibid.,* 106.

85 ABC cuts into its regularly scheduled programming: Garrow, *Bearing the Cross, op. cit.,* 399.

85 Valeriani, back on the civil rights beat: Valeriani, Richard. Interview with Mary Morin. *Syracuse University Knight Chair in Political Reporting, Prof. Charolotte Grimes.* Web. 1 Nov. 2014. And, Valeriani, Richard. Personal Interview. 31 Oct. 2013.

86 "Naturally Bloody Sunday rendered": *Civil Rights Movement Veterans, op. cit.*

86 "The people of Selma will struggle on": *Ibid.*

Chapter 5: "How Do You Murder People?"

87 "Grant us peace fearlessly to contend against evil": Mendelsohn, Jack. *The Martyrs: Sixteen Who Gave their Lives for Racial Justice.* New York: Harper & Row, 1966. 159. Print.

88 Over the next few hours: *Ibid.,* 164.

88 "I am speaking as a Negro": Howlett, Duncan. *No Greater Love: The James Reeb Story.* New York: Harper & Row, 1966. 195. Print.

88 Reeb next speaks with John Sullivan: *Ibid.,* 195–196.

88 He warns Reeb: Mendelsohn, *op. cit.,* 165.

89 "a rambling old frame dwelling": *Ibid.,* 159.

89 "There are others to go": Morrison-Reed, *op. cit.,* 188.

89 "I want to be part of it": *Ibid.*

89 "I know you'll be all right": Howlett, *op. cit.,* 198.

89 Reeb's flight to Atlanta: *Ibid.,* 199.

90 "unofficial chaplain": Mendelsohn, *op. cit.,* 153.

90 "Inside all was blackness": Howlett, *op. cit.,* 21.

91 "a literalist as far as belief in the Bible was concerned": *Ibid.,* 33.

91 He refused to study on Sundays: *Ibid.,* 38.

91 "The Lutherans are not sufficiently involved": *Ibid.,* 30.

91 "All the Bible minutiae": *Ibid.,* 57.

91 Reeb had enjoyed doing fieldwork: *Ibid.*

92 Reeb had his doubts: *Ibid.,* 82.

92 "clearly progressed in my views": *Ibid.,* 87.

92 "inspire people to noble and courageous living": *Ibid.,* 86.

92 "Here were his own thoughts duplicated": *Ibid.,* 92.

93 "I do feel it": *Ibid.,* 109–110.

93 "Jim was singularly dedicated": Mendelsohn, *op. cit.,* 155.

93 Civil rights also became a priority: *All Souls Archives and History.* All Souls Church Unitarian. Web. 25 Sept. 2014.

94 Reeb quickly became involved in urban matters: Mendelsohn, *op. cit.,* 161.

94 "Once there, we paid our respects": Engel, Ronald J. "For the Love of the World: The Public Ministry of James Reeb." *Unitarian Universalism 1989: Selected Essays.* Ed. E. Gillis. Boston: Unitarian Universalist Ministers Association, 1990. 2. Print.

94 "caught up in this ecumenical movement": *Ibid.,* 6.

94 "We believed that the first word religion must speak": *Ibid.*

95 Reeb interviewed for a position there: Engel, Ronald, J. Personal Interview. 16 Oct. 2013.

95 "The emphasis was to be on working *with* people": Mendelsohn, *op. cit.,* 160.

95 "I have been primarily seeking": *Ibid.,* 158.

95 Reeb spoke of the current racial climate: Howlett, *op. cit.,* 176.

96 "show the folks what police brutality is": *Ibid.,* 186.

96 "Had the visitor seen to the heart of the man": *Ibid.*

96 "Jim was kind, very kind": Mendelsohn, *op. cit.,* 160.

96 He also observed: Reeb, James. "Community Relations Program Weekly Logs–Jim Reeb." Daily log of James Reeb. 9 Oct. 1964–9 Mar. 1965. American Friends Service Committee Archives. Print.

97–98 "4 Die in Roxbury Fire, Mother Killed in Leap With Baby", "details of family deaths after an apartment fire in January 1965", "A third Perry child, Emmet Jr., 1": *Boston Globe.* 31 Dec. 1964. Web. 16 Sep. 2014.

98 "We were mainly concerned": Reeb, *op. cit.*

98–99 Clougherty went on the offensive, "How do you murder people?", "So long as I may be 'murdered' ": *Ibid.*

99 One pamphlet was turned to a page: Howlett, *op. cit.,* 194.

99 Just a few weeks earlier Miller had told another clergyman: Morrison-Reed, *op. cit.*

99 "stand there on behalf of everyone in decency": Olsen, Clark. Personal Interview. 11 Oct. 2013.

99 Clergy of all faiths answer King's call: "The Central Points", *op. cit.*

100 "one of the doctors from King's party": Baker, *Diary of George Baker, op. cit.*

102 "integrating, scalawagging, carpetbagging liar": "The Central Points", *op. cit.*

103 "Democrats and Republicans complained": Robertson, Nan. "Johnson Pressed for a Voting Law; Members of Congress Voice Disgust at Selma Violence." *New York Times* 9 Mar. 1965. Web. 1 Nov. 2014.

103 "a disgraceful exhibition of arbitrary power", "Shame on you, George Wallace": "The Central Points", *op. cit.*

103 "indiscriminate use of [clubs] by forces of law": Internal undated FBI memorandum. "World Press Reaction to Selma." 2.

103 "bloody pogrom": *Ibid.,* 9.

103 "the law and the court are but an instrument": *Ibid.,* 10.

104 "editorials condemn police brutality in Selma, but point out that", "more immediate concern": *Ibid.,* 1.

104 Johnson's conversation with Ellington is recorded: "President Johnson to Buford Ellington." 8:29a.m. Tape *WH6503.03, #7032. Recordings of Telephone Conversations–White House Series, Recordings and Transcripts of Conversations and Meetings, Lyndon B. Johnson Library.* Accessed at Stephens, Alice Anne. "The President, the Wildcard, and the Link." *University of Virginia, Miller Center.* Web. 4 Nov. 2014.

105 "There's no telling what would have happened": Franklin, Ben A. "Wallace Says Police Saved Negro Lives." *New York Times* 9 Mar. 1965. Web. 1 Nov. 2014.

105 "We've gone too far to turn back": May, *op. cit.,* 100.

105 "more than one thousand, the veterans of the day before", "Although King did not explicitly say it": *Ibid.*

105 "There will be no irreparable harm", "hereby enjoined and restrained from attempting to march": "The Text of Judge's Order Banning Alabama March." *New York Times* 10 Mar. 1965. Web. 1 Nov. 2014.

106 "I am certain Americans everywhere join in deploring the brutality": Mohr, Charles. "Presidents Plea Curtails March." *New York Times* 10 Mar. 1965. Web. 1 Nov. 2014.

106 "whether that person is black or white, whether that person is rich or poor": "Transcript of Statewide TV-Radio Talk to the People of Florida on Race Relations by Governor Leroy Collins." 20 Mar. 1960. *University of Florida George A. Smathers Library Digital Collections.* Web. 4 Nov. 2014.

107 "I have no alternative but to lead a march": Sitkoff, Harvard. *King: Pilgrimage to the Mountaintop.* New York: Hill and Wang, 2008. 159. Print.

107 "Jim believed in a law that was higher than the law of the state": Howlett, *op. cit.,* 204.

107 "It seems if we wait two more days", "There is a higher law in God's universe": "The Central Points", *op. cit.*

108 "The civil rights movement owes its life", "If it were the truth that there were no hope": *Ibid.*

108 thousands in cities across North America march: *Ibid.*

109 In Beloit . . . and in Detroit: "Romney Leads a Protest." *New York Times* 10 Mar. 1965. Web. 2 Nov. 2014.

109 "We will go back to the church now", "astounded and bewildered", "Many thought that it was [King's] worst moment": May, *op. cit.,* 101.

109–110 "We decided we had to stand and confront the state troopers": *Ibid.,* 104.

110 Reeb puts his suitcase in the minister's car: Morrison-Reed, *op. cit.,* 105.

110 "This is Selma, where to respect the dignity of man": McGrath, Edward G. "A Reporter's Ordeal." *Boston Globe* 11 Mar. 1965. Web. 4 Nov. 2014.

110 "Do you prefer to eat with your own kind?": Howlett, *op. cit.,* 208.

110 After a long day of flying: Olsen, Clark. Personal Interview. 11 Oct. 2013.

111 At Walker's Café, "Lots of positive energy": *Ibid.*

111 "I stood outside the restaurant": Miller, Orloff. Interview with Blackside, Inc. *Eyes on the Prize: American's Civil Rights Years (1954–1965).* Washington University Libraries, Film and Media Archive, Henry Hampton Collection. 1985. Film.

Chapter Six: "They Just Flushed Out Like Birds . . ."

112 "It was getting to be that time": Olsen, Clark. Personal Interview. 11 Oct. 2013.

113 With its swinging doors and tin spittoons: Stanton, Mary. *From Selma to Sorrow: The Life and Death of Viola Liuzzo*. Athens, GA: University of Georgia Press, 1998. 47. Web. 4 Dec. 2013.

113 "We felt an atmosphere of hatred": Norsworthy, Richard. "Selma: The Witness." *The Liberal Context*. Spring, 1965. 5. Quoted in Howlett, Duncan. *No Greater Love: The James Reeb Story*. New York: Harper & Row, 1966. 209. Print.

113 Reeb and his companions are almost at the corner, "Hey you niggers": Olsen, Clark. Personal Interview. 11 Oct. 2013.

114 "Just keep walking": *Ibid*.

114 four "vicious and intense" faces: *Ibid*.

114 "I heard the sound it made": *Ibid*.

114 "Here's how it feels to be a nigger down here": *Ibid*.

114 the attack took no more than a minute, "basically okay": *Ibid*.

115 They speed to the infirmary: Mendelsohn, *op. cit.*, 169.

116 "Selma had to show its true colors": Greeley, Dana McLean. "The Reeb Martyrdom." *A Sheaf of Papers on Selma, 1965, and James Reeb collected by Homer A. Jack*. 11 Mar. 1993. 22. Print.

116 "Shey, you know who it was", "Of course he never did come back to my house": Webb and Nelson, *op. cit.*, 111.

117 "Police seem somewhat sympathetic": Mendelsohn, *op. cit.*, 169.

117 "Marie Reeb had to be notified": Jack, Homer A. "The Ordeal of James Reeb." *A Sheaf of Papers on Selma, 1965, and James Reeb collected by Homer A. Jack*. 11 Mar. 1993. 19. Print.

118 "At that point I became quite afraid": Olsen, Clark. Personal Interview. 11 Oct. 2013.

118 "Everything in me was saying, get out of this ambulance": *Ibid*.

119 "an interminable amount of time": *Ibid*.

119 "Hey, what ya doing in there?": *Ibid*.

119 "We'll radio ahead": Mendelsohn, *op. cit.*, 170.

119 "All I remember saying to him": Olsen, Clark. Personal Interview. 11 Oct. 2013.

119 Miller wants to tell their story: Miller, Orloff. Personal Interview. 17 Oct. 2014.

119 Miller's notes are simple: Mendelsohn, *op. cit.*, 170–171.

121 Olsen finds it difficult to feel completely safe: Olsen, Clark. Personal Interview. 11 Oct. 2013.

121 "We are making every effort to arrest the assailants": "3 Pastors Beaten." *Associated Press* 10 Mar. 1965. Web. 3 Nov. 2013.

121 "they just flushed out like birds": McGrath, Edward G. "Prosecution Loses 3 Witnesses in Reeb Case." *Boston Globe* 10 Dec. 1965. Web. 4 Nov. 2014.

121 He is well known to the police: Bickford, Daniel B. "Special Report: The Reeb Murder Trial." *Department of Social Responsibility, Unitarian Universalist Association.* Print.

122 Within twenty-four hours: "Massive Disorder Averted", *op. cit.*

122 "mean as a snake—all of them": Helman, Scott. "Letter from Selma." *Boston Globe Magazine* 25 June 2013. Web. 6 Dec. 2013.

122 "Cook wore a neat double breasted suit", "Cook said he liked black people": Dorsett, Bob. "A Black History Month Moment." *Players Magazine* Jan. 1999. Print.

122 "Their only knowledge of the assault": "Massive Disorder Averted", *op. cit.*

123 "Many marchers produced blankets": "Sylvan Street Demonstration Continues." *The Selma Times-Journal.* 7 Mar. 1965. Archived at Klann-Moren, Nancy. "March 6, 1965, Selma, Alabama, 48 Years Ago, today." *Nancy Klann-Moren, Author and Artist.* Web. 18 Oct. 2013.

123 "Lovemaking in open definitely occurred": "Lovemaking in open definitely occurred in Selma prayer vigil." *Birmingham News* 28 Mar. 1965. Print.

124 "It was ironic that as the plane stopped": Sullivan, John. "Reeb's Spirit Lives." *Boston Globe* 15 Mar. 1965. Web. 25 Oct. 2013.

124 "I will never forget": Mendelsohn, *op. cit.,* 171.

125 "preventing and discouraging Negroes from exercising their full rights": Pomfret, John D. "U.S. Sues to Void Ban on Marches." *New York Times* 11 Mar. 1965. Web. 4 Nov. 2014.

125 "7:30 A.M., cardiac arrest": Mendelsohn, *op. cit.,* 171.

125 "I was the last person Jim had contact with": Olsen, Clark. Personal Interview. 11 Oct. 2013.

125 "I had this question in mind": *Ibid.*

126 "There we saw him, lying on one of those rolling, stretcher-like beds": Howlett, *op. cit.,* 216.

126 "For a long time she remained there gazing at him": *Ibid.*

126 "He pointed out what we, isolated as we were, did not realize": *Ibid.,* 217.

126 Marie Reeb is understandably reluctant: *Ibid.*

126–27 Marie Reeb media Q&A, "I felt that hardened group": *Ibid.,* 218–220.

128 "When I looked at him, I knew he was done for": *Ibid.,* 220.

128 "Marie sat staring at them": *Ibid.*

128 "Marie, Jim was the right man, in the right place, at the right time": Miller, Orloff. Personal Interview. 17 Oct. 2014.

128 the FBI is investigating several events: Pomfret, *op. cit.*

129 "This minister is going to die, isn't he?": Branch, Taylor. *The King Years: Historic Moments in the Civil Rights Movement.* New York: Simon & Schuster, 2013. 119. Web. 10 Nov. 2013.

129 "All quiet on the civil rights front": Kotz, Nick. *Judgment Days: Lyndon Baines Johnson, Martin Luther King, Jr., and the Laws that Changed America.* New York: Houghton Mifflin Company, 2005. 300. Web. 20 Oct. 2013.

129 "Let them eat and drink": *Ibid.*

129 The event is noted in President Johnson's Daily Diary: Johnson, Lyndon Baines. *Lyndon B. Johnson's Daily Diary Collection.* 11 Mar. 1965. Web. 2 Nov. 2013.

130 he interviews several families who have been touched by James Reeb: Malin, Brenda. "'Jim Was My Friend,' says Boy of 8." *Boston Globe* 14 Mar. 1965. Web. 4 Nov. 2013.

130 "We loved to see him coming to the house": *Ibid.*

130 "He brought a new sense of hope": *Ibid.*

130 "Tell her about it in such a way": Howlett, *op. cit.,* 222.

131 "I will have a private plane waiting for you": *Ibid.,* 223.

132 "We've got a rope that's a Berlin Wall": Leonard, Richard D. *Call to Selma: Eighteen Days of Witness.* Boston: Skinner House Books, 2002. 28. Print.

132 "Reverend Reeb has died in the hospital in Birmingham": Herbers, John. "Clergyman Dies of Selma Beating." *New York Times* 12 Mar. 1965. Web. 20 Oct. 2013.

132 "Can you control your people when it happens?", "We can control ours", "We will hold one minute of silent prayer": *Ibid.*

132 they improvised songs to taunt the police: Leonard, *Call to Selma, op. cit.,* 28.

133 "Any contempt proceedings will be a matter between the court and the contemptor": Franklin, Ben A. "Dr. King Says He Did Not Intend to March to Montgomery Tuesday." *New York Times* 12 Mar. 1965. Web. 4 Nov. 2013.

133 "I was very upset": "The Central Points", *op. cit.*

134 "Is it correct to say", "Yes, it is", King's courtroom revelation:

Franklin, "Dr. King Says He Did Not Intend to March to Montgomery Tuesday", *op. cit.*

134   "Go get them goddam niggers!", "I'm a country boy": "The Central Points", *op. cit.*

134   The proceeding grows testy: *Ibid.*

134   "no marches or demonstrations will be held in Selma": "Mayor Rejects Request From Civil Rightists." *The Selma Times-Journal.* 12 Mar. 1965. Archived at Klann-Moren, Nancy. "March 12, 1965, Selma, Alabama, 48 Years Ago, today." *Nancy Klann-Moren, Author and Artist.* Web. 18 Oct. 2013.

135   "They were expressing their sorrow": "Praying Negroes Fill Reeb Yard." *Associated Press* 13 Mar. 1965. Web. 10 Nov. 2013.

135   The Boston Symphony changes its program: Jack, "The Ordeal of James Reeb", *op. cit., 21.*

135   "[Mrs. Reeb] is not a bitter woman": "Praying Negroes Fill Reeb Yard", *op. cit.*

Chapter Seven: "One Good Man . . ."

136   President Johnson meets in the Cabinet Room for over two hours: Pearson, Drew. "Civil Rights for LBJ's Girls?" *Boston Globe* 17 Mar. 1965. Web. 1 Nov. 2013.

137   "weren't able to study for their exams because of all those pickets": *Ibid.*

137   those assembled "go around the table": *Ibid.*

137   "I'm just so sorry your two little girls were upset, Mr. President": *Ibid.*

137   "You know Mr. President, there was a black boy killed down there, too": *Ibid.*

137   "The real moral fervor did not come until Rev. James Reeb died": Riley, David. "Who is Jimmie Lee Jackson?" *The New Republic* 3 Apr. 1965. Web. 8 Nov. 2013.

137–38   "There is a sense of national outrage and shame over Reeb's death", "This young Negro was killed": *Ibid.*

138   "You could put badges on the U.S. Marshals": Pearson, *op. cit.*

138   "upset and somewhat emotional", "has been working day and night": *Ibid.*

138   Johnson defends his record on civil rights: *Ibid.*

138   "He gave an impressive recitation": *Ibid.*

138 Later in the day, the civil right leaders brief four thousand clergy: Collins, George M. "Boston Clergy Decry LBJ's 'Inaction'." *Boston Globe* 13 Mar. 1965. Web. 15 Nov. 2013.

139 "It is wrong to do violence to peaceful citizens": Baker, Robert E. "Johnson Is Firm in Talk with Wallace." *Washington Post* 14 Mar. 1965. Web. 18 Oct. 2014.

139 "When the court has made its orders, it must be obeyed": *Ibid.*

140 "It was evident that Mr. Johnson was giving Wallace little comfort", "The president was a gentleman": *Ibid.*

140 "strike down all restrictions": *Ibid.*

140–41 Lingo, Johnson, Doar: Franklin, Ben A. "Official in Alabama Says Trooper Shot Negro Who Died." *New York Times* 14 Mar. 1965. Web. 20 Oct. 2014.

141 "full investigation", "massive infection": *Ibid.*

142 "detailed answers", "belong to many organizations that have been cited": Franklin, Ben A. "Wallace to Bar a Rights March Till Court Acts." *New York Times* 15 Mar. 1965. Web. 18 Oct. 2014.

142 "That's not Selma. That's New York": *Ibid.*

142 "the hundreds of ministers from other states", "they soiled the cloth and demeaned the pulpit": "I Am The Law." *Montgomery Advertiser.* 11 Mar. 1965. Web. 4 Nov. 2013.

142 "forty of the ministerial grenadiers", "where citizens won't phone the police", "gunfire erased Malcolm X", "the subways have to be policed": *Ibid.*

142 the editorial concludes with purple prose: *Ibid.*

143 "the ghetto in Roxbury and the ivy-covered homes in the Back Bay": Thomas, John C. "25,000 March on Boston Common in Tribute to Slain Minister." *Boston Globe* 14 Mar. 1965. Web. 9 Nov. 2013.

143 "The tempo of the demonstration varied", "It was a memorial service and a civil rights rally": *Ibid.*

144 "makes us all, North and South, remove every trace of hate": *Ibid.*

144 "James Reeb stirred the conscience": Sullivan, *op. cit.*

144 Nearby town councils, every mass includes a "Prayer for Selma", A Catholic newspaper in Worcester, Massachusetts, proposes Reeb for sainthood: "Hub Rally By 10,000 Due Today." *Boston Globe* 14 Mar. 1965. Web. 9 Nov. 2013.

144 "To disregard Alabama is to place all of America in jeopardy": Collins, George. "Why Go To Selma?" *Boston Globe* 15 Mar. 1965. Web. 9 Nov. 2013.

144 "to stiffen the spine of the President of the United States": "Would-Be Marchers Turned Back Again." *The Selma Times-Journal.* 15 Mar. 1965. Archived at Klann-Moren, Nancy. "March 6, 1965, Selma, Alabama, 48 Years Ago, today." *Nancy Klann-Moren, Author and Artist.* Web. 2 Nov. 2014.

144 "If they want to march, let them march": "Protests Spread over the Nation." *New York Times* 15 Mar. 1965. Web. 2 Nov. 2014.

144 Some gatherings are met with counterprotests: *Ibid.*

146 "I'm pledged to enforce the laws": Anglin, Robert. "Wreath Honoring Reeb Laid at Selma Courthouse." *Boston Globe* 16 Mar. 1965. Web. 7 Sept. 2014.

146 "And the Constitution of the United States is that not right?": *Ibid.*

146 "The world is on our side": *Ibid.*

146–47 "And one or two days later they allegedly assaulted Reverend Reeb?", "Our deputies had their hands full": "2 Reeb Killing Suspects Tied to Earlier Clash." *Washington Post* 16 Mar. 1965. Web. 10 Nov. 2013.

147 "From the moment the service began", "James Reeb's death was described": Leonard, Richard D. "The View from the Balcony: A Witness's Diary Captures the Torment and Magic of James Reeb's Euology." *UU World* 15 Mar. 1965. Web. 2 Nov. 2014.

148 "our fallen hero and martyr", "Truly they lie, black and white together": McGrath, Edward C. "US Judge Clears Road for Triumphant Rights March." *Boston Globe* 16 Mar. 1965. Web. 3 Nov. 2014.

148 "Who killed James Reeb?": *Ibid.*

148 "redeem the soul of our nation": *Ibid.*

148 "God has spoken from the federal court": *Ibid.*

149 "an experience he was willing to forego": Anglin, *op. cit.*

149 "We are here to reaffirm our commitment", "Here the spirit of James Reeb will dwell": Reed, Roy. "Selma March Held after U.S. Court Arranges Accord." *New York Times* 16 Mar. 1965. Web. 2 Nov. 2014.

149 "we shall overcome" America's "crippling legacy of bigotry and injustice": "Transcript of the Johnson Address on Voting Rights to Joint Session of Congress." As recorded by *New York Times* 16 Mar. 1965. Web. 4 Dec. 2013.

150 "At times history and fate meet": *Ibid.*

150 "His actions and protests, his courage to risk safety": *Ibid.*

150 "No other American President had so completely identified himself with the cause of the Negro": Wicker, Tom. "Johnson Urges

Congress at Joint Session to Pass Law Insuring Negro Vote." *New York Times* 16 Mar. 1965. Web. 6 Nov. 2014.

150–51 "the effort of American Negroes", "Should we defeat every enemy", "There is no constitutional issue here": "Transcript of the Johnson Address on Voting Rights to Joint Session of Congress", *op. cit.*

151 "We have already waited", "long hours, nights and weekends", "We cannot—we must not—": *Ibid.*

151 "Mr. Johnson's accent and emphasis imparted an unmistakable determination": Wicker, "Johnson Urges Congress at Joint Session to Pass Law Insuring Negro Vote", *op. cit.*

151 "there was jubilation": Miller, Orloff. Personal Interview. 17 Oct. 2014.

151 "Everyone in the room": Leonard, "The View from the Balcony", *op. cit.*

152 "There was din everywhere", "We were all jumping around": Vivian, Cordy Tindell. Personal Interview. 21 Aug. 2014.

152 "great and amazing understanding": "Dr. King Praises Voting Bill But Urges Continued Protests." *New York Times* 17 Mar. 1965. Web. 18 Nov. 2014.

152 King would later reflect on one omission: King, Martin Luther, Jr. *Where Do We Go From Here: Chaos or Community?* Boston: Beacon Press, 1968. 34. Print.

152 "Not that they felt": *Ibid.*
"a good strong bill": "Dr. King Praises Voting Bill But Urges Continued Protests", *op. cit.*

152 It will send federal registration officials to six states in the South: Wicker, "Johnson Urges Congress at Joint Session to Pass Law Insuring Negro Vote", *op. cit.*

153 Data showing that fewer than half: Kenworthy, E. W. "Johnson to Address Congress Tonight on Vote Rights Bill." *New York Times* 15 Mar. 1965. Web. 5 Nov. 2014.

153 "filibuster against it as long as god gives me breath": Kenworthy, E. W. "Congress Ready to Move Swiftly on Voting Rights." *New York Times* 17 Mar. 1965. Web. 2 Nov. 2014.

153 "Qualified citizens of Selma and Dallas County", "obey because it is the law": *Ibid.*

153 "We must keep the issue alive", "a tinkling empty symbol": Williams, Juan. *Eyes on the Prize: America's Civil Rights Years, 1954–1965.* New York: Penguin Books, 1988. Web. 15 Nov. 2014.

153 "spoiled a good song": May, *op. cit.,* 125.

153 "It was like you'd been struck by a dagger in your heart": Williams, *Eyes on the Prize, op. cit.*

154 A second demonstration is held after this debacle: Schutte, Hugh. "Eight Injured in Alabama Race Melee." *Washington Post* 17 Mar. 1965. Web. 4 Nov. 2013.

154 "a lanky boy": Thomas, John. "Only 13, He Blocks Tears" *Boston Globe* 17 Mar. 1965. Web. 1 Nov. 2013.

154 Rev. Duncan Howlett of All Souls remembers his colleague and friend: *Ibid.*

155 "James Reeb was one of the unusual": Jack, Homer A. "James Reeb: Civil Rights Martyr." *Friends Journal* March 1990. 10–11. Print.

155 The Quaker leader remembers his colleague: *Ibid.*

156 "There is a killer in the dark and racist streets of the South": *Ibid.*

156 Some years later Orloff Miller will tell Marie: Miller, Orloff. Personal Interview. 17 Oct. 2014.

Chapter Eight: "We Have a New Song to Sing"

157 "an almost continuous pattern of conduct": Franklin, Ben A. "U.S. Court Allows Alabama March." *New York Times* 18 Mar. 1965. Web. 3 Nov. 2013.

158 "I intend to call on the president": "Excerpts from Wallace's Speech on the Alabama Rights March." *New York Times* 19 Mar. 1965. Web. 10 Nov. 2014.

158 "Now why in the hell didn't you stand up like a man": "LBJ, Governor Wallace, and Buford Ellington in Selma, Alabama." 9:13 p.m. Tape WH6503.10, #7124. *Recordings of Telephone Conversations— White House Series, Recordings and Transcripts of Conversations and Meetings, Lyndon B. Johnson Library. Accessed at Stephens, Alice Anne. "The President, the Wildcard, and the Link." University of Virginia, Miller Center.* Web. 4 Nov. 2014.

158 Just hours before the march is to leave Selma, five time bombs are discovered in Birmingham: *Civil Rights Movement Veterans, op. cit.*

158 his "eyes were opened" by the death of Jimmie Lee Jackson: Dobyne, Walter. Personal Interview. 22 Oct. 2013.

159 "people, people, and more people": Baker, *Diary of George Baker, op. cit.*

160 "gave me the feeling of organizing a wagon train to go west": *Ibid.*

160 "I'm glad to get rid of the ones who are leaving": *Eyes on the Prize, op. cit.*

160 "I will be glad to get these people out of town": "King Allots 14 Miles Today For Marchers." *The Selma Times-Journal.* 22 Mar. 1965. Archived at Klann-Moren, Nancy. "March 6, 1965, Selma, Alabama, 48 Years Ago, today." *Nancy Klann-Moren, Author and Artist.* Web. 18 Oct. 2013.

160 "Priests, nuns, ministers and rabbis walked": *Ibid.*

160 "he is trying to divide our people", "crusaders", "There are certainly things that need correcting": Pearson, Ted. "Toolen rips King, says priests, nuns should go home." *Montgomery Advertiser* 18 Mar. 1965. Print.

160–61 "I see this march as doing a great disservice": "Bishop Goodson Deplores March to Montgomery." *Associated Press* 11 Mar. 1965. Print.

161 "return to their homes": *Ibid.*

161 "I left just before (the march) started": Baker, *Diary of George Baker, op. cit.*

161 "Martin always wore the good preacher blue suit": Young, Andrew. Interview with Blackside, Inc. *Eyes on the Prize: American's Civil Rights Years (1954–1965).* Washington University Libraries, Film and Media Archive, Henry Hampton Collection. 1985. Film.

162 "the promised land", "Everyone is tired, happy, joyous, and contented": Baker, *Diary of George Baker, op. cit.*

162 It is estimated that as many as eight thousand people, return to Selma before bedtime, sleeping bags in two tents, suffering a blister, protect the camp: "King Allots 14 Miles Today For Marchers", *op. cit.*

162 get out of the line: Evans, *op. cit.,* 174.

163 "kind of our leader", "So we boycotted": *Ibid.*

163 "Why can't all the white people go back?": "Rain Dampens March As Third Day Begins." *The Selma Times-Journal.* 23 Mar. 1965. Archived at Klann-Moren, Nancy. "March 6, 1965, Selma, Alabama, 48 Years Ago, today." *Nancy Klann-Moren, Author and Artist.* Web. 18 Oct. 2013.

163 "We must have at least a small group of white people": *Ibid.*

163 As in other counties throughout the South, the blacks in Lowndes suffered greatly: Jeffries, Hasan Kwame. *Bloody Lowndes: Civil Rights and Black Power in Alabama's Black Belt.* New York: New York University Press, 2009. 16–17. Print.

164 four African Americans attempted to register, two had won the right to vote, formed the Lowndes County Christian Movement for

Human Rights: Freeman, Jo. Review. "Making the Revolution–In One County." Book review of *Bloody Lowndes: Civil Rights and Black Power in Alabama's Black Belt.* Web. 10 Nov. 2014.

164 "unemployed agitator ceases to agitate": "King Allots 14 Miles Today For Marchers", *op. cit.*

164 his group plans to put up more than eight hundred of these billboards: *Ibid.*

164 "At about every intersection you passed": Dobyne, Walter. Personal Interview. 22 Oct. 2013.

164 "Along the road are Negroes who watch": Baker, *Diary of George Baker, op. cit.*

165 "to make a positive out of a negative", "Listen, we're going to stay": Carmichael, Stokely. Interview with Blackside, Inc. *Eyes on the Prize: American's Civil Rights Years (1954–1965).* Washington University Libraries, Film and Media Archive, Henry Hampton Collection. 1985. Film.

165 they will work through their Easter break: "King Allots 14 Miles Today For Marchers", *op. cit.*

165 "They can't accomplish a darned thing": "Rain Dampens March As Third Day Begins", *op. cit.*

166 "We have a new song": May, *op. cit.,* 138.

166 "battlefield wounds": Young, Quentin. *Everybody In, Nobody Out: Memoirs of a Rebel Without a Pause.* Friday Harbor, WA: Copernicus Healthcare, 2013. 61. Print.

166 "Why don't these people understand": *Ibid.*

166 "That's not a simple request": *Ibid.*

166 Baker marches the entire distance on day four: Baker, *Diary of George Baker, op. cit.*

167 "Negroes who watch", "Have the feeling": *Ibid.*

167 "Broadway Answers Selma" (footnote): Benjamin, Philip. " 'Broadway Answers Selma' Nets $150,000 for Civil Rights Fight." *New York Times* 5 Apr. 1965. Web. 15 Nov. 2013.

167 "I have blisters on my feet which cause me to limp": Baker, *Diary of George Baker, op. cit.*

168 "This is the greatest march on any capitol": Hagen, Ross. "Marchers Ready to End Lengthy Trek to Capitol." *The Selma Times-Journal.* 25 Mar. 1965. Archived at Klann-Moren, Nancy. "March 6, 1965, Selma, Alabama, 48 Years Ago, today." *Nancy Klann-Moren, Author and Artist.* Web. 18 Oct. 2013.

168 "You danged fool": *Civil Rights Movement Veterans, op. cit.*

169 looked like an occupied military zone: Hagen, *op. cit.*

169 "my boss told me if I ever got involved": Goode, Steve. "Lesson in Freedom." *Hartford Courant* 5 Feb. 2002. Web. 2 Dec. 2013.

169 "I tell you what, I never really thought about the weather": Dobyne, Walter. Personal Interview. 22 Oct. 2013.

170 "To me, there was never a march like this one before": Lewis, John. Interview with Blackside, Inc. *Eyes on the Prize: American's Civil Rights Years (1954–1965)*. Washington University Libraries, Film and Media Archive, Henry Hampton Collection. 1985. Film.

170 Amelia Boynton later remembered those final steps: Robinson, Amelia B. *Bridge Across Jordan*. Washington, DC: Schiller Institute, 1991. 200. Print.

171 "I look worse than anybody": Adler, Renata. "Letter From Selma." *The New Yorker* 27 Mar. 1965. Web. 15 Oct. 2014.

171 Dr. King now addresses "all the freedom-loving people": King, Martin Luther, Jr. "Our God Is Marching On." *Stanford University Martin Luther King, Jr. Research and Education Institute*. Web. 3 Oct. 2014.

171 "The real victory": Webb and Nelson, *op. cit.,* 126.

172 "interested in what black people were doing": Dees, Morris, with Steve Fiffer. *A Season for Justice*. New York: Charles Scribner's Sons, 1991. 91. Print.

172 "He loved me like a son": *Ibid.*

172 "I oughta take this gun": *Ibid.*

172 "In these changing times": *Ibid.,* 92.

173 Afraid, she starts singing: "Viola Liuzzo." *Dictionary of Unitarian and Universalist Biography*. Web. 5 Oct. 2014.

173 Moton, who has not been hit: *Civil Rights Movement Veterans, op. cit.*

174 When he awakens, Moton climbs to the roadside: Reed, Roy. "Witness to Slaying Cites Harassment on Road Earlier." *New York Times* 27 Mar. 1965. Web. 4 Oct. 2014.

174–75 "a tragedy and horrible stain", "Mrs. Liuzzo went to Alabama", "bring the activities of the Klan under effective control of the law": "Transcript of Johnson's Statement on the Arrests in Alabama." *New York Times* 27 Mar. 1965. Web. 2 Oct. 2014.

175 "not connected in any way", "trumped up Communist plot", "How are we to know": Franklin, Ben A. "Klan Chief Calls 2 Rights Deaths Part of Red Plot." *New York Times* 28 Mar. 1965. Web. 5 Oct. 2014.

175 "freedom fighter": Jones, David R. "4 Rights Leaders Attend Funeral." *New York Times* 31 Mar. 1965. Web. 5 Oct. 2014.

175 "The cost for freedom just might be another life": Reed, Roy. "Wallace Meets a Biracial Group." *New York Times* 31 Mar. 1965. Web. 20 Nov. 2013.

176 The petition calls for removal of the poll tax: *Ibid.*

176 The grand jury does not indict Rowe: Associated Press. "U.S. Jury Indicts 3 Liuzzo Suspects." *New York Times* 8 Apr. 1965. Web. 5 Oct. 2014.

176 When a state grand jury hands down indictments: Graham, Fred. "Liuzzo Witness an F.B.I. Informer." *New York Times* 21 Apr. 1965. Web. 5 Oct. 2014.

177 "Well, God bless you, boys": May, *op. cit.,* 200.

177 Wilkins' attorney Matt Murphy: Reed, Roy. "Liuzzo Case Jury Retires for Night." *New York Times* 7 May 1965. Web. 5 Oct. 2014.

177 Murphy's sixty-seven-minute closing argument: *Ibid.*

178 "snuggling up pretty close": May, *op. cit.,* 168.

178 "The press was starting to ask": *Ibid.,* 146.

178 "What sorely troubles me": "Was FBI Man an Accessory to Murder of Mrs. Liuzzo?" *El Paso Herald-Post* 14 May 1965. Web. 5 Oct. 2014.

178 "But, gentleman, she was here": Reed, "Liuzzo Case Jury Retires for Night", *op. cit.*

179 A mistrial is declared: Reed, Roy. "A Mistrial in Liuzzo Case." *New York Times* 8 May 1965. Web. 5 Oct. 2014.

Chapter Nine: "He Had to Die for Something . . ."

180 Cager Lee reflected on his grandson's death: Chapman, William, and Thomas R. Kendrick. "3000 Start Alabama March Along U.S.-Guarded Route." *Washington Post* 22 Mar. 1965. Web. 10 Nov. 2013.

181 "triumphant evidence of this nation's resolve": Kenworthy, E. W. "Senate Approves Voting Right Bill in 77-to-19 Ballot." *New York Times* 27 May 1965. Web. 4 Nov. 2013.

181 the House version bans state and local poll taxes: *Ibid.*

181 Dr. King announces the creation of SCOPE: "Dr. Martin Luther King Jr. Commemorated." *UCLA Newsroom* 19 May 2011. Web. 1 Oct. 2014.

182 As with the Freedom Summer, the work is dangerous: *Civil Rights Movement Veterans, op. cit.*

182 "We were part of a history-making enterprise": *Ibid.*

182   the Lowndes registrar eliminates the literacy test and extends office hours: *Ibid.*

183   When released six days later, Coleman aims his shotgun: "Jonathan Myrick Daniels, Seminarian." *Biographical Sketches of Memorable Christians of the Past.* Web. 1 Nov. 2014.

183   The judge shows no sympathy: Thomas, Robert McG. Jr. "Thomas Coleman, 86, Dies; Killed Rights Worker in '65." *New York Times* 22 Jun. 1997. Web. 17 Sept. 2014.

184   The final bill is similar to: Kenworthy, E. W. "Voting Measure Passed By House." *New York Times* 4 Aug. 1965. Web. 4. Nov. 2013.

184   Liberals did not like the compromise, but agreed to it: *Ibid.*

185   "Why are we going up to the halls of Congress", "We're going up", "Some who are here": Smith, Evan. "Luci Baines Johnson on Her Father's Legacy." *Texas Monthly* Aug. 2008. Web. 1 Nov. 2014.

185   "is a triumph for freedom": Kilpatrick, Caroll. "Vote Rights Bill Signed in Ceremony at Capitol." *Washington Post* 7 Aug. 1965. Web. 4 Nov. 1965.

185   Johnson also issues several challenges: *Ibid.*

186   "I didn't have to convince": Johnson, Luci Baines. "Lessons from My Father, LBJ." *CNN Opinion* 8 Apr. 2014. Web. 15 Sept. 2014.

186   "eloquent and persuasive", "all the obstacles to the right to vote", "celebrating another step in the disintegration": Kilpatrick, Caroll. "Vote Rights Bill Signed in Ceremony at Capitol." *Washington Post* 7 Aug. 1965. Web. 4 Nov. 1965.

186   The federal government wastes no time: *Ibid.*

187   the government sends examiners to nine counties: Mintz, Morton. "Vote Examiners Sent to 9 Counties." *Washington Post* 10 Aug. 1965. Web. 10 Nov. 2013.

187   "I think a good many politicians in the south will rethink some of their positions": *Ibid.*

187   Cager Lee returns: Branch, *Pillar of Fire, op. cit.,* 124.

187   Jack Nelson speculates: Nelson, Jack. "Political Shakeup Seen in South." *Washington Post* 8 Aug. 1965. Web. 20 Oct. 2013.

187   the number of blacks who register increases, but intimidation remains: *Civil Rights Movement Veterans, op. cit.*

188   By March 1966, there are more than 235,000 black voters: *Ibid.*

189   Democrats slate about seventy-five black candidates: Freeman, Jo. "The 1966 Macon County Alabama Campaign." Web. 10 Dec. 2013.

189   emboldens SNCC and the Lowndes County Freedom Organization: "Lowndes County Freedom Organization." *Encyclopedia of*

Alabama. Alabama Humanities Foundation, Auburn University, The University of Alabama, and Alabama State Department of Education. Web. 20 Nov. 2014.

189 Prospects for success appear good: "Lowndes County Negroes Work to Take Over County." *The Movement.* June 1966. Web. 7 Dec. 2013.

189 "fighting for life or death": "Lowndes County Freedom Organization", *op. cit.*

189 "That's okay, baby": "Lowndes County Negroes Work to Take Over County", *op. cit.*

189 "not to start any trouble": *Ibid.*

190 "have no illusion that whites will turn over their power peacefully": *Ibid.*

190 Lucius Amerson wins the Democratic nomination for sheriff: Freeman, "The 1966 Macon County Alabama Campaign", *op. cit.*

190 Before the VRA, fewer than 1,000 blacks were registered: Konieczko, Jill. "Alabama Primary Facts and Figures." Web. 10 Dec. 2013.

190 When Clark runs as an independent: Thornton, *op. cit., 498.*

190–91 tries to exclude primary votes cast in black precincts: *Ibid.*

191 "The choice of Mrs. George Wallace": "Lowndes County Negroes Work to Take Over County", *op. cit.*

191 because white landowners threatened their black sharecroppers: "Lowndes County Freedom Organization", *op. cit.*

191 "The new Southern Negro vote will have a marked effect": Wicker, Tom. "Negroes and Conservatives in the New South." *New York Times* 7 Aug. 1966. Web. 3 Oct. 2013.

191 In the twelve months following passage of the VRA: "New Law Spurs Negro Vote Rolls." *New York Times* 5 Aug. 1966. Web. 10 Oct. 2013.

191 "We are firmly convinced": *Ibid.*

192 "eyes of the black community", "It made everybody have respect": Ruane, Michael E. "Sheriff Made History Simply by Doing His Job." *Washington Post* 14 Aug. 2008. Web. 10 Dec. 2013.

Chapter Ten: "A Most Unusual Occurrence . . ."

193 "If it should appear from the evidence": Bickford, *op. cit.*

194 "I have a very weak case": Graham, Fred P. "Prosecutor for Reeb Trial Says Case in Selma Slaying is Weak." *New York Times* 28 Oct. 1965. Web. 15 Dec. 2013.

194   "We have a man that had been in an asylum": *Ibid.*

195   "If I hadn't indicted them, what would you newspaper people have said?": *Ibid.*

195   deputized hundreds of citizens: Thornton, *op. cit.,* 411.

195   "We must meet force with force": Thornton, J. Mills, III. *Dividing Lines: Municipal Politics and the Struggle for Civil Rights in Montgomery, Birmingham, and Selma.* Tuscaloosa, AL: University of Alabama Press, 2002. 411. Print.

195   "any intention of forcefully and aggressively prosecuting the case": Helman, *op. cit.*

195   "Selma is getting ready for Christmas": Jones, Walter Royal Jr. "Justice in an Alienated Community." *Department of Social Responsibility, Unitarian Universalist Association.* Print.

196   "violating the code of Southern hospitality": Olsen, Clark. Personal Interview. 11 Oct. 2013.

197   "Many self-anointed saints": Stanton, *op. cit.,* 48.

197   "a straight shooter": McGrath, Edward G. "Reeb jury selection to begin in Selma." *Boston Globe* 7 Dec. 1965. Web. 9 Sept. 2013.

197   "It took me some time to figure out who the judge was": Bickford, *op. cit.*

198   The lack of formality: McGrath, Edward G. "Defendant Linked to Attack on Rev. Reeb." *Boston Globe* 8 Dec. 1965. 9 Sept. 2013.

198   a section separate from their white counterparts: Bickford, *op. cit.*

198   Defense attorney Joe Pilcher explains, The State's list: McGrath, "Defendant Linked to Attack on Rev. Reeb", *op. cit.*

198   the judge addresses the potential jurors: *Ibid.*

198   Jones will insist: Jones, "Justice in an Alienated Community", *op. cit.*

198   "No Negro has sat as a juror": Graham, "Prosecutor for Reeb Trial Says Case in Selma Slaying is Weak", *op. cit.*

199   "conduct or activity" made him "a low person": Bickford, *op. cit.*

199   ordered the prosecution to make this inquiry: McGrath, "Defendant Linked to Attack on Rev. Reeb", *op. cit.*

199   "I am sure that experience must show": Bickford, *op. cit.*

199   "I am sick of civil rights": *Ibid.*

199   "I am prejudiced against a man", "I feel Reeb didn't belong down here": *Ibid.*

200   all-white, all-male panel: *Ibid.*

200   the prosecution will prove that the defendants "did the killing": *Ibid.* "Leading doctors from the university hospital": McGrath, "Defendant Linked to Attack on Rev. Reeb", *op. cit.*

201　"bizarre twist": *Ibid.*

201　"You are all aware", "unfriendly press", "because the basic rights", "shout about civil rights": *Ibid.*

201　Clark Olsen will be the first witness for the prosecution: Olsen, Clark. Personal Interview. 11 Oct. 2013.

201　"He didn't know he was going to be killed", "His life was sacrificed": Niebuhr, *op. cit.*

201–02　Olsen finds some solace, "That was me": Olsen, Clark. Personal Interview. 11 Oct. 2013.

202　"Four or five men", "They shouted at us": McGrath, "Defendant Linked to Attack on Rev. Reeb", *op. cit.*

202　"Miller crouched down": *Ibid.*

202　Ashworth questions Olsen: *Ibid.*

203　Olsen describes how he and Miller helped Reeb: *Ibid.*

203　Pilcher questions Olsen: *Ibid.*

204　"I respected his conscientious approach": *Ibid.*

204　The next day's proceedings seem to solidify the case against Cook: Bickford, *op. cit.*

204　Rev. Miller takes the stand: McGrath, "Defendant Linked to Attack on Rev. Reeb", *op. cit.*

204–05　"He was in the lead that night", "The other two defendants": McGrath, Edward G. "Reeb Defendants Placed Near Scene." *Boston Globe* 9 Dec. 1965. Web. 10 Sept. 2013.

205　Pilcher asks Miller: Bickford, *op. cit.*

205　"It was brought up that the injured man": *Ibid.*

206　"an attractive blonde", She remembers serving them coffee: McGrath, "Reeb Defendants Placed Near Scene", *op. cit.*

206　"part of the scuffle", "small, swarthy man", "His right hand trembled": "Selma Prosecution to Call Kelly to Witness Stand." Associated Press. *The Gadsden Times* 8 Dec. 1965. Web. 15 Sept. 2013.

206　"persons who have not the use of reason": Bickford, *op. cit.*

206　Pilcher calls witnesses: *Ibid.*

207　Dr. P. Caldwell DeBardeleben, an internist, takes the stand: *Ibid.*

207　"The State made no attempt": *Ibid.*

207　"I realize that it is a serious thing": *Ibid.*

207　The remainder of the second day: *Ibid.*

208　"seriously impaired": *Ibid.*

208　the minister died due to irreversible brain damage: *Ibid.*

208　identified two other men who witnessed the attack: McGrath, "Prosecution Loses 3 Witnesses in Reeb Case", *op. cit.*

208 Kelley, a 30-year-old Selma television repairman: Bickford, *op. cit.*

209 "at midnight last night": Waldron, Martin. "Selma Judge Bars Plea to End Trial." *New York Times* 10 Dec. 1965. Web. 15 Sept. 2013.

209 "The state has made every effort", "He is out of the jurisdiction of this court": McGrath, "Prosecution Loses 3 Witnesses in Reeb Case", *op. cit.*

209 "The state rests": *Ibid.*

209 "He would not talk to us": "Breach of Faith; Murder in Selma; A New York State of Mind." *CNN Transcripts.* 5 Mar. 2000. Web. 16 Sept. 2013.

209 "The record is completely devoid of evidence": McGrath, "Prosecution Loses 3 Witnesses in Reeb Case", *op. cit.*

210 "I'm going to leave with this jury": *Ibid.*

210 "it was to the advantage of certain civil rights movements to have a martyr": Waldron, *op. cit.*

210 The judge allows Baker: McGrath, "Prosecution Loses 3 Witnesses in Reeb Case", *op. cit.*

210 Pilcher calls five witnesses: *Ibid.*

211 "I can't see how he could have got across the street": *Ibid.*

211 Vardaman does not testify: Bickford, *op. cit.*

211 "The State should have known": *Ibid.*

211 Pilcher questions Bowden: *Ibid.*

212 Pilcher questions Foreman: *Ibid.*

212 Pilcher questions South: *Ibid.*

213 Pilcher questions Boddiford: *Ibid.*

213 Judge Moore instructs the prosecution: *Ibid.*

213–14 no one has definitively identified, "grossly negligent": McGrath, Edward G. "Reeb Acquittals Stir Ire." *Boston Globe* 11 Dec. 1965. Web. 10 Sept. 2013.

214 "knowingly and deliberately": *Ibid.*

214 "The law of the state of Alabama": *Ibid.*

214 "He also instructed", "who struck the fatal blow": *Ibid.*

214 goes into the jury room for five minutes: *Ibid.*

215 "We have": *Ibid.*

215 "He left the big question mark until last", "Evidence against the Hoggle brothers", "groaned, rose in their seats, and broke for the doors": *Ibid.*

215 "Your verdict is in form": *Ibid.*

215 "No comment", "Don't tell 'em nothing, Pa", "not surprised": *Ibid.*

216 "a most unusual occurrence", "There was no real defense": Bickford, *op. cit.*

216 "What happened in the jury room will stay in the jury room": Anonymous Interview A. 8 Dec. 2013.

216 "I wouldn't swear to it on a bible": Anonymous Interview B. 8 Dec. 2013.

216 "I feel all that should have been done": McGrath, "Reeb Acquittals Stir Ire", *op. cit.*

216 "failure or refusal", "prosecutors did not follow his orders", "sweep it under the rug": "Prosecution Hit in Reeb Trial." *United Press International. The Pittsburgh Press* 18 Dec. 1965. Web. 15 Sept. 2013.

216–17 Flowers says he is shocked by: "Flowers Charges Faulty Prosecution in Reeb Death Trial." *United Press International. New York Times* 18 Dec. 1965.

217 "there is little protection under Southern justice": Bickford, *op. cit.*

217 "Of course revenge is not what anyone seeks": *Ibid.*

Chapter Eleven: "He's Gonna Have to Go to Jail . . ."

219 "find out exactly what really happened": Cornish, Audie. "Alabama to Revisit Civil-Rights Era Killing." *National Public Radio* 10 May 2007. Web. 22 Sept. 2014.

219 "Jimmie Lee Jackson was a young guy who didn't ever think first of himself": Jackson, Michael. Personal Interview. 18 Aug. 2014.

219 "To this day, there are two big opposite views": *Ibid.*

219 "I think it helps heal the country": *Ibid.*

220 Born in 1963, the prosecutor understands that he would not be where he is: *Ibid.*

220 "I figured this Fowler guy was dead": *Ibid.*

221 "James Bonard Fowler is a man given to frankness": Fleming, "The Death of Jimmie Lee Jackson", *op. cit.*

221 Fowler tells Fleming, "where there were reports of people throwing bottles": *Ibid.*

222 "We headed up the stairs": *Ibid.*

222 "Jimmie Lee Jackson was not murdered": *Ibid.*

222–23 "rails against police", "Ms. Bessie Swear", "always fared better when they stayed in their place": *Ibid.*

223 "incited to riot": *Ibid.*

223 "No one from the DA's office": *Ibid.*

223 Fleming's ability to find and report an important story: Fleming, John. "Re: Jimmie Lee Jackson." Message to the authors. 26 Nov. 2014. Email.

223 At the same time, he joined two other crusading journalists: *Ibid.*

223 "Fowler wants his side of the story to be told": Fleming, "The Death of Jimmie Lee Jackson", *op. cit.*

224 "I had a lot of witnesses": Jackson, Michael. Personal Interview. 18 Aug. 2014.

224 The governor of Alabama offers: Johnson, Bob. "Governor posts $5,000 reward in civil rights-era shooting death." *The Gadsden Times* 29 Aug. 2006. Web. 5 Oct. 2013.

224 "You get a belief in your head": Jackson, Michael. Personal Interview. 25 Oct. 2013.

224 Then the prosecutor speaks with Vera Booker: FBI memorandum. SA Archibald L. Riley, *op. cit.*

225 "the final piece to the puzzle", "We have enough to go to a grand jury": Jackson, Michael. Personal Interview. 18 Aug. 2014.

226 "Justice was never brought about": Sanders, Hank. Personal Interview. 25 Oct. 2013.

226 He presents them with a range of evidence: Jackson, Michael. Personal Interview. 18 Aug. 2014.

226 "You don't put on your whole case for the grand jury", "Half the battle", "Fowler never denied that he shot Jimmie Lee Jackson": Jackson, Michael. Personal Interview. 18 Aug. 2014.

227 "I think somebody is trying to rewrite history": Rawls, Phillip. "Indictment in Civil Rights-Era Killing." *Washington Post* 9 May 2007. Web. 5 Oct. 2014.

227 "I think that we have to be real careful": Cornish, *op. cit.*

227 "they kept it smothered down", "it would still have been swept under the rug": "Trooper James Bonard Fowler is a Racist Murderer." *Police Crimes Forum.* 19 Dec. 2010. Web. 1 Oct. 2014.

227 "a lot of things could have been different in my life": Cornish, *op. cit.*

228 "give the wound a little more healing": "My Name is Emma Jackson." *Alabama Blogs and Bloggers.* Alabama Media Group. Web. 10 Sept. 2013.

228 "he is not a man of means": Fleming, John. "Jury returns indictment in 1965 civil-rights killing." *Anniston Star* 10 May 2007. Web. 5 Oct. 2013.

228 the trooper was fired in September of 1968: *Ibid.*

228–29 "He later worked with military prosecutors": Fleming, John. "McCain wrote on behalf of ex-trooper Fowler." *Anniston Star* 7 Oct. 2008.

229 "poor medical treatment and a mistake", "a survivable injury": Fleming, John. "Former Trooper arraigned in 1965 murder case." *Anniston Star* 11 July 2007. Web. 4 Nov. 2013.

229 "there was a botched medical procedure": *Ibid.*

230 "It's a tough defense to use": *Ibid.*

230 filed several motions before Circuit Court Judge Tommy Jones: *Ibid.*

230 "all persons presently known to the district attorney's office": Petition for Writ of Mandamus: *State of Alabama v. James Bonard Fowler.* Perry Circuit Court, CC-07-17. Special Term, 2009. *Alabama Appellate Watch.* Alabama Appellate Courts. 3. Web. 2 Nov. 2014.

231 Judge Jones issues a ruling: *Ibid.,* 4.

231 "I want the record to be very clear": *Ibid.*

231 Jackson finds the order "outrageous": Jackson, Michael. Personal Interview. 18 Aug. 2014.

232 "and he's embarrassed by it": Fleming, John."McCain wrote on behalf of ex-trooper Fowler", *op. cit.*

232 "I see George Beck has started the spinning": *Ibid.*

232 "Fowler had lived all this time", "I just felt like he needed to spend some time behind bars": Jackson, Michael. Personal Interview. 18 Aug. 2014.

232 "They were all looking to see whether I won re-election": *Ibid.*

233 "Well, he's gonna have to go to jail": *Ibid.*

233 the two lawyers begin negotiating: *Ibid.*

233 "He wants to put it behind him": "Trooper James Bonard Fowler is a Racist Murderer", *op. cit.*

233 "I was coming over here to save lives": Brown, Robbie. "45 Years Later, an Apology and 6 Months." *New York Times* 15 Nov. 2010. Web. 15 Nov. 2013.

233 "perhaps the most significant of all the civil rights cold cases", "The more important verdict": "Former state trooper, 77, pleads guilty in civil rights case." *CNN Justice* 10 Nov. 2010. Web. 1 Nov. 2013.

233 "One thing we've never experienced", "What happened today": Brown, *op. cit.*

234 "a slap in the face of the people of this county": *Ibid.*

234 "enough effort and resources into it": Sanders, Hank. Personal Interview. 7 Oct. 2014.

234 "We try not to be hateful": Lauderdale, Florence. Personal Interview. 25 Oct. 2013

234 "Time was starting to run out": Jackson, Michael. Personal Interview. 18 Aug. 2014.

235 "In a lot of these cases": "Former state trooper, 77, pleads guilty in civil rights case", *op. cit.*

235 "Fowler admitted his guilt", "We feel the family showed more mercy": *Ibid.*

235 "Obviously everybody would like to have had him serve more time", "left a bitter taste": Jackson, Michael. Personal Interview. 18 Aug. 2014.

235 "No matter what happened": *Ibid.*

235 "This is supposed to be closure": Rawls, Phillip. "James Bonard Fowler Pleads Guilty to Manslaughter in Death That Sparked Selma March." *Huffington Post* 15 Nov. 2010. Web. 5 Oct. 2013.

Chapter Twelve: "A Dagger into the Heart . . ."

236 "ridiculous, devastating" decision: Avery, Willie Nell. Personal Interview. 22 Aug. 2014.

237 "We issue no holding on Section 5 itself": Berman, Matt, and Brian Resnick, Matt Vasilogambros, and Brian Fung. "Supreme Court Shreds Key Provision of the Voting Rights Act." *National Journal* 25 Jun. 2013. Web. 11 Sept. 2013.

237 "[The decision] basically gives a green light": Mears, Bill, and Greg Botelho. " 'Outrageous' or overdue?: Court strikes down part of historic voting rights law." *CNN Politics* 26 Jun. 2013. Web. 15 Nov. 2013.

238 "I'm just not aware": McAuliff, Michael. "Voting Rights Claim by Jeff Sessions Hammered by Black Lawmakers." *Huffington Post* 25 Jun. 2013. Web. 15 Nov. 2013.

238 "The justices correctly acknowledged that the covered jurisdictions": Mears and Botelho, *op. cit.*

238 "In my judgment the Court errs egregiously", "Hubris is a fit word": Shelby County, Alabama v. Holder, Attorney General, et al. Supreme Court of the United States. United States Court of Appeals for The District of Columbia, 12–96. October Term, 2012. 30. Web. 15 Nov. 2014.

238 "a dagger into the heart", "These men never stood": Jeltsent, *Melissa*. "John Lewis on Voting Rights Act: Supreme Court 'Put a

Dagger in the Heart' of the Law." *Huffington Post* 25 Jun. 2013. Web. 11 Sept. 2014.

239 "risks denying the right to vote to hundreds of thousands": Liptak, Adam. "Supreme Court Allows Texas to Use Strict Voter ID Law in Coming Election." *New York Times* 18 Oct. 2014. Web. 10 Nov. 2014.

239 "A decrease of some 271,000 total voters": Friedman, Brad. "Texas GOP's voter ID ploy 'worked': Turnout way down, provisional ballots way up." *Salon* 13 Nov. 2014. Web. 15 Nov. 2014.

239 Voters can no longer present utility bills or Social Security cards: Brandeisky, Kara, and Hanquing and Mike Tigas. "Everything That's Happened Since Supreme Court Ruled on Voting Rights Act." *ProPublica* 4 Nov. 2014. Web. 15 Nov. 2014.

240 "The lawmakers said they had no choice": "Race, Politics and Drawing Maps: The Supreme Court Hears an Alabama Case on the Voting Rights Act." *New York Times* 13 Nov. 2014. Web. 15 Nov. 2014.

241 "The weakening of the Voting Rights Act": Ellwanger, Joseph. "Re: Supreme Court Decision and VRA." Message to the authors. 17 Nov. 2014. Email.

241 "I do believe that voting rights have been undermined": Lauderdale, Florence. Personal Interview. 4 Sept. 2014.

241 "I was crushed by the action of the Supreme Court": Baker, George. "Re: Supreme Court Decision." Message to the authors. 13 Nov. 2014. Email.

242 "Anybody on the Supreme Court knows what the Voting Rights Act did": Vivian: Vivian, Cordy Tindell. Personal Interview. 21 Aug. 2014.

242 "The Supreme Court was full of shit": Dobyne, Walter. Personal Interview. 22 Oct. 2013.

242 "Hundreds and even thousands of Americans": Olsen, Clark. "Re: Supreme Court Decision and Voting Rights." Message to the authors. 18 Nov. 2014. Email.

242 "a self-indictment of that Court": Miller, Orloff. "Re: Supreme Court Decision and VRA." Message to the authors. 11 Nov. 2014.

244 "a cloud of witnesses", "We must lay aside", "Don't let the assault": Medley, Keith Weldon. "Civil Rights Memorial in Montgomery: A New Awakening of Conscience?" *Writers Net*. Web. 1 Dec. 2013.

244 "Most of those who made the movement", "As the old Freedom Song reminds us": Bond, Julian. "Civil Rights Memorial Dedication Speech." Southern Poverty Law Center, Montgomery, AL. 5 Nov. 1989. Web. 24 Oct. 2014.

INDEX

ABC-TV, 85, 126, 141
Abernathy, Ralph, 12, 61–62, 76, 123, 147, 148,
    158–59, 166
activism
    calls for modern-day, 244
    See also specific person, organization, or protest
Alabama
    blacks election to legislature of, 192
    constitutional convention in, 5
    Democratic Party in, 188–89, 190–91, 192,
        239–40
    disenfranchising of blacks in, 5
    elections of 1966 in, 188
    redistricting in, 239–40
    return to normalcy for, 171
    voter registration in, 4–7, 188, 239–40
    Wallace (Lurleen) election as governor of, 191
Alabama Court of Criminal Appeals, 231–32
Alabama Department of Public Safety, 223
Alabama Project, 10, 11
Alabama State College
    petition of students from, 154
    sit-ins at, 195
Alabama State Supreme Court, 232
All Souls Church (Washington, D.C.), 89, 90,
    93–94, 95–96, 154–55
Allen, Thomas, 208
ambulance ride, Reeb's, 116–17, 118–20, 203,
    205, 207–8, 212–13, 214
American Baptist Theological Seminary, 10,
    21, 59
American Friends Service Committee (AFSC),
    16, 87, 95, 99
American Nazi Party, 217*n*
American Revolution, 62
Amerson, Anthony, 192
Amerson, Lucius, 190, 192
Anderson, L.L., 61
Andrews, R.C., 36–37, 40
Anglin, Robert J., 149
Anniston, Alabama
    Brewster murder in, 194
    Freedom Riders in, 194

Anti-Defamation League of B'nai Brith,
    167*n*
Argires, James, 208
Arizona State University: voter fraud study at,
    239
Arlington Street Church (Boston): Reeb funeral
    at, 155–56
Army, U.S.: and March to Montgomery, 158,
    161, 168, 169
Ashworth, Virgis: and trial of Reeb assailants,
    200–204, 208–15
Associated Press (AP), 123, 135, 161*n*, 206
Atlanta, Georgia: King in, 75
Attucks, Crispus, 62
Avery, James, 2, 3–4, 7, 82
Avery, Willie Nell
    Bloody Sunday and, 81–82
    and children's protest, 14
    Foster's description by, 57
    and non-violence strategy, 23
    and plans and preparations for March to
        Montgomery, 78
    and Voting Rights Act, 236
    voting rights movement and, 1, 2–4, 5–6,
        7, 17, 27
    and women's contributions to civil rights
        movement, 101
Ayers, Brandt "Brandy," 223

Baez, Joan, 167, 170
Baker, Ella, 11, 101
Baker, George
    arrest of, 26–27, 60
    background of, 16
    and Bloody Sunday, 82–83, 100
    commitment of, 159
    and Freedom Day in Selma, 60
    and Jimmie Lee's death/funerals, 59, 62
    joins SNCC, 16
    and March to Montgomery, 159, 160, 161,
        162, 164, 166, 167–68, 169, 173
    and plans and preparations for March to
        Montgomery, 59, 60, 74, 76

Baker, George (*cont.*)
  and Selma white power structure–civil rights
    leaders meeting, 53, 54
  and voting rights movement, 16–17, 18–19,
    24, 26–27, 53, 58, 241
Baker, Wilson
  and attack on ministers, 121, 149
  and attempts at civil rights marches in Selma,
    154
  beginning of March to Montgomery and, 79
  Bloody Sunday and, 80, 83
  and Brown Chapel–Dallas County
    Courthouse march, 123, 131, 146, 148–49
  Clark and, 73, 74, 190, 191
  and Clark's election defeat, 190, 191
  and CWCA protest march, 65, 72, 73
  King and, 73–74
  media and, 74
  and plans and preparations for March to
    Montgomery, 75
  Reeb's death and, 132
  and Selma prayer vigil, 123, 131
  songs about, 133
  trial of Reeb assailants and, 206–7, 210
Bamboo Club (Selma), 212
Bearing the Cross (Garrow), 76
Beck, George, 227, 228, 229, 230–32, 233
Belafonte, Harry, 167, 170–71
Bell, James, 42
Bennett, Tony, 167
Benson, Leeandrew, 44
Bernstein, Leonard, 167
Bevel, James
  and Alabama Project, 10
  background of, 11, 21
  and Birmingham Children's Crusade, 11, 12
  at Brown AME Chapel, 56
  and CWCA demonstration, 74
  and Jimmie Lee's death, 56
  Nash's marriage to, 11
  and plans and preparations for March to
    Montgomery, 56, 57, 63, 74, 75, 76, 78
  and voting rights movement, 10, 12, 240
  at Zion United Church, 58
Bibb, Leon, 170
Bickford, Daniel, 195, 197–98, 199, 205, 211,
  214, 216
Billingsley, Cordelia Heard, 51, 218, 219, 227,
  235
Birmingham, Alabama
  attack on King in, 217*n*
  black churches in, 135, 158
  Children's Crusade in, 11, 12, 13
  16th Street Baptist Church in, 10, 61, 70–72,
    172, 201, 210, 227, 234
  time bombs in, 158
  voter registration in, 188

Birmingham Council on Human Relations
  (BCHR), 64, 69
Birmingham News, 123
black churches, 67, 135, 158. *See also specific
  clergyman or church*
Black Panther Party, 165, 189–90, 191
Blackmon, Ulysses, 10
blacks
  disengagement and marginalization of,
    242–43
  IQ of Selma, 197
  as jurors, 183–84, 198
  as political force in South, 236
  See also specific person or topic
Blair, Joe Neal, 67
blame/finger-pointing
  of Fowler, 223
  for Jimmie Lee shooting, 45–47, 55–56, 62
  by *Montgomery Advertiser,* 142–43
  for Reeb murder, 148
  of Wallace, 142
Bloody Sunday
  and Alabama's return to normalcy, 171
  and Confederate flag, 100
  congressional reactions to, 103
  at Edmund Pettus Bridge, 79–86
  FBI investigation of, 128
  King's comments about, 133, 171
  and King's memorial service at Edmund
    Pettus Bridge, 109–10
  Lingo's testimony about, 140–41
  media and, 83–84, 85, 99, 103–4
  medical staff for, 75, 100
  and Selma prayer vigil, 133–34
  troopers at, 80, 81, 82, 85, 100, 105, 110,
    120, 141
  Wallace and, 86, 100, 105
  See also specific person
Boddiford, Paul, 213
Bogalusa, Louisiana, 49, 49*n*
Bolden, Willie, 16, 17, 19, 25, 26, 31, 175, 182
Bolton, Willie. *See* Bolden, William
Bond, Julian, 244
Booker, Vera, 44–45, 224–25, 227, 229
Boston Action Group, 96
Boston Globe, 130, 143, 144, 149, 201, 202–3
Boston, Massachusetts
  demonstrations in remembrance of Reeb in,
    143–44
  reactions to Reeb shooting in, 130, 135
  Reeb funeral service in, 131, 155–56
  Reeb's activities in, 87–89, 95, 96–99, 110
Bowden, Frances, 122, 211–12
Boynton, Amelia, 9–10, 12, 16, 57, 60, 79, 82,
  101, 160, 170
Boynton, Samuel, 9
Brand, Oscar, 170

Breland Saw Mill, 34*n*

Brewster, Willie Jr., 194

"Broadway Answers Selma" (benefit revue), 167*n*

Brown AME Chapel (Selma)
  and beginning of March to Montgomery, 79, 159–60
  Bloody Sunday and, 82, 85
  Jimmie Lee's funeral at, 60–61
  King at, 54, 105, 112, 115, 120, 202
  and King's Edmund Pettus Bridge compromise, 106–7, 134
  Malcolm X at, 52
  and Ministers March to Montgomery, 107
  and permission for March to Montgomery, 157
  and plans and preparations for March to Montgomery, 75, 76, 78, 102, 105
  rally at, 132
  Reeb memorial service at, 146, 147–49
  and return from King's memorial at Edmund Pettus Bridge, 109–10
  Selma police at, 115
  See also specific person

Brown Chapel–Dallas Courthouse march, 123, 131–33, 145–46

Brown, H. Rap, 137

Brown, Jerry, 34, 34*n*

Brown, Michael: shooting of, 226–27*n*

Brown v. Board of Education, 11

Bryant, Richard, 13

Buchanan, Charles, 213

Bunche, Ralph, 160

Burwell Infirmary (Selma), 45, 49, 115, 203, 207

Carmichael, Stokely, 86, 164–65, 182, 189

Catholics, 67–68, 144. *See also specific person or church*

Cavanaugh, Jerome, 109

CBS-TV, 85, 141, 171

Chandler, Len, 170

Chaney, James, 48, 118, 172

Chicago Freedom Movement, 143

Children's Crusade, Birmingham, 11, 12, 13

children's protests, 2, 12–14, 15–16, 17

China: reactions to Bloody Sunday in, 103–4

churches
  and civil rights movement, 18
  race relations and, 66–68
  and voting rights movement, 58–59
  See also black churches; clergy; *specific church*

Citizens Council of Louisiana Inc., 164

Civil Rights Act (1964), 11, 106, 125, 153

Civil Rights Cold Case Project, 223

Civil Rights Memorial (Montgomery, Alabama), 243–44

civil rights movement
  and churches, 18
  communism and, 47
  and LBJ–civil rights leaders White House meeting, 136–37, 138
  and LBJ legislation, 149–52
  media's relationship with, 29
  role of federal government in, 108
  strategy of, 20–21, 108
  voting rights campaign as central to, 243
  Wallace meeting with leaders of, 176
  women's contributions to, 101
  See also Voting Rights Act; voting rights campaign; voting rights legislation

Civil War, 9, 93, 186

Clark, James "Jim"
  and attack on ministers, 149
  and attempts at civil rights marches in Selma, 154
  Baker (Wilson) and, 73, 74, 190, 191
  and ban on marches, 125, 133, 145–46
  Bloody Sunday and, 80, 83, 86
  and Brown Chapel–Dallas County Courthouse march, 145–46, 149
  calls for removal of, 53
  conviction of, 240
  Cooper's punching of, 196
  and CWCA Selma protest march, 68, 73
  and Fowler–Jimmie Lee murder trial, 230
  freedom songs and, 84
  Harris compared with, 32
  and Johnson's permission for March to Montgomery, 157
  and King's Edmund Pettus Bridge compromise, 106–7
  March to Montgomery and, 158, 160
  and Marion civil rights movement, 30
  McLeod and, 194
  and memorial service at Edmund Petrus Bridge, 134
  and plans and preparations for March to Montgomery, 75
  Selma protest activities and, 73
  and strategy of civil rights activists, 108
  and trial of Reeb assailants, 214, 215
  Vivian and, 16, 19–22, 30, 196
  and voter rights/registration, 196, 240
  white support for, 53–54
  Williams' testimony about, 134

Clark, Joseph S. Jr., 103

clergy
  attack on, 112–16, 120–22, 123, 126–27, 132–33, 142, 149, 202
  civil rights leaders' briefing of, 138–39
  criticism of LBJ by, 139
  criticisms of, 142
  protests and demonstrations led by, 145
  and race relations, 66–72
  at Walker's Café, 110–11
  Washington meeting of, 138–39

clergy (*cont.*)
   See also Ministers March to Montgomery;
      specific person
Cloud, John, 80, 109, 140–41
Clougherty, John E., 98
CNN, 209
Cochran, Don, 235
Coffee Pot Café (Selma), 211
Cohen, Richard, 233
Coleman, Tom, 183–84
Collins, Addie Mae, 172
Collins, Donald E., 67
Collins, John F., 155
Collins, LeRoy, 106, 107, 148
communism, 47, 103–4, 164, 175
Concerned White Citizens of Alabama
   (CWCA): march of, 64–65, 66,
      68–69, 72–73, 74–75, 146–47, 196
Confederate flag: and Bloody Sunday, 100
Congress of Racial Equality (CORE), 97, 129,
   167*n*
Congress, U.S.
   LBJ address to, 149–52
   reactions to Bloody Sunday in, 103
   SCLC strategy and, 59
   See also specific legislation
Connor, Eugene "Bull," 11, 19–20, 133
Cook, Elmer
   charges against, 122–23, 132, 215–16
   and CWCA march, 146
   federal charges against, 122–23, 215–16
   indictment of, 179, 196–97
   Olsen's identification of, 125
   prosecution for Reeb murder of, 193–97, 199,
      200, 202–6, 210–16
   Rowe and, 177, 217
   Selma police arrest of, 121–22
   verdict about, 215
Cooke, Sam, 111
Cooper, Annie Lee, 20, 196
CORE. *See* Congress of Racial Equality
"Courageous Eight," 10. *See also specific person*
Crank, James, 126
Crocker, L.C., 55–56, 65
Cushing, Richard Cardinal, 144

Dallas County
   Lutherans in, 65
   voting in, 8, 12, 153, 187, 190
   See also Selma, Alabama
Dallas County Chamber of Commerce, 161*n*
Dallas County Courthouse
   Clark-Vivian incident at, 196
   CWCA march to, 72, 74, 146–47, 196
   King at, 53, 196
   march to, 123, 131–33, 145–46, 148–49
   and protest activities in Selma, 73

   Reeb vigil at, 196
   and trial of Reeb assailants, 196
   voting rights movement and, 16, 19–20,
      21–22, 196
Dallas County Democratic Executive
   Committee, 190–91
Dallas County Sheriff's Office, 119
Dallas County Voters League (DCVL), 8, 9, 10,
   68, 71. *See also specific person*
Daniels, Jonathan, 183, 241
Davies, A. Powell, 94
Davis, Mattie Campbell, 57–58
Davis, Ossie, 167
Davis, Sammy Jr., 167, 167*n*
DeBardeleben, P. Caldwell, 207
Dee, Ruby, 167
Dees, James, 172
Dees, Morris, 171–72
Democratic Party, Alabama, 4, 188–89, 190–91,
   192, 239–40
detention camps, 14–15
Dinkins, William, 45, 55, 55*n*, 115, 116, 117,
   118, 119, 207–8, 212
Dirksen, Everett, 181, 186
Doar, John, 47–48, 106, 140–41, 194
Dobyne, Walter
   Bloody Sunday and, 81, 83
   and civil rights/voting rights movement, 8,
      13, 242
   commitment of, 158–59
   Dobynes as cousin of, 17*n*
   and Jimmie Lee's shooting, 43
   and King's visit to Perry County, 8
   and March to Montgomery, 157, 158–59, 162,
      164, 169–70
   and plans and preparations for March to
      Montgomery, 78–79
Dobynes, James, 17, 17*n*, 23, 25–26, 27, 31
Dorsett, Robert, 122
Douglas, Emily Taft, 100, 100–101*n*, 107
Doyle, Earnest, 10
Dresner, Israel, 99–100, 107

Eaton, William, 174, 176–77, 194
Edmund Pettus Bridge
   Bloody Sunday at, 79–86, 87
   and compromise about March to
      Montgomery, 106–7, 109–10, 133–34
   memorial service at, 108–11, 133–34
Edwards, Billy Dowd, 208, 209
elections of 1966, 187, 188, 190–91
elections of 2014, 239
Ellender, Allen, 153
Ellington, Buford, 104
Ellis, Frank Jr., 238
Ellwanger, Joseph, 65, 66, 69–72, 136, 146–47,
   170, 176, 196, 241

Ellwanger, Joyce, 69
Engel, Ron, 94–95
Episcopal Society for Cultural and Racial
  Unity, 164
Evans, Ned Jr., 34*n*
Evers, Medgar, 48, 61, 172, 234
Eyes on the Prize (documentary), 55*n*, 73, 99,
  161, 229

Face the Nation (CBS-TV), 141
Fager, Chuck, 59, 73–74
Farmer, James, 52, 108, 175
Fathers of St. Edmund, 44, 67
Fauntroy, Walter, 136
FBI (Federal Bureau of Investigation)
  and attack on Reeb/ministers, 120–21, 122,
    125, 128, 204
  Bloody Sunday and, 128
  and foreign media comments about Selma
    events, 104
  and Jimmie Lee at Good Samaritan Hospital,
    39–40, 55
  Jimmie Lee interview by, 39–40
  and Jimmie Lee's background, 50
  and Jimmie Lee's shooting, 39–40, 50, 55,
    128, 219, 221, 224, 229
  Liuzzo murder and, 174, 175, 176–77, 178
  and Mack's Café events, 38, 39–41, 43, 44,
    47, 48, 50
  and Marion protest movement, 15, 16, 17, 18,
    25, 27, 28, 31, 32, 34, 128
  McLeod and, 195
  Rowe as informant for, 174, 176–77
  See also specific person
federal troops: and March to Montgomery, 103,
  138, 158, 161, 168, 169
Ferguson, Missouri: Brown shooting in,
  226–27*n*
Fifteenth Amendment, 4
Fifth Amendment, 209
First Methodist Church (Marion), 67
Fisher, Pete, 28
Fisk University, 10
Fitzgerald, Ella, 167
Fleming, John, 221–24, 226, 228–29, 233–34
Flowers, Johnny, 159, 162, 163
Flowers, Richmond, 145, 179, 183, 191, 199,
  216–17
Ford, Sandy, 81
Foreman, Lewis, 212
Forman, James "Jim," 52, 77, 86, 108, 153,
  185
Forrest, Nathan Bedford, 9
Foster, Lucy, 57, 64, 101, 240
Foster, Marie, 10, 79, 101
Foulkes, Robert, 91, 130
Fourteenth Amendment, 4

Fowler, James Bonard
  apology for shooting Jimmie Lee by, 233, 235
  decision not to indict and prosecute, 217
  finger-pointing by, 223
  Fleming interview with, 221–24, 226
  indictment and arraignment of, 220, 226–27,
    226*n*, 228, 230
  and Jackson's investigation of Jimmie Lee's
    murder, 219, 220
  and Jimmie Lee's shooting, 35, 36, 37–38, 40
  and Jimmie Lee's statement about shooting,
    224–25, 226, 229
  at Mack's Café, 35, 36, 37–38, 40
  personal and professional background of, 223,
    228–29
  plea agreement with, 232, 233–34, 235
  pre-trial actions concerning, 230–32
  statements about Jimmie Lee's shooting by,
    35, 37–38, 221–24
  surrender of, 228
Freedman's Relief Union, 93
Freedom Day, in Selma, 53, 59–60
Freedom Rides, 9, 59, 86, 100, 171, 194
freedom songs, 13, 18, 23, 84, 160, 244
Freedom Summer, 61, 182
Friedman, Brad, 239
Frye, Robert, 48
Fuller, Millard, 172

Gamble, Arthur, 178
Gandhi, Mahatma, 10, 78
Garrow, David, 76
George Washington Carver Homes (Selma
  housing project), 151
Gielgud, John, 167*n*
Gildersleeve, James E., 10
Gingras, George, 100
Ginsburg, Ruth Bader, 238
Golson, Billy, 130
Good Samaritan Hospital (Selma)
  FBI–Jimmie Lee interview at, 39–40
  founding of, 44, 67–68
  Jimmie Lee at, 39–40, 41, 43–45, 48, 50, 54,
    55, 224–25
  Jimmie Lee's death at, 55–56
  Lewis (John) at, 84
  Sisters of St. Joseph staff at, 44
Goodman, Andrew, 48, 118, 172
Goodson, W. Kenneth, 160–61, 161*n*
Graham, Stanley, 208
Gray, Fred, 192
Great Society, 11
Greeley, Dana McLean, 146, 148, 149, 154, 217
Greenberg, Jack, 134
Gregory, Dick, 167
Grooms, Floyd, 213
Gustafson, Bob, 88

Hall family, 162
Hall, Peter, 146–47
Hamer, Fannie Lou, 101–2, 240
Hamm, George, 210–11
Hammond Street Fire (Roxbury, Massachusetts), 97–99, 110
Hampton, Henry, 99
Hare, James J., 10, 33, 73, 196–97
Harris, T.O., 17, 25, 26, 31–34, 80, 230
Heard, Addie, 51
Herbers, John, 32, 49–50
Heschel, Abraham, 160
Higginbotham, Frank E., 36, 41, 43
Higgs, William, 137, 138
Highlander Folk School, 59, 164
Hill, Lister, 104
Hillman, Herbert, 88
Hoggle, Namon O'Neal "Duck"
    charges against, 122–23, 132, 215–16
    federal charges against, 122–23, 215–16
    indictment of, 179, 196–97
    prosecution of, 193, 199, 200, 204, 205, 206, 209–10, 211–12, 214
    Selma police arrest of, 122
    verdict about, 215
Hoggle, William "Stanley"
    charges against, 122, 132, 215–16
    FBI arrest of, 122–23
    federal charges against, 122–23, 215–16
    indictment of, 179, 196–97
    prosecution of, 193, 199–200, 204, 205, 206, 209–10, 212, 214
    Selma police arrest of, 122
    verdict about, 215
Homrighausen, Edgar, 66
Hoots, B.J., 35–36
Hoover, J. Edgar, 47, 48, 120, 174–75, 178
Horton, Myles, 59
House Un-American Activities Committee, 142
Howlett, Duncan, 90, 92, 93, 94, 96, 107, 125–26, 128, 130, 136, 137, 154–55
Hulett, John, 189–90, 192
Humphrey, Hubert, 131, 136, 138, 154, 175, 186
Hunter, J.D., 10

"I Am the Law" (*Montgomery Advertiser* editorial), 142–43
"I Have a Dream" speech, King's, 94
Iakovos, Archbishop, 148, 149
Ian & Sylvia, 59
Ickes, Jane Dahlman, 100, 101*n*

Jack, Homer, 115–16, 117, 133
Jackson, Albert, 28
Jackson, Cordelia (daughter). See Billingsley, Cordelia Heard

Jackson, Emma Jean (sister), 17, 38, 40, 51, 56, 218, 219, 228
Jackson, Jimmie Lee. See Jimmie Lee Jackson
Jackson (Jimmie Lee) family, financial contributions to, 167*n*
Jackson, Mahalia, 167
Jackson, Michael (district attorney)
    and cause of Jimmie Lee's death, 229–30
    elections as district attorney of, 220, 232–33
    and FBI files of Jimmie Lee's shooting, 219, 229
    and Fowler's indictment, 226–27
    Fowler's plea agreement and, 232, 233–34, 235
    and goals for Jimmie Lee murder case, 235
    investigation of Jimmie Lee's murder by, 218–20, 224–26
    personal and professional background of, 220–21
    and pre-trial actions, 230–32
    and witnesses in Fowler–Jimmie Lee murder trial, 230–32
Jackson, Viola (mother), 17, 38, 39, 40, 49, 51, 56, 61, 218, 224
Jackson, Mississippi: Evers assassination in, 48
Jimmie Lee Jackson
    and Alabama's return to normalcy, 171
    autopsy on, 55, 229–30
    background of, 50–51, 243
    blame for shooting of, 45–47, 55–56, 62
    cause of death of, 229–30
    commitment of, 219, 243
    death of, 55–56, 55*n*
    as dying for something, 180
    FBI and, 39–40, 50, 55, 128, 219, 221, 224, 229
    funerals for, 57, 58, 60–62
    in Good Samaritan Hospital, 39–40, 41, 43–45, 48, 50, 54, 55, 224–25
    headstone for, 62
    ignorance about shooting of, 138*n*
    impact of death of, 137–38, 138*n*, 180, 228
    Justice Department's report about, 47–48
    King's eulogy/comments about, 62, 148, 152, 171
    King's visit with, 54
    and LBJ, 150, 152
    and LBJ–civil rights leaders White House meeting, 137
    Lee's (Cager) comments about, 180
    and March to Montgomery, 57–58, 63, 76, 220, 228, 233
    as martyr, 201
    at Perry County Hospital, 43, 44
    Reeb compared with, 243–44
    and Selma prayer vigil, 132
    shooting of, 35–41, 42–43, 47–48, 119, 128, 141

songs about, 133
statement about shooting by, 45, 224–25, 226, 229
and voting rights movement, 17, 18, 51, 241
warrant for, 41
white perspectives about, 219
Jimmie Lee Jackson—investigation and trial for shooting of
and decision not to prosecute Fowler, 217
and Fowler's apology, 233
and Fowler's indictment, 226–27, 226n, 228
and Fowler's plea agreement, 233–34
and Fowler's statements about shooting, 35, 37–38, 221–24
and Fowler's surrender, 228
Jackson's (Michael) goals for, 235
Jackson's (Michael) investigation of, 218–20, 224–26
and pre-trial actions, 230–32
reward for conviction in Jimmie Lee's case, 224
and witnesses to shooting, 230–32
Johnson, Elbert, 31
Johnson, Frank M. Jr.
and ban on marches, 102, 105–6, 107, 109, 125, 133–34, 139, 140–41, 146–47
and Liuzzo murder convictions, 194
and permission for March to Montgomery, 157–58, 159
Johnson, J.T., 62
Johnson, Lady Bird, 129, 131
Johnson, Luci Baines, 137, 185, 186
Johnson, Lynda Bird, 137
Johnson, Lyndon "LBJ"
Amerson's meeting with, 190
and ban on marches, 124–25
civil rights leaders White House meeting with, 136–37, 138
and civil rights legislation, 149–52
criticisms of, 139, 145
Ellington's conversation with, 104
Great Society of, 11
and Jimmie Lee's death, 137, 150, 152
King and, 12, 19, 103, 147–48, 152
and King's memorial service at Edmund Pettus Bridge, 109
Ku Klux Klan comments of, 175
Lewis's comments about, 84
and Liuzzo murder, 174–75, 178
and March to Montgomery, 103, 106–7, 109, 165
nationalization of Alabama National Guard by, 158
and Reeb's death, 128–29, 131, 135, 136, 137, 150, 152
and SNCC-CORE sit-in at White House, 129
songs about, 133

"two little girls" comment of, 137
and voting rights legislation, 11–12, 19, 21, 103, 106, 136, 138, 140, 147–53, 175, 181, 185–86, 240
Wallace and, 104–5, 139–40, 141–42
"We Shall Overcome" speech of, 149–53
Jones, Tommy: as judge in Fowler–Jimmie Lee murder trial, 230, 231–32, 233
Jones, Walter Roy Jr., 195–96, 198
jury/jurors
blacks as, 183–84, 198
and Fowler's indictment, 226–27, 226n
grand, 225, 226–27, 226–27n
and Jimmie Lee shooting, 225, 226–27, 226–27n
for trial of Reeb assailants, 193–94, 198, 199–200, 211, 214–15, 216, 217, 217n
and voter registration efforts, 183–84
See also specific trial
Justice Department, U.S.
and ban on marches, 106, 124–25
and Black Panther Party, 189
investigations by, 47–48, 128–29
and Jimmie Lee's murder, 47–48, 223
and March to Montgomery, 106
McLeod and, 195
and PCCL lawsuit, 7
and Reeb shooting, 122–23
and trial of Reeb assailants, 215
voting rights and, 7, 185, 186, 187, 237, 238
Wallace comments about, 142
See also specific person

Katzenbach, Nicholas, 47, 48, 103, 128–30, 136, 181, 185, 187, 188, 223
Kelley, R.B., 122, 197, 208–9, 215–16
Kennedy, Edward, 154
King, Coretta Scott, 47, 52–53, 166
King, Martin Luther Jr.
in Atlanta, 75
and attack on ministers, 116, 120, 125, 202
attacks on, 72, 142, 217n
awards for, 165
Baker (Wilson) and, 73–74
Baker's (George) comments about, 16
and ban on marches, 54, 102–3, 105–6, 107, 124–25, 133–34, 140
in Birmingham, 217n
Bloody Sunday and, 86, 108–9, 133, 171
Bolden's meeting with, 19
Boynton and, 10
at Brown Chapel, 54, 105, 112, 115, 120, 202
and Brown Chapel–Dallas County Courthouse march, 148, 149
and Chicago, 143
at Dallas County Courthouse, 53, 196
documentary about, 202

King, Martin Luther Jr. (*cont.*)
Fowler as blaming, 223
Hoover and, 47, 120
"I Have a Dream" speech of, 47, 94
influence on Dobyne of, 158–59
in jail, 12, 52, 66
and Jimmie Lee's death, 46–47, 148, 152, 171
Jimmie Lee's eulogy by, 62, 148
Jimmie Lee's visit with, 54
Katzenbach wire of, 47
Lawson and, 10
LBJ and, 12, 19, 103, 147–48, 152
"Letter from a Birmingham Jail" of, 66
and Liuzzo murder, 175
and Mack's Café shooting, 47
and Malcolm X's death, 52
in Marion, 8, 54
media and, 152
and Miller (Orloff), 149
in Montgomery, 133, 149
Montgomery Advertiser views about, 46–47
Nash and, 10
non-violence commitment of, 66, 171
"Our God is Marching On" speech of, 171
in Perry County, 8
and poll taxes, 184
and Reeb eulogy/memorial service, 146, 147, 148
and Reeb prayers, 121
and Reeb's death, 133, 152, 171
and SCLC strategy, 77
SCOPE and, 181, 182
security for, 168
and segregation in North, 143
in Selma, 12, 15, 54, 60, 72, 73, 146
Selma comments by, 154
and Selma voting rights movement, 16
Smitherman meeting with, 54
songs about, 133
Sparkman's comments about, 153
theological background of, 66
threats against, 75, 161, 168
and trial of Reeb assailants, 210
trooper comments of, 54
UCLA speech of, 181
and voter registration efforts, 181, 182
and Voting Rights Act, 184, 185, 186
and voting rights legislation, 11–12, 19, 147–48, 152–53, 171, 240
Wallace and, 54, 142, 169
Williams' relationship with, 77
Young as personal physician for, 166
at Zion United Methodist Church, 54
King, Martin Luther Jr.—and March to Montgomery
and beginning of March to Montgomery, 159–60

call for Minister's March to Montgomery, 86, 87, 88–90, 99–100
and compromise about March to Montgomery, 106–7, 109–10, 133–34
and Foster's proposal for Walk to Montgomery, 57
King as participant in, 162, 164, 165, 166, 168, 169
King's address for, 171, 172–73
as leader of March to Montgomery, 63
and plans and preparations for March to Montgomery, 54, 57, 75, 76
and postponement of March to Montgomery, 102–3, 105–6, 107
King, Rodney, 222
kiss, interracial, Travers-Belafonte, 170–71
Klibanoff, Hank, 223
Know Alabama textbook, 46
Knox, John B., 5
Krick, Gerald, 111, 144
Ku Klux Klan
Baker (Wilson) as member of, 73
in Birmingham, 69, 70–71
in Bogalusa, Louisiana, 49n
Clark's recruitment of members of, 20
founding of, 9
Freedom Riders and, 171
LBJ comments about, 175
and Reeb ambulance incident, 118
Rowe as betrayer of, 177–78
in Selma, 9, 113
Silver Moon Café as hangout for, 113
textbook comments about, 46
and trial of Reeb assailants, 209, 217n
and voter registration effort, 182–83
See also specific person
Kwame Ture. *See* Carmichael, Stokely

Lackeos, Peter, 207
Lafayette, Bernard, 9, 10, 12, 16, 56, 58–59, 75
Lafayette, Colia, 9
Larson, Ouida, 206
Lauderdale, Florence, 50, 51, 234, 241
Lawson, James, 10, 11, 14, 21, 22, 59
Lecky, W.E.H., 155
Lee, Cager
death of, 218
and impact of Jimmie Lee's death, 180
Jimmie Lee as protector of, 51
at Jimmie Lee's funeral, 61
at Mack's Café, 34, 38, 40, 224
and March to Montgomery, 56, 159, 160
media interview of, 49–50
and voting rights movement, 17–18, 49–50, 51, 187
Lee, Hampton, 29
Leonard, Richard, 132–33, 147, 151–52

"Letter from a Birmingham Jail", King's, 66
Lewis, John
  background of, 10, 21
  and beginning of March to Montgomery, 79
  Bloody Sunday and, 79–80, 84
  at Brown Chapel, 59–60
  comments about LBJ of, 84
  and Fowler-Jimmie Lee murder trial, 228
  and Freedom Day in Selma, 59–60
  jailing of, 182
  and Liuzzo murder, 175
  at Malcolm X's funeral, 52
  and March to Montgomery, 160, 165, 170
  in Marion, 60
  and Nashville Student Movement, 10
  and plans and preparations for March to
    Montgomery, 77–78
  and Reeb's death, 132
  in Selma, 59–60, 132
  voter registration efforts of, 182
  and Voting Rights Act, 185, 238
Lewis, John C., 30–31
Lin, Maya, 243
Lincoln, Abraham, 61, 186
Lingo, Al, 48, 80, 106–7, 125, 133, 140–41,
  221
Liuzzo, Viola
  arrests and indictments of suspects in murder
    of, 174–75, 176–77
  funeral for, 175–76
  impact of murder of, 179, 180
  and March to Montgomery, 159, 169
  murder of, 173–74, 178
  trials of suspects in murder of, 177–79, 194,
    217
  and voting rights movement, 241
Loftis, William, 25, 31–32, 41, 45
Lord, John Wesley, 100, 108
Los Angeles Times, 187
Lowery, Joseph, 125, 176, 244
Lowndes County
  black candidates for office in, 189–90, 191,
    192
  Liuzzo murder and, 173–74
  and March to Montgomery, 59, 158, 159,
    162–66
  trial of Liuzzo murder suspects in, 177–79
  voter registration in, 164, 182–83, 187,
    189
Lowndes County Christian Movement for
  Human Right, 164
Lowndes County Freedom Organization
  (LCFO), 189, 192
Lum, Sister Barbara, 55, 67–68
Lutheran Church Missouri Synod (LCMS), 66
Lutherans, 64–65, 66
Lynch, John, 32

Mack's Café (Marion)
  blame for events at, 45–47, 55–56, 62
  events during, 34–41, 42–43, 221–22
  FBI investigation of, 38, 39–41, 43, 44, 47,
    48, 50
  Justice Department's report about, 47–48
  King and, 47
  media and, 49–51
  See also Jimmie Lee Jackson
Macon County: election of black candidates
  in, 190
MacPherson, James, 9
Malcolm X, 52–53, 142
Malone, Vivian, 185
Manchester Guardian, 103
Mandela, Nelson, 222–23
Mansfield, Mike, 180–81
Mants, Bob, 79
March to Montgomery
  accommodations for marchers on, 158
  ban on, 65, 75, 102, 105–6, 107, 109, 124–25,
    133–35, 139, 140–41, 146–47
  beginning of, 79, 157, 159–60
  Bevel's announcement about, 56, 57, 63
  campsites for, 159, 161
  and City of St. Jude, 166–67, 168
  compromise about, 106–7, 109–10, 134
  federal troops and, 103, 138, 158, 161, 168,
    169
  final hours/rally of, 168–73
  final night of, 167–68
  flags/banners for, 76, 160
  Jimmie Lee's death and, 76, 220, 228, 233
  King and, 54, 57, 63, 76, 105, 106–10, 162,
    164, 165, 166, 168, 169, 171, 172–73
  length of, 78
  Lowndes County and, 59, 158, 159, 162–66
  media and, 65, 78, 160, 161*n,* 169, 171
  ministers, 86, 87, 88–90, 99–100, 108–10
  and National Guard and, 158, 162, 164, 169
  and non-violence, 59, 163, 171
  number of participants in, 162, 166–67, 170
  permission for, 157–58, 159
  plans and preparations for, 54, 56, 57–58, 59,
    63, 65–66, 74–79, 138, 159
  postponement of, 102–3, 105–6
  proposal for, 57
  reason for, 57–58, 63, 78
  responsibilities of marchers on, 78
  and SCLC non-violent strategy, 59
  SCLC plans for, 159
  and security/protection of marchers, 138,
    157–58, 161, 162, 164, 168, 169
  supplies for, 159
  Uniontown participants in, 162–63
  Vaughn and Davis comments about, 57–58
  Wallace and, 63, 65, 158, 168–69

March to Montgomery (*cont.*)
  and women, 100–101, 100–101*n*
  See also Bloody Sunday; Edmund Pettus
    Bridge; *specific person*
March on Washington (1963), 47, 94
Marion, Alabama
  ban on nighttime marches in, 54
  boycott of white-owned business in, 2
  children's protests in, 2, 12–14, 15–16, 17
  churches in, 67
  detention camps in, 14–15
  Jimmie Lee's funeral in, 62
  Lewis in, 60
  nighttime protests in, 2, 54
  racial tensions in, 2
  voting rights movement in, 1–2, 5–6, 12–13,
    15–16, 20, 24–34, 51, 128
  See also Mack's Café; Perry County; Police
    Department,
    Marion; Zion United Methodist Church;
    specific person
Marion Drugs: segregation at, 13
Martin, Willie, 227
May, Gary, 105, 109, 178
McCormack, John, 103
McGrath, Edward, 202–3, 204, 215
McKinnie, Lester, 136
McLeod, Blanchard, 56, 194–95, 199, 200, 204,
    206, 209, 211
McNair, Chris, 70, 71
McNair, Denise, 70, 71, 172
media
  and attack on ministers, 120, 122, 125,
    126–28
  Baker (Wilson) and, 74
  and Bloody Sunday, 83–84, 85, 99, 103–4
  civil rights movement's relationship with, 29
  and CWCA protest march, 72
  foreign, 103–4
  and Jimmie Lee shooting, 49–51, 60, 61,
    226, 227
  and Katzenbach press conference, 129–30
  King and, 152
  and LBJ-Wallace meeting, 139
  Liuzzo murder and, 178
  March to Montgomery and, 65, 78, 160,
    161*n*, 169, 171
  and Marion voting rights movement, 25,
    28–29, 32
  and nonviolent protest strategy, 14
  Reeb shooting and, 120, 122, 126–28
  Reeb's (Marie) meeting with, 126–28
  and Rowe case, 177
  Selma voting rights movement and, 53–54
  and Travers-Belafonte kiss, 171
  and trial of Reeb assailants, 194–95, 201, 209,
    215, 216–17

Vivian-Clark confrontation and, 21–22
Wallace and, 141–42
  See also specific person or organization
Medical Committee for Human Rights
    (MCHR), 75, 100, 159, 166
Mendelsohn, Jack, 89, 95, 117, 124, 130
Meredith, James, 48
Michael Ann, Sister, 44, 55
Middlebrooks, Asbury, 146–47
Millard, Richard, 160
Miller, Orloff
  attack on, 112–16
  and Brown Chapel–Dallas Courthouse
    march, 149
  FBI interviews with, 120–21, 125
  and identification of assailants, 125
  and Jimmie Lee's shooting, 138*n*
  King and, 149
  and King's call for Ministers March to
    Montgomery, 99
  and King's prayer vigil at Edmund Pettus
    Bridge, 109
  and March to Montgomery, 170
  reaction to LBJ speech by, 151
  and Reeb as a martyr, 128
  and Reeb's injuries/death, 115, 117, 119,
    120–21, 125, 128
  and Reeb's petrified log, 156
  trial of Reeb assailants and, 194, 198, 202,
    203, 204–5, 208–12, 215, 216
  and voting rights movement, 242
  at Walker's Café, 110, 111, 144
Ministers March to Montgomery, 86, 87,
    88–90, 99–100, 108–10
Mississippi Freedom Summer, 101–2, 181
Mitchell, Chad, 167
Mitchell, Jerry, 223
Montgomery Advertiser, 46–47, 142–43
Montgomery, Alabama
  Bus Boycott in, 67
  Civil Rights Memorial in, 243–44
  demonstrations in, 154
  King in, 133, 149
  voter registration in, 188
  Wallace–civil rights leaders meeting in, 176
Montgomery Improvement Association, 201
Moore, Jeff, 39
Moore, L.S.: and trial of Reeb assailants, 197–99,
    201, 204, 206, 207, 209, 210, 213–17
Moore, William, 172–73
Morrisroe, Richard, 183
Moton, Leroy, 16, 169, 173–74, 177
Moultrie, Carl, 137
Murphy, Matt, 177–78

Nash, Diane, 10–11, 12, 102, 110, 115, 117
Nashville Student Movement, 10–11, 102

Nation of Islam, 52
National Association for the Advancement of Colored People (NAACP), 103. *See also specific person*
National Council of Churches, 139
National Guard, Alabama, 105, 158, 162, 164, 169
National Public Radio (NPR), 227
National States' Rights Party, 194
NBC-TV, 28, 43, 85
Needham, Edgar, 126
Nelson, Jack, 187
Nelson, William Stuart, 155
New Republic: Riley article in, 137–38
New York City
    criticisms of activities in, 142
    demonstrations/protests in, 144–45
New York Times—stories in
    and Alabama elections of 1966, 191
    and Alabama redistricting plan, 240
    and blacks on juries, 198
    and Bloody Sunday, 83–84
    and Jimmie Lee's funeral, 60
    and Jimmie Lee's shooting, 141
    and King's compromise, 134
    and LBJ and civil rights, 150
    and Mack's Café events, 49–50
    and Marion civil rights protest, 32
    Orange article in, 13
    and tensions in Selma, 53–54
    and trial of Reeb assailants, 194–95
    and voter registration in Selma, 15
    and voting rights legislation, 103
    See also specific journalist
News21: voter fraud study by, 239
Nichols and May, 167
1984 (Orwell), 99
non-violence
    as community movement, 13–14
    King's commitment to, 66, 171
    and March to Montgomery, 59, 163, 171
    Marion voting rights movement and, 23, 27, 48–49
    and SCLC strategy, 59
    and strategy of civil rights activists, 108
    and voting rights campaign, 23, 27, 48–49, 243
Norsworthy, Richard, 113
North: *Montgomery Advertiser* criticisms of activities in, 142–43

Oakes, James W., 51
Odetta, 167, 170
Olsen, Clark
    attack on, 112–16
    and Brown Chapel–Dallas Courthouse march, 148

FBI interviews with, 125
    and identification of assailants, 125
    and King's call for Ministers March to Montgomery, 99
    reason for coming to Selma of, 203
    and Reeb's injuries/death, 115, 116, 117, 118, 119, 120, 121, 125, 128
    and trial of Reeb assailants, 194, 196, 198, 201–4, 205, 208, 209–12, 215, 216
    and Voting Rights Act, 201
    and voting rights movement, 242
    at Walker's Café, 110, 111, 144
Orange, James
    arrest and jailing of, 2, 13, 15–16, 19
    children's protests and, 2, 12–14, 15–16
    and Marion voting rights movement, 2, 12–13, 15–16
    and Reeb's death, 132
    SCOPE and, 182
    and voting rights legislation, 240
Orwell, George, 99
"Our God is Marching On" speech, King's, 171

Parks, Rosa, 101, 160, 185
Patterson, John, 200
Pearson, Drew, 138
Pegues, R.L., 45
Perkins, Vernetta, 225
Perkins, William, 42–43
Perry, Anna Lou, 98
Perry County, Alabama, 3–4, 7, 8, 171, 187, 192
    See also Marion, Alabama
Perry County Civic League (PCCL), 7, 8, 48, 62
Perry County Courthouse: and Marion voting rights movement, 1, 24
Perry County Hospital
    Higginbotham at, 36
    Jimmie Lee at, 43, 44
    Valeriani in, 67
Perry County Sheriff Department, 1, 24, 26
    See also Loftis, William
Perry, Emmet Jr., 98
Peter, Paul & Mary, 167, 170–71
Philadelphia General Hospital (PGH): Reeb at, 91, 92
Pike, James, 100, 145
Pilcher, Joe, 198, 200–207, 209–15
Pitts, W. McLean, 133, 134
police. *See specific person or department*
Police Department, Marion
    and Mack's Café events, 40–41, 43
    voting rights movement and, 1, 17, 23, 24, 26, 27, 30, 34
    See also Harris, T.O.

Police Department, Selma
and attack on ministers, 117, 121, 123, 204
Baker's (Wilson) influence on, 74
and beginning of March to Montgomery, 79
Bloody Sunday and, 80, 82, 83
at Brown Chapel, 115
and Brown Chapel–Dallas Courthouse
march, 131
and CWCA protest march, 72, 73
and plans and preparations for March to
Montgomery, 75
poll taxes, 5, 163, 176, 181, 184, 186
Powell, Colin, 222–23
"Prayer for Selma" (Cushing), 144
Princeton Theological Seminary, 90
Pritchett, Laurie, 74
protests/demonstrations
prevalence of, 143–45
See also specific protest or demonstration
Pryor, Charles, 38–39, 42

race relations
churches/clergy and, 66–68
prevalence of tensions in, 143
among women, 101
Rae, George, 97
Randolph, A. Philip, 160
Reconstruction, 4, 46
Reeb, Anne (daughter), 89, 96
Reeb, Harry (father), 90, 118, 128, 130, 131,
135, 154
Reeb, James
ambulance ride of, 116–17, 118–20, 203, 205,
207–8, 212–13, 214
attack on, 112–16, 130, 146–47, 202
and ban on March to Montgomery, 107
Boston activities of, 87–89, 95, 96–99,
110
at Burwell Infirmary, 203, 207
commitment of, 243
injuries of, 115–17
Jimmie Lee compared with, 243–44
and King's call for Ministers March to
Montgomery, 86, 87, 88–90, 99
as martyr, 128, 201, 212, 214
personal and professional background of,
90–96, 243
petrified log of, 156
and Roxbury fire, 97–99, 110
in Selma, 107, 108, 109, 110–11
SNCC and, 97
trial concerning civil rights of, 216
at University Hospital, 116, 120, 124, 125,
126, 130–31, 207, 208
and voting rights movement, 241
at Walker's Café, 110–11, 127*n*
See also trial, Reeb murder

Reeb, James—death of
and Alabama's return to normalcy, 171
announcement of, 130–31
arrests for, 121–23
blame for, 148
and Brown Chapel–Dallas County
Courthouse march, 146, 149
as communist plot, 175
Dallas County Courthouse vigil for, 196
demonstrations in remembrance of,
143–44
funeral services for, 131, 146, 147–49,
154–55
impact of, 137–38, 180
King's comments about, 152, 171
King's condolences on, 133
and LBJ–civil rights leaders White House
meeting, 136, 137
LBJ comments about, 150, 152
and memorial fund for Reeb family, 135
and memorial service at Edmund Pettus
Bridge, 108, 109
prosecution of assailants for, 193–217
Selma memorial service/prayer vigil for, 131,
132, 146, 147–49
See also trial, Reeb murder
Reeb (James) family, 117–18, 124, 127, 135,
155, 156, 167*n*
Reeb, John (son), 89, 91, 96, 124, 127, 154
Reeb, Karen (daughter), 89, 96
Reeb, Mae (mother), 90, 154
Reeb, Marie (wife), 89, 91, 96, 111, 117–18,
121, 124, 126–31,
127*n*, 135, 136, 154, 155, 156, 240
Reeb, Steven (son), 89, 96
Reed, Roy, 60, 61, 83–84
Reed, Thomas, 192
Reese, Frederick Douglas, 9, 10, 12, 84, 160,
216
Reformed Baptist Church (Selma), 72
Reuther, Walter, 148, 149
Reynolds, Charles, 108
Richardson, Dan, 88
Richardson, Elliot, 143–44
Riley, Archibald, 15, 16, 18, 19, 27
Riley, David, 137–38
Robb, Inez, 178
Roberts, John, 237
Robertson, Carol, 172
Robinson, Jimmy George, 72
Romney, George, 109
Rongstad, James, 66
Roosevelt, Eleanor, 93–94
Rowe, Gary Thomas, 174, 176–78, 179
Rowe, Tommy, 217
Roxbury, Massachusetts: fire in, 97–99,
110

Rusk, Dean, 131
Russell, Nipsey, 167
Rustin, Bayard, 52, 145

Saltonstall, Leverett, 155, 156
Sanders, Hank, 138n, 225–26, 234
Savio, Mario, 111
Sawyer, George, 31
Schwerner, Michael, 48, 118, 172
SCLC (Southern Christian Leadership
    Conference)
  and Alabama's return to normalcy, 171
  and attack on ministers, 115, 117
  Baker's (George) comments about, 59
  and banning of nighttime marches, 54
  and Birmingham Children's Crusade, 11
  Bloody Sunday and, 86
  Chicago Freedom Movement and, 143
  and contributions of women to civil rights
    movement, 101
  "Courageous Eight" and, 10
  financial contributions to, 167n
  and Hare's injunction, 73
  Malcolm X and, 52–53
  and March to Montgomery, 59
  and Marion voting rights movement, 1, 2, 16,
    24, 26, 28, 51
  and Ministers March to Montgomery, 107
  Montgomery Advertiser views about, 46
  and plans and preparations for March to
    Montgomery, 75, 76, 159
  Selma headquarters of, 16, 19, 24, 29–30, 76
  and 16th Street Baptist Church bombing, 10
  SNCC relationship with, 77
  St. Augustine Movement and, 11
  strategy of, 59, 77
  voter registration efforts of, 10, 12, 51, 59,
    163–64, 167n, 181, 187
  See also specific person
SCOPE (Summer Community Organization
    and Political Education
    Project), 181–82
Seeger, Pete, 167
Selma, Alabama
  and ban on marches, 54, 134–35
  boycott of white businesses in, 53
  and Brown Chapel–Dallas Courthouse
    march, 123, 131–33, 145–46, 148–49
  Catholics in, 67–68
  civil rights marches in, 154
  in Civil War, 9
  CWCA protest march in, 64–65, 66, 68–69,
    72–73
  DCVL in, 8
  Freedom Day in, 53, 59–60
  history of, 8–9
  IQ of blacks in Selma, 197

King in, 12, 52, 54, 60, 72, 73, 146
  King's comments about, 154
  Ku Klux Klan in, 9
  LBJ comments about, 150
  Malcolm X in, 52
  and Marion voting rights movement, 16
  and plans and preparations for March to
    Montgomery, 74–75
  and prayer vigil at "Selma Wall," 123,
    131–33, 135, 145–46
  reaction to LBJ speech in, 151–52
  Reeb memorial service in, 131, 146, 147–49
  voter registration in, 12
  voting rights movement in, 10, 12, 16–17,
    19–20, 53–54
  white power structure–civil rights leaders
    meeting in, 53, 54
  See also specific person, organization, or event
The Selma Campaign, 1963–1965 (Vaughn and
    Davis), 57–58
Selma Chamber of Commerce, 161n
Selma Lord, Selma (Webb), 84
Selma Teachers Association, 9
Selma Times-Journal, 54n, 65, 72, 80–81, 83, 123,
    125, 160, 169, 197
Senate Internal Security Committee, 142
Sessions, Jeff, 238
Shabazz, Betty, 52
Shannon, Henry Jr., 10
Shaw, Bernard, 209
Shelby County v. Holder, 236–44
Shelton, Robert, 175
Shoffeitt, Paul, 55
Silver Moon Café (Selma), 113, 114, 121, 177,
    179, 202, 206, 207, 210–11, 213
Simone, Nina, 167
Sisters of St. Joseph, 44, 67
16th Street Baptist Church (Birmingham)
  bombing of, 10, 61, 70–72, 172, 201, 210,
    227, 234
  Children's Crusade and, 11
Smith, Willie Lee, 39
Smitherman, Joseph, 54, 54n, 65, 73, 75, 134,
    149, 153, 160, 240
SNCC (Student Nonviolent Coordinating
    Committee)
  and Alabama's return to normalcy, 171
  Bloody Sunday and, 86
  and contributions of women to civil rights
    movement, 101
  "Courageous Eight" and, 10
  and CWCA protest march, 72
  educational interests of, 77
  financial contributions to, 167n
  founding of, 9, 11
  and Hare's injunction, 10, 73
  Malcolm X and, 52

SNCC (Student Nonviolent Coordinating
    Committee) (*cont.*)
    and March to Montgomery, 77, 103, 161*n*,
        162
    and Marion voting rights movement, 16
    and Montgomery demonstrations, 154
SNCC (Student Nonviolent Coordinating
    Committee) (*cont.*)
    political party of, 189
    Reeb and, 97
    SCLC relationship with, 77
    in Selma, 9, 86
    strategy of, 77
    voter registration efforts of, 9, 163–64, 167*n*,
        181, 182, 183, 188
    White House sit-in by, 129
    See also specific person
Sojourn to the Past Project, 242
"The Songs of Selma," 8–9
South, J., 212–13
Southern Christian Leadership Conference.
    See SCLC
Southern Poverty Law Center, 172, 243
Southern Regional Council, 188
Soviet Union: reactions to Bloody Sunday in,
    103
Sparkman, John, 153
Sperry, Kris, 229, 230
Sprott Estate, 8, 43
St. Augustine (Florida) Movement, 11, 19, 21
St. James Baptist Church (Marion), 50
St. John's Lutheran Church (Selma), 66
St. Jude, City of: and March to Montgomery,
    166–67, 168
St. Paul's Lutheran Church (Birmingham), 65,
    69, 70
Star: articles about Jimmie Lee's murder in,
    221–24, 226, 228–29, 234
Steele, Rosie, 165
Strange, Herbert, 194
Streisand, Barbra, 167*n*
Stripling, Edgar, 194, 198, 206–7, 208
Student Nonviolent Coordinating Committee.
    See SNCC
Sturgeon, Kelso, 123
Sullivan, John, 88, 124, 126, 135, 144, 155–56
Supreme Court, U.S.
    and Alabama redistricting plan, 239–40
    and *Shelby County v. Holder,* 236–39
    and Texas photo ID rules, 239
    Voting Rights Act and, 236–40
Swear, Bessie, 223
sympathy marches, 108–9

Thirteenth Amendment, 4
Thomas, Daniel, 148
Thomas, Eugene, 174, 176–77, 194

Thomas, Jimmy, 225
Thomas, John C., 143
Thurmond, Strom, 186, 187
Till, Emmitt, 61
Time magazine, 109, 134
Tobey, Lillian Crompton, 100, 101*n*
Toobin, Jeffrey, 237
Toolen, Thomas Joseph, 67–68, 160, 161*n*
Touchstone, Ned, 164
Travers, Mary, 170–71
trial, Reeb murder, 193–217
    altered-wounds defense in, 200–201, 203, 214
    closing arguments in, 213–14
    defense case in, 210–14
    grand jury for, 196–97
    and indictments of suspects, 179
    jurors for, 193–94, 198, 199–200, 211,
        214–15, 216, 217, 217*n*
    medical testimony during, 207–8, 216
    onlookers at, 198
    opening of, 197–98
    opening statements in, 200–201
    prosecution case in, 201–10
    reactions to, 215–17
    and Reeb as "low person," 199
    request for dismissal of charges in, 209–10
    verdict in, 214–17
    witnesses at, 198, 201–13, 216
    See also Cook, Elmer; Hoggle, Namon
        O'Neal "Duck"; Hoggle, William
troopers, Alabama state
    and blame for Jimmie Lee's shooting, 46,
        59, 62
    Bloody Sunday and, 80, 81, 82, 85, 100, 105,
        110, 120, 141
    and Brown Chapel–Dallas Courthouse
        march, 123
    intimidation by, 192
    and Jimmie Lee's shooting, 34–41, 42, 43, 44,
        45, 56, 119, 141, 221–22
    Justice Department interviews of, 48
    King's comments about, 54
    at Mack's Cafe, 34–41, 42, 43, 47–48
    and Marion voting rights movement, 1–2,
        17, 19, 20, 24, 25, 26, 27–28, 29, 30–31,
        32, 34
    and memorial service at Edmund Pettus
        Bridge, 109
    and Orange's protest march, 13
    as patrolling Selma, 53
    and plans and preparations for March to
        Montgomery, 75
    and Reeb's ambulance ride, 119–20
    and Selma voting rights movement, 53
    songs about, 133
    See also specific person
Truman, Harry, 165

Tubbs, Robert, 43–44
Turner, Albert
  background of, 22–23
  and ban on nighttime marches, 54
  and beginning of March to Montgomery, 79
  Foster and, 57
  and March to Montgomery, 160, 162, 163,
    165, 171
  and Marion voting rights movement, 17, 18,
    22–23, 25, 26, 27, 29, 31, 49
  and PCCL, 7
  and plans and preparations for March to
    Montgomery, 76, 79
  SCOPE and, 182
  and voting rights/registration, 7, 23, 240
Turner, Albert Jr., 234
Turner, Robert Jr., 23
Turner, Robert Sr., 51
Twenty-Fourth Amendment, 181
"two little girls" comment, LBJ's, 137

Uniontown participants: in March to
    Montgomery, 162–63
Unitarian Universalists, 88–89
Unitarians, 68, 88–90, 92–93, 107, 116, 117,
    135, 144, 195–96,
    217. *See also specific person*
United Press International (UPI), 28, 32,
    216–17
University of Alabama
  Harris speech at, 33–34
  Malone as first black enrolled at, 185
University of California at Los Angeles
    (UCLA): King speech at, 181
University Hospital (Birmingham)
  Reeb and, 116, 120, 124, 125, 126, 130–31,
    200, 207, 208
  and trial of Reeb assailants, 200, 207, 208
University of Mississippi, 48

Valenti, Jack, 129
Valeriani, Richard, 28, 43, 67, 85
Vardaman, Edgar, 211, 212
Vardaman, Harry, 211
Vaughan, William, 214–15
Vaughn, Wally G., 57–58
Vivian, C.T.
  arrest and jailing of, 16, 19–20
  and attack on ministers, 125
  background of, 10, 21
  and ban on marches, 146
  and Brown Chapel–Dallas County
    Courthouse march, 123, 146
  Clark and, 19–20, 21–22, 30, 196
  and CWCA demonstration, 74
  and Jimmie Lee's death, 56
  and LBJ speech, 152

Nashville Student Movement and, 10
and plans and preparations for March to
    Montgomery, 65, 74
voting rights movement and, 12, 16, 17,
    19–20, 21–22, 29–30, 241–42
voter registration
  in Alabama, 239–44
  black, 152–53
  and election of black candidates, 191–92
  and elections of 1966, 187, 188, 190
  and elections of 2014, 239
  federal role in, 187–88
  financial contributions toward efforts at, 167*n*
  impact of Voting Rights Act on, 191
  and intimidation, 188, 191
  juries and, 183–84
  Justice Department complaint about, 125
  King and, 181
  in Lowndes County, 182–83
  SCLC and SNCC efforts at, 163–64, 167*n*
  SCOPE and, 181–82
  and *Shelby v. Holder* case, 237–39
  and voter fraud, 239
  and Wallace–civil rights leaders meeting, 176
  See also Voting Rights Act; *specific person or
    organization*
voting rights
  and Brown Chapel–Dallas County
    Courthouse march, 123
  churches and, 58–59
  King and, 11–12, 19, 152–53, 171
  LBJ and, 11–12, 19, 21, 103, 106, 136, 138,
    140, 147–53, 175, 181, 185–86
  and LBJ–civil rights leaders White House
    meeting, 136, 137, 138
  non-violence and, 243
  passage of, 180–81, 182, 184
  Senate commitment to, 165
  and threats against blacks, 8
  See also Voting Rights Act (1965); *specific
    person or organization*
Voting Rights Act (1965)
  and black candidates in Alabama, 189
  CWCA protest and, 66
  and elections of 1966, 187, 188, 190–91
  Ellwanger's plea for need for, 66
  Jackson (Michael) and, 220
  Jimmie Lee's death and, 228
  Olsen's views about, 201
  passage of, 184–86
  Section 4 of, 237
  Section 5 of, 236–44
  and *Shelby County v. Holder*, 236–44
  weakening of, 236–44

Walk to Montgomery. *See* March to
    Montgomery

Walker's Café (Selma): clergy at, 110–11, 127n,
    144
Wallace, George
  Alabama State College students petition to,
    154
  and ban on marches, 54, 124–25, 141–42
  Bevel's comments about, 59
  Bloody Sunday and, 86, 100, 105, 140
  civil rights leaders meeting with, 176
  and congressional reactions to Bloody
    Sunday, 103
  demonstrations against, 143
  and Fowler–Jimmie Lee murder trial, 230
  freedom songs and, 84
  Johnson's (Frank) relationship with, 102
  King and, 54, 142, 169
  LBJ and, 104–5, 139–40, 141–42
  and Lurleen's election as governor, 191
  and Malone as first black enrolled at
    University of Alabama, 185
  and March to Montgomery, 158, 168–69
  and Marion voting rights movement, 25
  media and, 141–42
  and plans and preparations for March to
    Montgomery, 57, 58, 63, 65, 75, 102
  songs about, 133
  and voting rights/registration, 187, 240
Wallace, Lurleen, 191
Ware, Virgil Jr., 176
Washington, D.C.
  clergy meeting in, 138–39
  demonstrations/protests in, 144
  Reeb funeral in, 131
  See also All Souls Church
Washington Post, 139, 140
Washington University: FBI files about Jimmie
    Lee shooting at, 229
"We Shall Overcome"
  and CWCA march, 72
  and Jimmie Lee's funeral, 61
  and LBJ speech, 149–53
  Liuzzo murder and, 173
  and March to Montgomery, 164, 166
  and Reeb's funeral, 155
Webb, Sheyann, 84–85, 116, 159, 171
Wesley, Cynthia, 172
West, Alice, 151
West, Ben, 102
West, Lonzy, 151
West, Rachel, 85, 159
When the Church Bells Rang Racist (Collins), 67
White Citizens' Action Inc. of Tuscaloosa, 164
White Citizens' Council, 64, 190–91, 195
White House
  LBJ–civil rights leaders meeting at, 136–37, 138
  sit-in at, 129

White, Lee, 154
white supremacists, 145, 177
Wicker, Tom, 150, 151, 191
Wilcox County, Alabama
  Lutherans in, 65
  voter registration efforts in, 182
Wilkerson, Arthur, 43
Wilkins, Collie, 174, 176–79, 194
Wilkins, Roy, 144, 175, 185, 191
Williams, Griffith, 90
Williams, Hosea
  background of, 76–77, 84
  and beginning of March to Montgomery, 79
  Bloody Sunday and, 80, 84
  King's relationship with, 77
  and memorial service at Edmund Petrus
    Bridge, 134
  and plans and preparations for March to
    Montgomery, 75, 76, 77–78
  SCOPE and, 182
  testimony in Johnson court by, 134
  and voting rights efforts, 12, 17, 182, 240
Wilson, Darren, 226–27n
Wilson, James H., 9
women
  contributions to civil rights movement of,
    101
  and March to Montgomery, 100–101,
    100–101n
  racial relations among, 101
  See also specific person
women's rights, 93–94
Wood, Virgil, 88
Woods, Herbert, 137
Woodson, Paul, 212
Working Families Party, 241

Yarborough, Ralph, 103
Young, Andrew, 12, 16, 52, 65–66, 76, 148,
    161, 163, 165
Young, Quentin, 166
Zion United Methodist Church (Marion)
  Bevel at, 58
  as center of civil rights protests, 67
  Clark at, 20
  Jimmie Lee's funeral at, 62
  King at, 54, 62
  King's eulogy for Jimmie Lee at, 62
  and Mack's Cafe shooting, 43
  and Marion voting rights movement, 2, 7,
    15, 17, 18–19, 20, 22–23, 24, 27–28, 29,
    31, 32, 34
  PCCL meetings at, 7
  and plans for March to Montgomery, 58
  post–Jimmie Lee shooting meeting at,
    48–49